Real Estate
STUDY GUIDE

SEVENTEENTH EDITION

Fillmore W. Galaty

Wellington J. Allaway

Robert C. Kyle

This publication is designed to provide accurate and authoritative information in regard to the subject matter covered. It is sold with the understanding that the publisher is not engaged in rendering legal, accounting, or other professional service. If legal advice or other expert assistance is required, the services of a competent professional should be sought.

President: Roy Lipner
Vice President of Product Development & Publishing: Evan M. Butterfield
Managing Editor: Kate DeVivo
Senior Development Editor: Tony Peregrin
Instructional Designer: Catherine M. Izor
Production Editor: Karen Goodfriend
Creative Director: Lucy Jenkins
Typesetter: Todd Bowman

Published by Dearborn Real Estate Education

30 South Wacker Drive
Chicago, Illinois 60606-7481
(312) 836-4400
www.dearbornRE.com

Printed in the United States of America

06   07   10   9   8   7   6   5   4   3   2   1

Library of Congress Cataloging-in-Publication Data

Galaty, Fillmore W.
    Study guide for Modern real estate practice / Galaty, Allaway, Kyle.
        p. cm.
    Supplement to Modern real estate practice.
    ISBN-13: 978-1-4195-2194-2
    ISBN-10: 1-4195-2194-2
    1. Real estate business—Law and legislation—United States. 2. Vendors and purchasers—United States. 3. Real property—United States. I. Allaway, Wellington J. II. Kyle, Robert C. III. Galaty, Fillmore W. Modern real estate practice.17th ed. IV. Title.

    KF2042.R4G34 2006 suppl.
    346.7304'37—dc22

                                                              2006007593

Contents

Preface   iv
Instructions How To Use This *Study Guide*   vi

CHAPTER **1**   Introduction to the Real Estate Business   1

CHAPTER **2**   Real Property and the Law   7

CHAPTER **3**   Concepts of Home Ownership   15

CHAPTER **4**   Agency   23

CHAPTER **5**   Real Estate Brokerage   33

CHAPTER **6**   Listing Agreements and Buyer Representation   43

CHAPTER **7**   Interests in Real Estate   55

CHAPTER **8**   Forms of Real Estate Ownership   67

CHAPTER **9**   Legal Descriptions   77

CHAPTER **10**   Real Estate Taxes and Other Liens   83

CHAPTER **11**   Real Estate Contracts   91

CHAPTER **12**   Transfer of Title   103

CHAPTER **13**   Title Records   113

CHAPTER **14**   Real Estate Financing: Principles   121

CHAPTER **15**   Real Estate Financing: Practice   133

CHAPTER **16**   Leases   145

CHAPTER **17**   Property Management   157

CHAPTER **18**   Real Estate Appraisal   165

CHAPTER **19**   Land-Use Controls and Property Development   177

CHAPTER **20**   Fair Housing and Ethical Practices   187

CHAPTER **21**   Environmental Issues and the Real Estate Transaction   197

CHAPTER **22**   Closing the Real Estate Transaction   205

Preface

M ost students find their real estate principles class to be a challenging, rewarding, and traumatic experience, all at the same time. For some, mastering the basic jargon of the real estate industry can be as demanding as learning a foreign language. Students who have not attended classes or studied for exams for several years sometimes find it difficult to get back into the habit—particularly when they have other important demands on their time, and homework is just another responsibility among many. Dearborn™ Real Estate Education is aware of the particular challenges that face today's real estate students. This *Study Guide* was written with your needs in mind.

ABOUT THIS BOOK

This *Study Guide* is designed to be used as a supplement to your prelicense education. It can be used in conjunction with any of the following textbooks:

- *Modern Real Estate Practice*
- any state-specific *Modern Real Estate Practice*
- state-specific *Practice & Law* or *Basics*
- *Mastering Real Estate Principles*
- *Real Estate Fundamentals*

It can even be used on its own as a review or refresher. Each chapter in the *Study Guide* corresponds to a chapter in one of the three main Dearborn™ real estate prelicensing textbooks. Check the inside front cover for a handy correlation table.

The *Study Guide* is intended to reinforce and elaborate on the basic information provided in your main textbook. Specifically, it is designed to help you master the three fundamental goals vital to academic success, which are to

1. **recognize** important terms and concepts;
2. **evaluate** your understanding of basic real estate issues; and
3. **apply** learned principles to real-world practice.

The preceding goals form the basis for the basic learning objectives of the *Study Guide*, which are to

- **define and explain** fundamental concepts and vocabulary terms of the real estate industry;
- **identify and discuss** the characteristics of various legal and financial relationships; and
- **perform and apply** basic financial and property-related calculations.

To help you along the way, the *Study Guide* uses several different learning strategies: an approach called **multitesting.** Each of the styles of self-testing included here has been proven effective in helping students not only to memorize factual information, but actually to retain the material in a constructive way. By working through the various components of each chapter, you will be reinforcing your real estate knowledge as well as your test-taking skills.

WHY A MULTITESTING APPROACH?

The advantage of the multitesting approach is that the same material is tested repeatedly, but in different styles. While the real estate examination itself is exclusively in multiple-choice format, the use of other testing styles helps reinforce your understanding of the subject matter. The stronger your basic understanding of basic terms and concepts, the more prepared you'll be for possible exam curveballs.

NOTE	This *Study Guide* is NOT a substitute for attending class or reading the main text! Rather, it is a tool to help you understand and retain what you've learned and read.

ACKNOWLEDGMENTS

The following individuals provided professional guidance and real-world expertise in the development of this edition of the *Study Guide:*

- Eileen Cahill, assistant director, Weichert Real Estate School
- Edith Lank, columnist and author of *Essentials of New Jersey Real Estate* and *Modern Real Estate Practice in New York.*
- Jean Ritter, Coldwell Banker Residential Brokerage School of Real Estate (Pasadena, Maryland).
- John Theis, Instructor with the Frederick Academy of Real Estate (Front Royal, Virginia).

Instructions
How to Use This *Study Guide*

This Section includes complete instructions for all the exercises contained in the *Study Guide*. You may refer to these instructions at any time as you work through the various exercises of each chapter. In addition, the instructions include **Study Strategies:** tips and tools you can use to make the *Study Guide* exercises as effective as possible. The chapters in this *Study Guide* include the following sections: "Before You Start . . ." (a post-study assessment tool), key term matching, true or false, multiple-choice review, fill-in-the-blanks, illustrations, logic problems, math problems, and an answer key.

BEFORE YOU START . . .

New! The post-study assessment questions in "Before You Start . . ." help you evaluate how well you've grasped the general concepts covered in each chapter of the text. We encourage the student to review each chapter's "Before You Start . . ." section before attempting to answer the questions in this *Study Guide*.

STUDY STRATEGY Before answering the Key Term Matching, True/False, Multiple Choice, and Fill in the Blank questions in each chapter, quickly review the "Before You Start . . ." section. If you can answer most of the questions in this section, you are ready to move forward in the *Study Guide*. If not, please review that chapter's content in the textbook.

KEY TERM MATCHING

Test yourself to see how many of the key terms and other important real estate words you can match with their correct definitions. In some chapters, we've split this section into two parts to make it easier for you to use. Each part is completely self-contained. Simply write the letter of the key term in the blank next to the definition.

STUDY STRATEGY First fill in the blanks and check your answers. Then later, you can also use this section for more study by covering the answer you have written in and verbally (or mentally) give the definition, or cover the definition and pronounce the term. Both exercises will reinforce your basic knowledge of key definitions.

TRUE OR FALSE

This section helps you prepare for the multiple-choice questions used on most exams. You are presented with a series of statements based on material in the main text. Determine whether the statement is true or false, and circle the T or F accordingly.

STUDY STRATEGY   Be careful! These statements are designed to test how closely you can read and how clearly you understand what you've read: They may be tricky. There may be only one word that makes the entire statement false. The answer key provides explanations for all the questions with False as the answer.

Here's an example:

14. T   F   A real estate appraiser is licensed by the state to buy, sell, exchange, or lease real property.

*The statement is clearly **False**. Circle the **F**. In the Answer Key, you would find:*

14. False. A real estate *broker* is licensed by the state to buy, sell, exchange, or lease real property.

The focus of the preceding question is clearly on the *characteristics of a real estate broker,* not what an appraiser can do. The better choice is to stick to the question's main idea. As a rule, the smaller the changes you have to make to create a true statement, the better. In this example, changing only one word (appraiser to broker) makes the statement true.

MULTIPLE-CHOICE REVIEW

Each chapter includes a section of multiple-choice questions. It may help to recognize that each multiple-choice question is actually four true or false statements. The question formats used in the *Study Guide* help you retain information as well as help you prepare for the format and structure of the licensing exam.

STUDY STRATEGY   Most multiple-choice questions will consist of three false statements (answers) and one true statement. Circle the letter of the answer that makes a true ending to the question. For study purposes (and rarely on official exams), we ask you to compile a list of information. These questions consist of three true statements and one false answer. These are characterized by these words . . . "All of the following are true . . . *EXCEPT* . . ." In this situation, you choose the exception to the list.

FILL-IN-THE-BLANK

New! Many chapters include a Fill-in-the-Blank section. This new question format re-emphasizes key terms and concepts and prepares the student for taking the licensing exam.

STUDY STRATEGY   Read the entire sentence or phrase and determine the meaning and/or purpose of the statement. Then insert the term that best completes the sentence from the list provided.

ILLUSTRATIONS

Many people remember information visually. In these sections, you are asked to complete an illustration of one or more basic concepts. Some illustrations ask you simply to label certain elements; for others, you may need to analyze information and fill in a practice-related form.

STUDY STRATEGY   Try to visualize the concepts presented in the illustrations. Creating a useful mental picture may be very helpful to recall during the exam.

LOGIC PROBLEMS

When working on a complicated fact-pattern problem (whether in this *Study Guide* or on the real estate licensing examination), draw a picture. Make a chart or diagram of the transactions involved in the problem. Label each actor by identifier and illustrate the role he or she plays in the event. For instance, if the problem is "F conveyed Blueacres to G, who conveyed a life estate pur autre vie to H, measured by the life of Y, retaining a reversionary interest," you might draw a diagram like this:

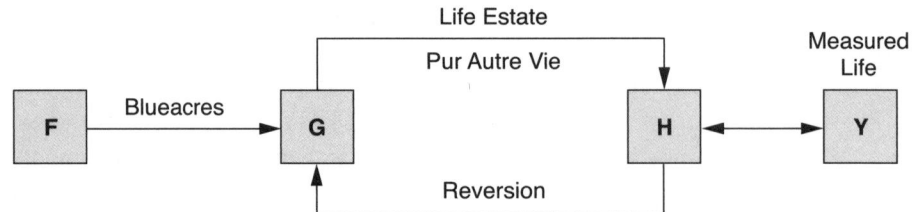

MATH PROBLEMS

When you're faced with a math problem, read the whole question carefully! Sometimes testers (and even this *Study Guide*) will include distracting or irrelevant facts or numbers to make sure you know not only how to perform certain calculations but know what information you need to do it. For example, if a question wants you to calculate a broker's commission on a sale, you can disregard information about the asking price or mortgage.

Never assume! You should be able to answer a question based only on the facts you're given. Be sure to pay attention to what you're really being asked to do. Don't make the mistake of trying to rewrite the question instead of choosing the correct answer to the given question.

ANSWER KEY

The *Study Guide* includes a complete set of answers at the end of each chapter so that you can assess your comprehension before proceeding to the next chapter.

Look at the answers only after you've completed all the sections in the chapter! If you check your answers after each section, you might accidentally peek at the correct responses for the next section. While that might improve your overall scores in the *Study Guide*, it won't help your score where it counts . . . on the licensing exam.

1

Introduction to the Real Estate Business

BEFORE YOU START...

After completing Chapter 1 of the textbook, you should be able to answer the following "learning assessment" questions. If you are able to answer these questions, then you are ready to move ahead with this chapter of the *Study Guide!* If, however, you are having some difficulty answering any of these learning assessment questions, we advise you to reread key sections of the textbook before attempting to answer the questions in this chapter of the *Study Guide*.

- Can you describe the activities involved in at least seven types of real estate specialization?

- Do you know why there is specialization in the real estate business?

- Are you able to list examples of the five types of real property?

- What does the word *market* mean?

- How would you explain the function of markets?

- Why does the value of real property go up and down?

- Can you name at least three factors that affect supply of real property?

- Can you name at least three factors that affect demand for real property?

MATCHING   *Write the letter of the matching term on the appropriate line.*

a. *home inspection*

b. *salesperson*

c. *appraisal*

d. *market*

e. *brokerage*

f. *demand*

g. REALTOR®

h. *supply*

i. *broker*

j. *property management*

1. ____ A place where goods can be bought and sold and a price for goods established

2. ____ The amount of goods available in the market to be sold at a given price

3. ____ Person who performs real estate activities while employed by or associated with a licensed real estate broker

4. ____ In real estate, a licensed person who acts as a go-between on behalf of others for a fee or commission

5. ____ Maintaining and administering another's property for a fee

6. ____ Process of using established methods and good judgment to estimate the value of a property

7. ____ The bringing together of parties interested in making a real estate transaction

8. ____ The amount of goods people are willing and able to buy at a given price

9. ____ Report based on visual survey of property structure, systems, and site conditions

10. ____ Person who adheres to the Code of Ethics of the National Association of REALTORS® (NAR)

TRUE OR FALSE   *Circle the correct answer.*

1. T F The five classes of real estate mentioned in the main textbook are residential, commercial, rental, agricultural, and special purpose.

2. T F The real estate market is generally slow to adjust to the changing forces of supply and demand.

3. T F The supply of labor and the cost of construction generally have a direct effect on the demand for real estate in a market.

4. T F Real estate agents generally tend to specialize in one activity or class of real estate.

5. T F Warehouses, factories, and power plants are examples of commercial property.

6. T F Members of the National Association of Real Estate Brokers are known as REALTORS®.

7. T F In general, the most widely recognized real estate activity is brokerage.

8. T F Finding funds to put together real estate transactions is called *appraising*.

9. T F Market trends in supply and demand can be overturned by a natural disaster, such as a hurricane or earthquake.

10. T F The rental market is characterized by space used temporarily by lease.

MULTIPLE CHOICE   *Circle a, b, c, or d.*

1. Office buildings and retail space are examples of
   a. commercial real estate.
   b. special-use real estate.
   c. residential property.
   d. industrial property.

2. A person who advises a real estate client who is making a purchase to use or invest in real estate is called a(n)
   a. educator.
   b. mortgage broker.
   c. counselor.
   d. subdivider.

3. All of the following factors will tend to affect demand for real estate *EXCEPT*
   a. transfer taxes.
   b. employment levels.
   c. wage rates.
   d. demographics.

4. When the population of a town suddenly increases, which of the following is *MOST LIKELY* to occur?
   a. Rental rates fall due to increased competition.
   b. Demand for housing decreases.
   c. New housing starts will decrease.
   d. Real estate prices will increase.

5. Property management, appraisal, financing, and development are all
   a. specializations directly linked to state and federal government financial policies.
   b. separate professions within the real estate industry.
   c. real estate brokerage professions.
   d. demographic factors that affect demand for real property in a commercial market.

6. The idea that no two parcels of land are exactly alike is called
   a. immobility.
   b. subdivision.
   c. uniqueness.
   d. location.

7. All of the following factors can affect the supply of real estate *EXCEPT*
   a. demographics.
   b. labor force.
   c. construction costs.
   d. government controls.

8. A property owner who does not want to deal with the everyday tasks of managing a rental property can hire a(n)
   a. property manager.
   b. appraiser.
   c. home inspector.
   d. developer.

9. When the supply of a certain commodity decreases while demand remains the same, the price of that commodity will tend to
   a. remain the same.
   b. increase.
   c. decrease by 10%.
   d. decrease by 20%.

10. All of the following are examples of government policies that can affect the real estate market *EXCEPT*
    a. the Federal Reserve Board's discount rate.
    b. a shortage of skilled labor or building materials.
    c. land-use controls such as zoning.
    d. federal environmental regulations.

FILL-IN-THE-BLANK   *Select the word or words that best complete the following statements:*

agricultural

appraiser

continuing education

demographic

go down

go up

industrial

licensing

market

remain the same

residential

salesperson

subdivision

valuation

1. A person who conducts activities on behalf of a broker is called a(n) _____.

2. Appraisers must have detailed knowledge of the methods of property _____.

3. Real estate licensees keep their skills and knowledge current by obtaining _____.

4. A single-family home is a type of _____ property.

5. If the supply of single-family homes goes up and a major local employer lays off a large number of workers, the price of real estate tends to _____.

6. The splitting of a single piece of property into smaller parcels is called _____.

7. *Niche marketing* refers to the targeted marketing of specific _____ _____ populations.

8. Farms and timberland are considered to be _____ property.

9. A community implements land-use restrictions so that less vacant land is available for residential development. At the same time, demand for housing increases due to higher population. Prices for real estate will tend to _____.

10. The function of a(n) _____ is to provide a setting in which supply and demand can establish the value of real property.

ANSWER KEY

Key Term Matching

1. d   **2.** h   **3.** b   **4.** i   **5.** j   **6.** c   **7.** e   **8.** f
9. a   **10.** g

True or False

1. **False.** The five classes of real estate mentioned in the text are residential, commercial, industrial, agricultural, and special-purpose. Rental is *not* a class of real estate.

2. **True**

3. **False.** Supply of labor and the cost of construction generally have a direct effect on the *supply* of real estate in a market.

4. **True**

5. **False.** Warehouses, factories, and power plants are examples of *industrial* property.

6. **False.** Members of the National Association of Real Estate Brokers are known as Realtists. REALTORS® are members of the National Association of REALTORS®.

7. **True**

8. **False.** Finding funds involves *financing*; estimating the value of property is *appraising*.

9. **True**

10. **True**

Multiple Choice

1. **a.** Special use includes churches and dormitories; industrial includes warehouses and factories.

2. **c.** An educator provides education; a mortgage broker searches for financing; and a subdivider splits larger properties into smaller ones.

3. **a.** Transfer taxes affect the supply; the other factors affect demand.

4. **d.** Rental rates will increase; demand for housing will increase; and more new homes will be started to satisfy demand.

5. **b.** Property management, appraisal, financing, and development are not linked to the government, and they are not all linked to real estate brokerage.

6. **c.** Another word for uniqueness is *nonhomogeneity*.

7. **a.** Demographics affects the *demand* for real estate.

8. **a.** An appraiser estimates value; a home inspector looks for problems with the property; and the developer improves the property.

9. **b.** When consumers continue to demand a product and there isn't enough to go around, the price generally increases.

10. **b.** A shortage of skilled labor will affect the supply of real estate, and this labor shortage is not generally associated with governmental policies.

Fill-in-the-Blank

1. A person who conducts activities on behalf of a broker is called a *salesperson*.

2. Appraisers must have detailed knowledge of the methods of property *valuation*.

3. Real estate licensees keep their skills and knowledge current by obtaining *continuing education*.

4. A single-family home is a type of *residential* property.

5. If the supply of single-family homes goes up and a major local employer lays off a large number of workers, the price of real estate tends to *go down*.

6. The splitting of a single piece of property into smaller parcels is called *subdivision*.

7. Niche marketing refers to the targeted marketing of specific *demographic* populations.

8. Farms and timberland are considered to be *agricultural* property.

9. A community implements land-use restrictions so that less vacant land is available for residential development. At the same time, demand for housing increases due to higher population. Prices for real estate will tend to *go up*.

10. The function of a *market* is to provide a setting in which supply and demand can establish the value of real property.

2

Real Property and the Law

After completing Chapter 2 of the textbook, you should be able to answer the following "learning assessment" questions. If you are able to answer these questions, then you are ready to move ahead with this chapter of the *Study Guide!* If, however, you are having some difficulty answering any of these learning assessment questions, we advise you to reread key sections of the textbook before attempting to answer the questions in this chapter of the *Study Guide*.

- Can you define and describe *land, real estate,* and *real property?*

- Can you explain the concept of the *bundle of legal rights* in the ownership of real property?

- Do you know the differences among *surface rights, subsurface rights,* and *air rights?*

- What are the differences between *real property* and *personal property?*

- How would you describe the differences between a *fixture* and a *trade fixture?*

- What are the legal tests of a fixture and how are they applied?

- Can you explain the economic and physical characteristics of *real property?*

MATCHING   *Write the letter of the matching term on the appropriate line.*

a. *annexation*

b. *bundle of legal rights*

c. *improvement*

d. *surface rights*

e. *emblements*

f. *fixture*

g. *subsurface rights*

h. *real estate*

i. *real property*

j. *severance*

k. *personal property*

l. *water rights*

m. *chattels*

n. *trade fixture*

o. *air rights*

1. _____ An article installed by a tenant under a commercial lease and removable before the lease expires

2. _____ Any property that is not real property

3. _____ Conversion of personal property to real property

4. _____ Ownership of all legal rights to the land: control, possession, exclusion, enjoyment, and disposition

5. _____ The interests, benefits, and rights automatically included in the ownership of land and real estate

6. _____ The right to use the open space above the surface of a property

7. _____ A portion of the earth's surface extending down to the center and up into space, including all natural and artificial attachments

8. _____ Ownership rights in the water, minerals, gas, and oil that lie beneath a parcel of land

9. _____ Personal property that is converted to real property by being permanently attached to the real estate

10. _____ Any structure or modification erected or imposed on a site to enhance the value of the property

11. _____ Changing an item of real estate to personal property by detaching it from the land

12. _____ Ownership rights excluding air or mineral rights

13. _____ Common law right of owners of land next to rivers, lakes, or oceans

14. _____ Another name for personal property

15. _____ Growing crops such as corn or soybeans that remain personal property

---

TRUE OR FALSE   *Circle the correct answer.*

1. T F The terms *land*, *real estate*, and *real property* are interchangeable; they all refer to the same thing.

2. T F *Real property* is defined as the earth's surface extending downward to the center of the earth and upward to infinity, including permanent natural objects such as trees and water.

3. T F The term *real property* includes land, rights, and real estate.

4. T F The transfer of the right to use the surface of the earth always includes the right to the natural resources that lie beneath the surface of the earth.

5. T F Trees, perennial shrubbery, and grasses that do not require annual cultivation are considered personal property.

6. T F The process by which personal property becomes real property is called *annexation*.

TRUE OR FALSE (continued)

7. T F A *trade fixture* is an article owned by a tenant and attached to a rented space or building used in conducting a business.

8. T F The economic characteristics of real estate are scarcity, improvements, permanence of investment, and uniqueness.

9. T F Immobility, indestructibility, and scarcity are physical characteristics of real property.

10. T F The image of a bundle of sticks is the traditional illustration of the set of legal rights of ownership.

11. T F When determining if an item is a fixture, you should decide whether the item is actually being used as real or personal property.

12. T F The economic characteristic of *permanence of investment* refers to the concept that the total supply of land is limited.

13. T F One of the rights of real property ownership is the right of enjoyment, or the right to use the property in any legal way.

14. T F A property's air rights extend upward into outer space.

15. T F Trade fixtures are typically excluded from a mortgage.

REAL PROPERTY OR PERSONAL PROPERTY?

Enter check marks in the appropriate columns to indicate whether each item is real or personal property, and whether it is a fixture or a trade fixture (if applicable).

Property Description	Type of Property		Fixture	Trade Fixture
	Real	Personal		
1. Sidewalks and sewers in a subdivision				
2. Bushes surrounding a residence				
3. Wheat or corn crops on a farm				
4. Kitchen sink installed in a home				
5. Booths in a restaurant installed by tenant				
6. Curtains installed by a tenant				
7. Pumps installed by a gas station tenant				
8. Water well pump installed by the landowner				
9. Crystal chandelier hung from the ceiling				
10. 80-gallon water heater with fiberglass insulating jacket				

MULTIPLE CHOICE *Circle a, b, c, or d.*

1. Land, mineral, and air rights in the land are included in the definition of

a. attachments.
c. subsurface rights.
b. real property.
d. improvements.

2. Which of the following is an example of an economic characteristic of land?

a. Immobility
c. Uniqueness
b. Indestructibility
d. Scarcity

3. Another word for *uniqueness* is

a. scarcity.
c. fructus industrials.
b. nonhomogeneity.
d. immobility.

4. All of the following are included in the bundle of rights *EXCEPT*

a. possession.
c. exclusion.
b. control.
d. expansion.

5. The right to dispose of real property by will or deed is contained in the

a. bundle of rights.
b. deed.
c. statutory law of the federal government.
d. statutory law of the state.

6. Growing trees, fences, and buildings would all be considered

a. chattels.
c. fixtures.
b. land.
d. real estate.

7. The most important economic characteristic of land is

a. permanence.
c. uniqueness.
b. location.
d. possession.

8. A tenant farmer built a chicken coop and a tool shed. These buildings belong to the

a. tenant.
b. owner of real estate.
c. owner, but the owner must reimburse the tenant.
d. tenant, but the tenant must pay additional rent for them.

9. The developer added sewer lines, utilities, and built two streets. What are these items called?

a. Fixtures
b. Additions
c. Improvements
d. Permanence of investment

10. The new owner received the land, a garage, and the right to drive on his neighbor's driveway. This right is an example of a(n)

a. improvement.
c. appurtenance.
b. fixture.
d. chattel.

11. Method of annexation, adaptation, and agreement are the legal tests for determining whether an item is

a. a chattel or an emblement.
b. real property or personal property.
c. land or real estate.
d. fructus naturales or fructus industriales.

12. After suffering through a tornado and then flooding from the river, the buildings were gone. The land was still there. This is an example of

a. uniqueness.
b. scarcity.
c. location.
d. indestructibility.

13. The seller asked the real estate agent to draw up several documents relating to seller financing. Under these circumstances, the agent should

a. ask the broker for assistance.
b. draw up the documents.
c. ignore the instructions.
d. refer the seller to an attorney.

MULTIPLE CHOICE (continued)

14. Brad particularly liked the ornate brass lighting fixtures in Hannah's house and immediately made an offer, which Hannah accepted. On moving day, Brad discovered that Hannah had replaced all the ornate brass fixtures with plain steel ones. Which of the following is MOST LIKELY a correct assumption?

    a. Hannah: "As long as I replaced them with something of comparable value, I can take them with me."

    b. Brad: "Lighting fixtures are normally considered to be real property."

    c. Hannah: "The lighting fixtures were personal property when I bought them at the store, so they're personal property forever."

    d. Hannah: "The lighting fixtures belong to me because I installed them."

15. The farmer has posted a number of "No Trespassing" and "No Hunting" signs on the property. Which *stick* in the bundle of rights gives the farmer this authority?

    a. Exclusion   c. Control

    b. Enjoyment   d. Disposition

16. A right or privilege tied to real property, although not necessarily part of the property is called a(n)

    a. emblement.   c. appurtenance.

    b. trade fixture. d. deed.

17. An important characteristic of personal property is that it is

    a. small enough to be carried by a person.

    b. movable.

    c. alive.

    d. less than 100 years old.

18. *Mobile home*, rather than *manufactured housing*, is the term used for a factory-built home that was built before

    a. 1976.   c. 1987.

    b. 1980.   d. 1990.

19. To determine whether an item is a fixture, the MOST important test is whether the

    a. effort needed to remove the item is significant.

    b. item must be dismantled for removal.

    c. value of the item is high.

    d. person who installed it intended for it to be permanent.

20. Brittany planted a rose bush on her property and plans to dig it up and take it with her when her house is sold. The sales contract explicitly excludes the rose bush from the sale. This provision is necessary because the rose bush is considered to be

    a. a trade fixture.   c. an emblement.

    b. personal property. d. real estate.

ANSWER KEY

Key Term Matching

1. n **2.** k **3.** a **4.** b **5.** i **6.** o **7.** h **8.** g
9. f **10.** c **11.** j **12.** d **13.** l **14.** m **15.** e

True or False

1. **False.** The terms *land, real estate,* and *real property* are not interchangeable. They refer to different aspects of the same thing.

2. **False.** *Land* is defined as the earth's surface extending downward to the center of the earth and upward to infinity, including permanent natural objects such as trees and water. *Real property* is defined as the interests, benefits, and rights that are considered part of the ownership of land and real estate.

3. **True**

4. **False.** The transfer of the surface does not necessarily include the rights to the subsurface rights, the natural resources that lie beneath the surface.

5. **False.** Trees, perennial shrubbery, and grasses that do not require annual cultivation are considered *real estate*.

6. **True**

7. **True**

8. **False.** Economic characteristics of land include scarcity, improvements, permanence of investment, and *area preference*.

9. **False.** Physical characteristics of land include immobility, indestructibility, and *uniqueness*.

10. **True**

11. **True**

12. **False.** *Permanence of investment* refers to the concept that the return on investment in real estate tends to be long term and relatively stable. *Scarcity* refers to the concept that the total supply of land is limited.

13. **True**

14. **False.** Property air rights began to be limited when air travel became common. Now, light and solar rights may limit air rights in certain areas.

15. **True**

Multiple Choice

1. **b.** Subsurface rights and improvement are included in the definition of real estate. Real property also includes rights and privileges.

2. **d.** Immobility, indestructibility, and uniqueness are physical characteristics while scarcity is an economic characteristic.

3. **b.** Uniqueness, or nonhomogeneity, indicates that no two parcels of land are alike.

4. **d.** The bundle of rights includes possession, control, exclusion, but not the right to expand.

5. **a.** *Real property* is described as a bundle of legal rights that contains the right of disposition.

6. **d.** The definition of *real estate* includes fences, buildings, and growing trees. *Chattels* are personal property. The definition of *land* would not include fences and buildings.

7. **b.** Location is sometimes referred to as *area preference* or *situs*.

8. **a.** The coop and tool shed would be considered trade fixtures, and the tenant has the right to remove them up to the end of the lease.

9. **c.** Human-made permanent attachments are called *improvements*.

10. **c.** *Appurtenances* are rights that travel with the property ownership.

11. **b.** Whether or not an item is a fixture or personal property may be determined by method of annexation, adaptation, or agreement of the parties.

12. **d.** Land cannot be destroyed although the improvements might be removed, as they are in this case.

13. **d.** Real estate licensees should be careful not to "practice" law unless they are, in fact, licensed attorneys.

14. **b.** While Hannah might say the other things, Brad is correct in assuming that lighting fixtures are normally part of the real property. If Hannah had wanted to remove the fixtures, she should have done so before she put the house on the market or have written her intention to remove them into the agreement of sale.

15. **a.** A real estate owner has the inherent right to exclude others from the property, although this right is not absolute. An adjacent property owner may have an easement right to use the property.

16. **c.** An *emblement* or *trade fixture* is a tangible item on the property. The *deed* is a document that transfers title.

17. **b.** Personal property can be transported even though it can be large and antique.

18. **a.** The term *mobile home* was phased out with the passage of The National Manufactured Housing Construction and Safety Standards Act of 1976 when manufactured homes became federally regulated.

19. **d.** The *intent* of the person who installed the item is the most important test of whether the item is a fixture.

20. **d.** Because the rose bush is a perennial shrub, it is considered real estate.

REAL PROPERTY OR PERSONAL PROPERTY?

Property Description	Type of Property		Fixture	Trade Fixture
	Real	Personal		
1. Sidewalks and sewers in a subdivision	✓			
2. Bushes surrounding a residence	✓			
3. Wheat or corn crops on a farm		✓		
4. Kitchen sink installed in a home	✓		✓	
5. Booths in a restaurant installed by tenant		✓		✓
6. Curtains installed by a tenant		✓		
7. Pumps installed by a gas station tenant		✓		✓
8. Water well pump installed by the landowner	✓		✓	
9. Crystal chandelier hung from the ceiling	✓		✓	
10. 80-gallon water heater with fiberglass insulating jacket	✓		✓	

3

Concepts of Home Ownership

BEFORE YOU START...

After completing Chapter 3 of the textbook, you should be able to answer the following "learning assessment" questions. If you are able to answer these questions, then you are ready to move ahead with this chapter of the *Study Guide!* If, however, you are having some difficulty answering any of these learning assessment questions, we advise you to reread key sections of the textbook before attempting to answer the questions in this chapter of the *Study Guide*.

■ Can you describe the types of housing referred to in the chapter?

■ Are you able to itemize the factors that influence home ownership and identify the tax benefits of home ownership?

■ What do the words *capital gain* and *equity* mean when talking about real property ownership?

■ Do you know about the protections offered by homeowners' insurance?

■ Why was the Federal Flood Insurance Program established and how does this program apply to your geographical area?

MATCHING   *Write the letter of the matching term on the appropriate line.*

a. *apartment complex*	**1.** ____ A group of lowrise or highrise rental residences that may include parking, security, etc.
b. *actual cash value*	**2.** ____ A multiunit residential building owned by a corporation and operated on behalf of stockholder-tenants who hold proprietary leases
c. *coinsurance*	**3.** ____ A package insurance policy against loss due to fire, theft, and liability
d. *planned unit development*	**4.** ____ Cost of repairing damaged property without deduction for depreciation or annual wear and tear
e. *cooperative*	**5.** ____ A multiunit development in which owners own their units separately and share ownership of common facilities
f. *mixed-use development*	**6.** ____ A merger of diverse land uses into a subdivision or development
g. *condominium*	**7.** ____ Interest or value an owner has in property over and above any indebtedness on that property
h. *replacement cost*	**8.** ____ Clause in an insurance policy that requires the property to be insured for at least 80 percent of its replacement cost
i. *broker*	**9.** ____ In insurance, replacement value minus depreciation
j. *homeowner's insurance*	**10.** ____ Highrise development that combines commercial and residential uses in a single structure

TRUE OR FALSE   *Circle the correct answer.*

1. T F One way that some lenders evaluate whether a prospective buyer can afford a home is by setting a limit on PITI of 28 percent of gross monthly income, and on total debt payments of 36 percent of gross monthly income.

2. T F When lenders evaluate whether or not a prospective buyer can afford a home, expenses such as utilities and routine medical care are excluded from the calculation of debt payments.

3. T F A *cooperative* is a form of residential ownership in which residents share ownership of common areas while owning their own units individually.

4. T F A *planned unit development* is a type of property in which warehouses, factories, office buildings, hotels, and other structures have been converted to residential use.

5. T F Single taxpayers are allowed to exclude $250,000 from capital gains tax for profits on the sale of a principal residence.

6. T F A taxpayer can use the exclusion from capital gains tax for profits on the sale of a principal residence only once in a lifetime.

TRUE OR FALSE *(continued)*

7. T F First-time homebuyers can withdraw up to $10,000 (for a down payment) from their tax-deferred IRAs without a tax penalty.

8. T F Under most homeowners' insurance policies, the insured is usually required to maintain insurance equal to at least 41 percent of the replacement cost of the dwelling, including the price of the land.

9. T F If a borrower's property is located in a designated flood area, there are no exemptions from the flood insurance requirement under the National Flood Insurance Act.

10. T F Equity represents the *paid-off* share of a property, held free of any mortgage.

CHECK THE ADS

On the numbered lines below write the type of housing indicated by each ad.

Good view, quiet, roof new, garage, and security, furniture for sale. Easily refinanced if wish. $286,000 .
Call 773-555-5873

1 HERE'S A TIP—BUY STOCK IN YOUR HOME

Select units are now available in Gleason Tower: Lavish 4 & 5-bedroom apartments with all the extras! Approved buyers become stockholders in Gleason Tower Corp. From $260,000.
Call 312-555-9887

OPEN HOUSE 1-3
6033 OAK HILLS DR
Executive 2 story townhouse. 3 bed, 4 bath, 2 car, appliances free! Other features include: rec room with wetbar, open kitchen with appliances, great room with fireplace, walk out to heated swimming pool, convenient to I-80. $280's. R.E.G. 815-555-2600, Pennie Long, 815-555-0123. Do not miss out, come by TODAY!

OPEN SUN 1-4
10728 BERRY PLAZA
By owner. Applewood Townhomes. Huge beautiful townhome, 1504

pool. Near park, tennis court, schools location in the west.

2 CLOCK TOWER LOFTS

The old Mennsen-Hart Watch Factory is now 20 fabulous luxury lofts above the exclusive Watchmaker Mall! Studios, 1&2 BR; security. From $1,900/mo.
773-555-5678

WILLOW WOOD CONDO
12889 Burdette Circle Wonderful condition, 2 bedrooms, 2 baths, 2 car garage. Sits on cul-de-sac. Only $189,900.
Hurry—708-555-3241

6 1275 OAKVIEW TERRACE

3 bedroom, 2 bath unit; dining room, pool, 24-hour doorman. Great downtown location close to subway and bus routes. $275,000 Monthly assessment only $880.
312-555-7890

Cabin Rental by day or week. **5** Near Fort Robinson, Wisconsin, along the Scenic Fox River. Fishing and hiking. No Pets. Call 608-555-3826

LOOKING FOR A QUALITY TOWN HOME?

both only 3 minutes from train station and mall. Call Jeff 630-555-2837

Love where you work:

LOGAN VILLAGE

This quiet, tree-lined new community features lots of open space. Shops, schools and recreation: Logan village has it all! Townhomes start in the mid-180s; residences from $235,000.
773-555-0372

Elkhorn North   212
21586 Arabian Rd. By owner, 3 bed, 2 bath, 2 car garage. Elkhorn School District. See for yourself, (No Brokers please). 312-555-7864 leave message.

HICKORY HILLS
VILLAGE

2 bedroom, 2 bath unit with balcony. Utilities included. No pets. Pool, tennis, golf and health club. Located on private forest preserve. $1,900 per month; available May 1st.

E-Z access to all amenities, 4BR, 2.5BA, office, full bsmt, all appliances stay, motiv seller, a must see $380,000. 630-555-4736.

3 AURORA FSBO. OAKHURST OPEN SAT/SUN 1-4 2331 Waterbury Cir. Naper Dist 204 schools. 4BR, w/1st floor den. Gorgeous traditional w/ cherry kit & hwd floors. Brick FP, crown moldings, custom ceilings, finished bsmt. Fully landscaped. Located on quiet circle on oversized lot. 630-555-3456

4 THE SKY IS YOUR LIMIT

Fabulous downtown building offers stunning views super amenities, 5 world-class restaurants, great shopping and lifestyle services under one 85th floor rooftop garden. Residences start on the 62nd floor Priced from mid- 900's.
Call 312-555-9275

1. _____

2. _____

3. _____

4. _____

5. _____

6. _____

MULTIPLE CHOICE   *Circle a, b, c, or d.*

1. What is equity?
   a. Profit realized from the sale or exchange of real property
   b. Total amount of principal and interest plus tax and insurance
   c. Difference between the amount owed on a mortgage and the property's market value
   d. Amount of gain that may be deferred for income tax purposes

2. Which of the following may be deducted from a homebuyer's gross income for income tax purposes?
   a. Appraisal fee
   b. Mortgage insurance premiums
   c. VA funding fees
   d. Loan discount points

3. Kent's homeowners' insurance policy contains a coinsurance provision; the house is insured for replacement cost. If Kent's home burns down, which of the following statements is *TRUE?*
   a. Kent's claim will be settled for the actual cash value of the damage.
   b. Kent's claim will be prorated by dividing the percentage of replacement cost by the minimum coverage requirement.
   c. Kent may make a claim for the full cost of the repair without deduction for depreciation.
   d. Kent may make a claim for the depreciated value of the damage.

4. Mr. and Mrs. Jones purchased their home in the year 2000 for $250,000. Now, they are being transferred to a new city and must sell their home, currently valued at $400,000. They are 52 and 53 years old respectively and are concerned about paying capital gains on their apparent profit of $150,000. Which of the following statements is important to them?
   a. No taxes are due because they have lived there for the required time period and the gain is under the allowed amount.
   b. There is no problem as long as they purchase a new home for $400,000 or more within the next 24 months.
   c. They will have to pay taxes on their gain because the amount is more than the excluded amount.
   d. They will have to pay taxes on the amount of the gain if they decide to rent rather than buy a new home.

5. A highrise building that includes office space, stores, and residential units is an example of a
   a. loft building.
   b. master planned community.
   c. planned unit development.
   d. mixed-use development.

6. Randy, a single person, was born on July 10, 1949, and has lived in the same house for the past four years. When Randy sells the house on July 12, 2006, how will taxes be determined on any gain from the sale of the home?
   a. The gain will be taxed at a lower rate because of Randy's age.
   b. Taxes will need to be paid because Randy has lived in the house for less than the required time period.
   c. The gain is excluded from taxation if it is less than $250,000.
   d. The gain is excluded from income taxation up to $125,000 at most because of Randy's age and time-in-residence.

MULTIPLE CHOICE (continued)

7. All of the following are examples of items that a monthly condominium assessment would cover *EXCEPT*
   a. real estate taxes on individual units.
   b. management fees.
   c. maintenance of building exteriors.
   d. maintenance of common facilities.

8. Maria's house is constructed so that the floor of her home is built several inches above the 100-year flood mark. If Maria applies for a federally related mortgage loan, how will Maria's mortgage lender apply flood insurance rules?
   a. It may exempt Maria's house from the flood insurance requirement.
   b. It must require flood insurance.
   c. It is prohibited by federal law from requiring flood insurance.
   d. It may invoke the National Flood Insurance Act for properties lying inside, or within 500 feet of, a designated flood-prone area.

9. Ben, a prospective buyer, wants to purchase a house. His gross monthly income is $6,500. Ben wants to estimate how much he can reasonably afford to pay for a monthly PITI payment. What is the maximum monthly PITI payment that Ben can afford based on the past *rule* for this calculation?
   a. $1,635
   b. $1,775
   c. $1,820
   d. $2,340

10. All of the following expenses may be deducted from a homeowner's gross income for income tax purposes *EXCEPT*
    a. loan-repayment penalties.
    b. loan discount points.
    c. interest paid on overdue real estate taxes.
    d. real estate taxes.

11. A married couple is planning to purchase a house. She earns $45,000 and he earns $37,500 per year. Their college loan payments total $350 per month and a car payment is $375 per month. Using the old *rules* for calculating maximum monthly debt payment and PITI, what is the maximum amount of PITI they estimate they can afford?
    a. $1,750
    b. $1,925
    c. $2,475
    d. $2,818

12. The buyers just paid $465,000 for their new home. The lot is valued at $100,000 and the mortgage loan is $410,000. How much equity do they have in this home?
    a. $35,000
    b. $55,000
    c. $310,000
    d. $365,000

13. A broad-form homeowners' insurance policy generally covers all of the following *EXCEPT*
    a. frozen pipes.
    b. vandalism.
    c. flooding.
    d. theft.

14. The reason that homeowners buy homeowners' insurance is to
    a. be reimbursed for financial losses suffered because of events such as fire or theft.
    b. pay for replacing the furnace or roof because of age.
    c. be reimbursed for monetary losses due to a defect in the title.
    d. protect the homeowner for accidents on other people's property.

15. Which of the following is a characteristic of penalty-free IRA withdrawals for first-time homebuyers?
    a. The limit on the withdrawn amount is $15,000.
    b. The withdrawn amount must be spent entirely within 120 days on a down payment.
    c. The buyer must be no more than 30 years old.
    d. The withdrawn amount is not subject to income tax.

MULTIPLE CHOICE   *(continued)*

16. People buy homes for all of the following reasons *EXCEPT*

    a. homes can appreciate in value.

    b. they can provide federal income tax deductions.

    c. home ownership gives a sense of belonging to the community.

    d. home ownership usually gives residents more leisure time than renting provides.

17. Retirement communities are often developed as

    a. converted-use properties.

    b. planned unit developments.

    c. time-shares.

    d. industrial complexes.

18. In addition to examining the financial ability of applicants to handle loan payments, lenders also assign a key role in the loan decision to

    a. credit scores.

    b. the age of the home.

    c. whether the borrower is under age 55.

    d. the size of the property.

19. The decision to rent or buy a home is affected by all of the following factors *EXCEPT*

    a. mortgage interest rates.

    b. tax consequences.

    c. how long the person wants to live in a certain area.

    d. convenience of shopping.

20. A characteristic of both planned unit developments and condominiums is

    a. title to the units is held by a corporation.

    b. an association that collects fees from owners and maintains common areas.

    c. small lot sizes and street areas.

    d. conversion of a property from a prior use, such as a factory or warehouse, to residential use.

21. To insure against losses due to visitor injuries within the owner's unit, condominium owners typically obtain a policy that includes

    a. a basic form type of homeowners' insurance.

    b. a broad form type of homeowners' insurance.

    c. liability insurance.

    d. errors and omissions insurance.

22. A database of consumer claim history that makes it possible for insurance companies to access prior claim information is called the

    a. National and Fiduciary Insurance Program (NFIP)

    b. Comprehensive Loss and Underwriting Exchange (CLUE).

    c. Database of Prior Insurance Claims (DBPI).

    d. Fannie Mae Databank (FMD).

23. Why should agents note whether a property for sale is located on a flood plain?

    a. Buyers have lower expenses for insurance.

    b. Higher transfer fees are required to transfer title to the property.

    c. The federal government may require a house to be removed from the property.

    d. Property value is negatively affected.

24. A large tree on Scott's property died and slowly rotted. Eventually, a large branch fell off from its own weight and damaged the back porch roof. What type of homeowners' insurance policy would cover this damage?

    a. Liability insurance

    b. Basic-form policy

    c. Broad-form policy

    d. Emblements insurance

25. How is flood insurance coverage determined?

    a. It covers either the property value or mortgage loan amount (up to a limit).

    b. It is calculated as 80% of the property value.

    c. It is based on a table of standard values for properties in the flood-prone area.

    d. It depends on the income level of the property owners.

ANSWER KEY

Key Term Matching

1. a   **2.** e   **3.** j   **4.** i   **5.** g   **6.** d   **7.** h   **8.** c
9. b   **10.** f

True or False

1. True

2. True

3. False. A *condominium* is a form of residential ownership in which residents share ownership of common areas while owning their own units individually.

4. False. Warehouses, factories, office buildings, hotels, and other structures that have been remodeled to residential use are referred to as *converted use properties*.

5. True

6. False. The exemption may be used repeatedly, so long as the homeowners own and occupy the property as their primary residence for at least two of the past five years.

7. True

8. False. Under most homeowners' insurance policies, the insured is usually required to maintain insurance equal to at least 80 percent of the replacement cost of the dwelling, excluding the price of the land.

9. False. If a borrower's property is located in a designated flood area, it may be exempt from the National Flood Insurance Act's flood insurance requirement. However, the borrower needs to produce a survey showing that the lowest part of the structure is above the 100-year flood mark.

10. True

Check the Ads

1. cooperative

2. converted use

3. planned unit development

4. mixed-use development

5. apartment complex

6. condominium

Multiple Choice

1. **c.** *Equity* is the difference between market value and the money owed.

2. **d.** Appraisal fees, mortgage insurance premiums, and VA funding fees are not considered deductible interest, but they can be considered part of the acquisition cost and figured into the cost basis.

3. **c.** Because Kent has insured the property for replacement value and has a coinsurance clause, Kent may make a claim for the full cost of replacement without deduction for depreciation.

4. **a.** Because Mr. and Mrs. Jones have lived in the home at least two of the past five years and their capital gain is less than $500,000, they will not have to pay any capital gains tax.

5. **d.** A *planned unit-development* is also referred to as a *master plan community*. A loft building is a less-than-complete answer. A mixed-use development is usually a highrise offering a mixture of uses.

6. **c.** Under the Tax Reform Act of 1997, Randy will not have to pay any tax because he has lived there at least two of the past five years and the gain is less than $250,000.

7. **a.** Monthly assessments cover costs that all unit owners share as a group, such as management fees and maintenance of building exteriors and common facilities.

8. **a.** Because the lowest level is several inches above the 100-year flood mark, the owner may not be required to buy flood insurance.

9. **c.** Ben can afford a PITI payment of $1,820: $6,500 × 28% = $1,820.

10. **c.** Interest paid on overdue taxes may not be deducted from taxable income.

11. a. Five steps: (1) Calculate their total monthly income: $45,000 + $37,500 = $82,500 annual ÷ 12 = $6,875 monthly income. (2) Now, apply the old *rule* for maximum PITI: $6,875 × 28% = $1,925. (3) Then, apply the old *rule* for maximum total debt payments, including PITI: $6,875 × 36% = $2,475. (4) Then, subtract the debt payments to determine the estimated maximum PITI: $2,475 − $350 − $375 = $1,750. Because of the debts, they decide they are more likely to qualify for the lower amount.

12. b. The buyers have $55,000 in equity: $465,000 − $410,000 = $55,000.

13. c. Most homeowner's insurance policies cover many perils, but not flooding. Flood insurance generally must be purchased separately.

14. a. Homeowner's insurance is purchased to protect the property owner from financial losses caused by events such as fire, theft, or vandalism. It does not pay for routine maintenance, title defects, or accidents on other people's property.

15. b. The limit is $10,000, there is no age restriction, and the withdrawn amount is subject to income tax.

16. d. People buy homes for financial reasons, such as appreciation and federal tax deductions. They also buy them for psychological reasons such as a sense of belonging to the community. However, home ownership may require more time for management and maintenance than renting.

17. b. Converted-use properties are unlikely to be easily changed over to meet needs of retired individuals. Time-share ownership is not a long-term type of residential ownership. Industrial complexes are not residential in nature.

18. a. Condition, not age, is an important factor about the home. Lenders need to be concerned about age discrimination in terms of the borrower. The borrower's credit score is a key factor in whether a loan meets the standards for approval.

19. d. Mortgage interest rates affect whether a person can afford to buy a home. A short length of residence can negatively affect the tax benefits of home ownership. Shopping convenience is not usually affected by whether residential units are rented or owned.

20. b. Condominium units and PUD properties are individually owned. Lot size may not apply to a condominium if the development is set up as a multifloor apartment building. PUDs are usually developed as new construction.

21. c. Basic and broad forms of homeowners' insurance cover risk factors that don't apply to many individual condominium units, such as wind damage to a roof that is a common element.

22. b. CLUE contains five years of personal property claim history.

23. d. Because buyers are usually required to obtain flood insurance, costs are higher for buyers. Transfer fees are not increased.

24. c. A *broad-form* policy covers damage from falling objects such as a tree branch. *Basic-form* and *liability* insurance do not.

25. a. Policies are often purchased from a licensed property insurance broker or the National Flood Insurance Program and are written for the property value or mortgage loan amount, subject to the maximum limits available.

Agency

BEFORE YOU START...

After completing Chapter 4 of the textbook, you should be able to answer the following "learning assessment" questions. If you are able to answer these questions, then you are ready to move ahead with this chapter of the *Study Guide!* If, however, you are having some difficulty answering any of these learning assessment questions, we advise you to reread key sections of the textbook before attempting to answer the questions in this chapter of the *Study Guide*.

- Are you able to define the following terms: *agency, agent, principal, fiduciary, client,* and *customer.*

- Can you describe real estate agency and the meaning of fiduciary relationships?

- Are you able to define the different types of agency relationships?

- Do you know how agency relationships are created and terminated in the practice of real estate?

- How would you describe the fiduciary duties to the principal?

- Can you explain the differences between client-level and customer-level services as they relate to the seller and the buyer?

MATCHING A   *Write the letter of the matching term on the appropriate line.*

a. *nonagent*

b. *customer*

c. *fiduciary relationship*

d. *special agent*

e. *agent*

f. *general agent*

g. *implied agency*

h. *law of agency*

i. *puffing*

j. *principal*

1. _____ The basic framework that governs the legal responsibilities of an agent to a principal

2. _____ An agent who is authorized to represent the principal in one specific act or business transaction, under detailed instructions

3. _____ The individual who is authorized and consents to represent the interests of another person

4. _____ The establishment of an agency relationship as the result of the actions of the parties that indicate mutual consent

5. _____ The individual who hires and delegates to the agent the responsibility of representing his or her interests

6. _____ An affiliation of trust and confidence as between a principal and an agent

7. _____ Nonfraudulent exaggeration of a property's benefits or features

8. _____ An agent authorized to represent the principal in a broad range of matters related to a specific business or activity

9. _____ In a real estate agency relationship, the third party (or nonrepresented consumer) who receives some level of service and who is entitled to honesty and fair dealing

10. _____ An intermediary between a buyer and seller who assists both parties with a transaction, but who represents neither party

TRUE OR FALSE   *Circle the correct answer.*

1. T F The *fiduciary* is the individual who hires and delegates to the agent the responsibility of representing his or her other interests.

2. T F Examples of nonagents are facilitators, transactional brokers, transactional coordinators, and contract brokers.

3. T F An agent works with a client and for the customer.

4. T F Under the common law of agency, the agent owes his or her principal the six duties: care, obedience, loyalty, disclosure, accounting, and confidentiality, remembered by the acronym COLD AC.

5. T F The common law fiduciary duty of *obedience* obligates the agent to obey all the principal's instructions.

6. T F The common law duty of *loyalty* requires that an agent avoid disclosing material facts about the condition of the property.

7. T F The source of compensation is the key determining factor in whether or not an agency relationship exists.

8. T F Agents who work for a broker are considered to be subagents of the client.

TRUE OR FALSE *(continued)*

9. T F A real estate broker is usually the general agent of a buyer or seller.

10. T F The only difference between a buyer's agent and a seller's agent is that a buyer's agent owes the principal different fiduciary duties.

11. T F In a *dual agency* relationship, the agent represents two principals in the same transaction.

12. T F A dual agency relationship is legal if either the buyer or the seller consents to the dual representation.

13. T F An agent owes a customer the duties of reasonable care and skill, honest and fair dealing, and disclosure of known facts.

14. T F A negligent misrepresentation occurs when the broker makes a statement such as "This is the best-built house I've ever seen."

15. T F When a property has a hidden structural defect that could not be discovered by ordinary inspection, it is referred to as a *stigmatized property*.

MATCHING B *Write the letter of the matching term on the appropriate line.*

a. *disclosed dual agency*

b. *common law agent duties*

c. *buyers' agents*

d. *client*

e. *undisclosed dual agency*

f. *latent defect*

g. *stigmatized property*

h. *subagent*

i. *express agreement*

j. *errors and omissions insurance*

1. _____ An agency relationship in which the agent represents two principals simultaneously, without their knowledge or permission

2. _____ A contract in which the parties formally state their intention to establish an agency relationship

3. _____ Real estate licensees who represent buyers exclusively

4. _____ Type of insurance that covers liability for mistakes and negligence in the usual activities of a real estate office.

5. _____ A property that has been branded as undesirable because of the events that occurred in or near it

6. _____ The principal in a real estate agency relationship

7. _____ An agency relationship in which the agent represents two principals simultaneously, with their knowledge or permission

8. _____ Care, obedience, accounting, loyalty, and disclosure

9. _____ The party to whom an agent delegates some of his or her authority

10. _____ A hidden structural problem that would not be discovered by ordinary inspection

MULTIPLE CHOICE   *Circle a, b, c, or d.*

1. An individual who is authorized and consents to represent the interests of another person is a(n)

   a. customer.   c. agent.

   b. principal.   d. facilitator.

2. Broker Neil represents Carla but is currently working with Kristin to find a home. Assuming that no statute has replaced the traditional common law, which of the following correctly identifies the parties in this relationship?

   a. Neil is Kristin's agent; Carla is Neil's client.

   b. Kristin is Neil's client; Carla is Neil's principal.

   c. Carla is Neil's customer; Kristin is Neil's client.

   d. Neil is Carla's agent; Kristin is Neil's customer.

3. The agent's obligation to use his or her skill and expertise on behalf of the principal arises under which of the common-law duties?

   a. Care   c. Loyalty

   b. Obedience   d. Disclosure

4. An agent representing the seller has a duty to disclose to his or her principal all of the following *EXCEPT* the

   a. offers that are ridiculously low.

   b. buyer's financial ability to offer a higher price.

   c. agent's advertising budget.

   d. buyer's intention to resell the property for a profit.

5. Juan, a broker, has an agency agreement to represent the seller, Mel, in the sale of Grandview Mansion. The agreement's expiration date is June 10. On May 5, Grandview Mansion is struck by lightning and burns to the ground. Mel, overwhelmed by grief, dies. Based on these facts, which of the following is *TRUE*?

   a. The agency agreement was terminated by the fire, although Mel's death also would have done so.

   b. The agency agreement was not terminated until Mel's death on June 11.

   c. If Grandview Mansion had not been destroyed by the fire, Mel's death would not have terminated the agreement; Juan would become the broker for Mel's estate.

   d. Only the mutual agreement of the parties can terminate a valid agency agreement before its expiration date.

6. A person who is designated by the principal in a broad range of matters related to a particular transaction or activity is a

   a. subagent.   c. designated agent.

   b. special agent.   d. general agent.

MULTIPLE CHOICE   *(continued)*

7. Zeporah, a real estate broker, signed an agency agreement with a seller, Val. The asking price for Val's house was $799,000. A few days later, Zeporah met Seth at a charity dinner. Seth was interested in buying a home in the $780,000 to $810,000 price range. Zeporah agreed to help Seth locate such a property and to represent Seth in negotiating a favorable purchase price. Based on these facts, which of the following statements is *TRUE*?

   a. Zeporah's relationships and Seth and Val are separate issues, and no dual agency question arises.

   b. Val is Zeporah's client, and Seth is Zeporah's customer; there is no dual agency problem.

   c. Zeporah has created a potential undisclosed dual agency problem and should disclose the relationships to both parties before showing Val's home to Seth.

   d. Zeporah has created a dual agency problem and should immediately terminate the agreement with either Val or Seth.

8. Broker Tom is showing a house to a prospective buyer. Tom points out the "rustic charm" of the sagging front porch and refers to a weed-choked backyard as a "delightful garden." Tom is engaging in which of the following?

   a. Intentional misrepresentation

   b. Negligent misrepresentations

   c. Puffing

   d. Fraud

9. A house built over a ditch covered with decaying timber, or a house with ceilings that are improperly attached to the support beams are examples of

   a. stigmatized properties.

   b. environmental hazards.

   c. latent defects.

   d. conditions that need not be disclosed.

10. The seller's agent has certain duties to the client-principal. All of the following are duties of the principal *EXCEPT*

    a. cooperation.   c. marketing.

    b. compensation.   d. disclosure.

11. Every state has mandatory agency disclosure laws that stipulate

    a. how an implied agency may occur.

    b. when, how, and to whom licensees must reveal for whom they provide client-based services.

    c. restrictions on disclosure of confidential information.

    d. how a customer is differentiated from a client.

12. Who is the agent's principal?

    a. Seller

    b. Buyer

    c. Person who pays the commission

    d. Whoever hired the agent

13. The broker was hired to represent the seller, to market the property, and to solicit offers to purchase. The broker is called a

    a. general agent.   c. subagent.

    b. special agent.   d. nonagent.

14. The house was the scene of a drug arrest and a violent murder last year. When it was put on the market, many people considered it to be a

    a. latent property.

    b. stigmatized property.

    c. damaged property.

    d. property with a material defect.

MULTIPLE CHOICE   *(continued)*

15. All of the following will terminate an agency relationship *EXCEPT*

    a. death of either party.

    b. destruction of the property.

    c. offer made on the property.

    d. expiration of the agreement.

16. What is a seller's agent required to disclose to prospective buyers about material defects in the property?

    a. Only information about material defects the seller has given to the agent.

    b. Only information about material defects that the agent has personally observed.

    c. Both information the seller has given to the agent and material defects that the agent has personally observed.

    d. All information about material defects that the agent knows or should know.

17. Which of the following statements could be negligent misrepresentation?

    a. "The uneven floors just mean that the building dates to colonial times."

    b. "I think these low doorways are a charming part of the Cape Cod style."

    c. "The simple design is uncluttered and can give you many possibilities for decor."

    d. "The size of the bedrooms makes them wonderfully cozy and perfect for your children."

18. The seller's agent is aware of but does not disclose to a buyer that a new landfill has been approved for development on the adjacent property. This is an example of

    a. negligent misrepresentation.

    b. a latent defect.

    c. fraudulent misrepresentation.

    d. unnecessary disclosure.

19. A key element of an agent's fiduciary responsibility of loyalty is to

    a. report the status of all funds received from or on behalf of the principal.

    b. keep the principal's personal affairs confidential.

    c. obey the principal's instructions in accordance with the contract.

    d. reveal relevant information or material facts.

20. When a broker places trust funds of others into the company's operating account and then withdraws funds for the firm's use, what illegal practice has taken place?

    a. Escrowing

    b. DBA accounting

    c. Conversion

    d. Asset-liability management

FILL-IN-THE-BLANK *Select the word or words that best complete the following statements:*

accounting

buyer's agent

designated agent

fraud

implied agreement

listing agreement

loyalty

*negligent
misrepresentation*

obedience

operation of law

seller disclaimer

stigmatized property

1. The written employment contract that establishes the agency relationship between the seller and the broker is called a(n) _____.

2. The requirement that brokers promptly deposit funds entrusted to the broker in a special trust account is an example of how brokers fulfill the fiduciary duty of _____.

3. Even when a property is sold *as is* or with a(n) _____, the seller must have electrical, plumbing, and mechanical systems in working order unless the seller crosses out any printed provisions about these in the contract.

4. Although not available in all states, when a person is authorized by the broker to act as the agent of a specific principal-seller, this agent is called a(n) _____.

5. The intentional misrepresentation of a material fact in such a way as to harm or take advantage of another person is called _____ _____.

6. Discovery of a methamphetamine lab on a property can result in the property being regarded as a(n) _____.

7. Josh tells Sue, a real estate broker, that he has been thinking about selling his condominium. Sue contacts several buyers that she knows are looking for a condominium, and one makes an offer for the property. Sue presents the offer to Josh, and he accepts it. Although no documents were signed by Josh, an agency may have been created by _____.

8. If a buyer's agent reveals to the seller that the buyer must move within one month, this action would violate the agent's fiduciary duty of _____ to the buyer.

9. An agent who has a buyer as principal and the seller as a customer is called a(n) _____.

10. An agency is terminated by _____ when a principal declares bankruptcy and property title transfers to a court-appointed receiver.

ANSWER KEY

Key Term Matching (A)

1. h **2.** d **3.** e **4.** g **5.** j **6.** c **7.** i **8.** f
9. b **10.** a

True or False

1. **False.** The *principal* is the individual who hires and delegates to the agent the responsibility of representing his or her other interests.

2. **True**

3. **False.** An agent works *for* the client and *with* the customer. The client is the principal.

4. **True**

5. **False.** The common law fiduciary duty of *obedience* obligates the agent to obey all the principal's *lawful and ethical* instructions.

6. **False.** The common law duty of *loyalty* requires that an agent place the principal's interests above all others. However, the law of most states requires that the agent disclose material facts about the condition of the property.

7. **False.** The source of compensation is not the key determining factor in whether or not an agency relationship exists. An agent's commission may be paid, in whole or in part, by someone other than the agent's client-principal. Moreover, an agency can exist even when no fee is involved.

8. **True**

9. **False.** A real estate broker is usually the *special agent* of a buyer or seller.

10. **False.** A buyer's agent owes his or her principal the same fiduciary duties as a seller's agent owes a seller.

11. **True**

12. **False.** When *both* the buyer and the seller consent to it, the laws of some states permit dual representation.

13. **True**

14. **False.** *Puffing* occurs when the broker engages in exaggeration of a property's benefits or features. Brokers need to be careful about statements of fact or opinion. For example, if the broker knew that the seller had superficially patched and painted over serious cracks in the foundation, the broker's statement could then be interpreted as fraud or negligent misrepresentation.

15. **False.** When a property has a hidden structural defect that could not be discovered by ordinary inspection, it is referred to as having a *latent defect*.

Key Term Matching (B)

1. e **2.** i **3.** c **4.** j **5.** g **6.** d **7.** a **8.** b
9. h **10.** f

Multiple Choice

1. **c.** The agent is hired by the principal. The customer or facilitator is a third party.

2. **d.** Watch the terminology: The broker is working *for* (representing) Carla and is working *with* Kristin (a customer) to find a home.

3. **a.** *Care* requires skill and expertise; *obedience* requires following lawful instructions; *loyalty* is putting the client's interests above the agent's; and *disclosure* refers to material defects of the property.

4. **c.** The seller's (special) agent must present all offers and any facts about the buyers that would assist the seller in making a decision, including the fact that the buyer intends to resell the property.

5. **a.** Either destruction of the property or death of either party are a reason for termination of the agency agreement.

6. **d.** A *special agent* is given limited authority for a limited time. A *general agent* is given broad authority in a specific circumstance. A *subagent* is appointed by the agent.

7. **c.** Zeporah is representing the seller and now is at least implying that Zeporah will represent the buyer in locating a property: hence two clients. If Zeporah intends to show Val's property, Zeporah must disclose her relationship with both clients, gain their agreement to a dual agency, and only then proceed.

8. **c.** Because any prudent buyer can see the sagging porch and weed-choked garden, these are *puffing* statements. Agents must take care that they do not make statements in such a way as to harm the buyer or take advantage of the buyer's ignorance, which would constitute *fraud*.

9. **c.** Problems with the property that cannot be observed by the normal person are called *latent defects*.

10. **c.** Marketing is the agent's responsibility. The principal who hired the agent is responsible for cooperating with the agent, disclosing material defects, and compensating the agent.

11. **b.** In addition, state laws may require a particular type of written form be used and may require that all agency alternatives be explained.

12. **d.** The most complete answer is "whoever hired the agent." That could be either the buyer or the seller, but who pays the compensation is not the determining factor.

13. **b.** A *special agent* is one who is hired for a limited time and given limited authority. A broker taking a listing is generally a special agent.

14. **b.** Presuming that the property is physically intact, the drug arrest and violent murder may create psychological reactions to the property, rendering it *stigmatized*.

15. **c.** An offer on the property does not terminate the agency relationship, but the death of either party, destruction of the property, or expiration of the term will.

16. **d.** Agents are responsible for disclosing information they are told or discover on their own, plus information they should have known.

17. **a.** Presenting an opinion is acceptable as long as it is not presented as a fact. Uneven floors could mean a latent defect such as rotten supports.

18. **c.** This is an example of misleading a party by withholding a material fact. It is deliberate misrepresentation by silence. The proposed landfill adjacent to the property is not a latent defect because it does not threaten structural soundness or personal safety.

19. **b.** Reporting the status of funds is an accounting responsibility. Obeying the principal's instructions relates to obedience. Revealing relevant information relates to the responsibility of disclosure.

20. **c.** Both commingling the funds and the practice of conversion are illegal.

Fill-in-the-Blank

1. The written employment contract that establishes the agency relationship between the seller and the broker is called a *listing agreement*.

2. The requirement that brokers promptly deposit funds entrusted to the broker in a special trust account is an example of how brokers fulfill the fiduciary duty of *accounting*.

3. Even when a property is sold *as is* or with a *seller disclaimer*, the seller must have electrical, plumbing, and mechanical systems in working order unless the seller crosses out any printed provisions about these in the contract.

4. Although not available in all states, when a person is authorized by the broker to act as the agent of a specific principal-seller, this agent is called a *designated agent*.

5. The intentional misrepresentation of a material fact in such a way as to harm or take advantage of another person is called *fraud*.

6. Discovery of a methamphetamine lab on a property can result in the property being regarded as a *stigmatized property*.

7. Josh tells Sue, a real estate broker, that he has been thinking about selling his condominium. Sue contacts several buyers that she knows are looking for a condominium, and one makes an offer for the property. Sue presents the offer to Josh, and he accepts it. Although no documents were signed by Josh, an agency may have been created by *implied agreement*.

8. If a buyer's agent reveals to the seller that the buyer must move within one month, this action would violate the agent's fiduciary duty of *loyalty* to the buyer.

9. An agent who has a buyer as principal and the seller as a customer is called a *buyer's agent*.

10. An agency is terminated by *operation of law* when a principal declares bankruptcy and property title transfers to a court-appointed receiver.

5

Real Estate Brokerage

After completing Chapter 5 of the textbook, you should be able to answer the following "learning assessment" questions. If you are able to answer these questions, then you are ready to move ahead with this chapter of the *Study Guide!* If, however, you are having some difficulty answering any of these learning assessment questions, we advise you to reread key sections of the textbook before attempting to answer the questions in this chapter of the *Study Guide.*

■ How do you think the role of technologies, personnel, and license laws affect the operation of the real estate business?

■ What do the general term *brokerage* and the specific term *real estate broker* mean to you?

■ Do you know how the broker's and the salesperson's compensations are determined and the forms that such compensations may take?

■ Why do you think antitrust laws were passed; how do they relate to real estate brokerage practices; and what are the penalties for violating them?

■ Are you able to differentiate *employees* from *independent contractors* and explain why the distinction is important under IRS rules?

MATCHING   *Write the letter of the matching term on the appropriate line.*

a. *allocation of markets*

b. *antitrust laws*

c. *caveat emptor*

d. *commission*

e. *salesperson*

f. *brokerage*

g. *independent contractor*

h. *rules and regulations*

i. *employee*

j. *ready, willing, and able buyer*

k. *real estate broker*

l. *procuring cause*

m. *group boycotting*

n. *real estate license laws*

o. *sole proprietorship*

1. _____ The common law doctrine of *let the buyer beware*

2. _____ Statutes enacted by state legislatures to protect the public and ensure a standard of competence in the real estate industry

3. _____ The device by which a state licensing authority defines and enforces the statutory law

4. _____ The business of bringing parties together

5. _____ An individual who is licensed to buy, sell, exchange, or lease property for others, and to charge a fee for those services

6. _____ Company held by a single owner

7. _____ A person who is licensed only to perform real estate activities on behalf of a broker

8. _____ A salesperson whose activities are closely controlled, and who is entitled to benefits, unemployment compensation, and income tax withholding

9. _____ A licensee who works under the terms of a written contract and receives more than 90 percent of his or her income from sales production rather than hours worked

10. _____ A form of compensation computed as a percentage of the total sales price of a property

11. _____ The broker who starts an uninterrupted chain of events that results in the sale of a property

12. _____ A person who is prepared to buy on the seller's terms

13. _____ A conspiracy by two or more businesses against another

14. _____ An illegal division of territories to avoid competition

15. _____ Law that prohibits price fixing and tie-in agreements

TRUE OR FALSE   *Circle the correct answer.*

1. T F Only a few states regulate the activities of real estate brokers and salespeople.

2. T F The purpose of the real estate license laws is to regulate the real estate industry and protect the constitutional rights of property owners.

3. T F A real estate salesperson is licensed to buy, sell, exchange, or lease real property for others, and to charge a fee for those services.

4. T F The Internal Revenue Service has established criteria for determining whether a real estate licensee is classified as an employee or an independent contractor for income tax purposes.

TRUE OR FALSE   *(continued)*

5. T   F   The amount of a broker's compensation is always negotiable.

6. T   F   A real estate salesperson is an individual who is licensed to perform real estate activities on behalf of a licensed broker.

7. T   F   A broker is considered to be the procuring cause of a sale if he or she is present at the time the transaction closes.

8. T   F   Price-fixing, group boycotting, and allocation of markets are three examples of antitrust violations.

9. T   F   The practice of illegally setting standard prices for products or services is referred to as a *tie-in agreement.*

10. T   F   In a civil suit based on an antitrust violation by a real estate licensee, the injured party may recover three times the value of actual damages.

WHO'S WHO?

Based on their statements below, place each speaker's name in the appropriate box of Open Door Realty's organizational chart.

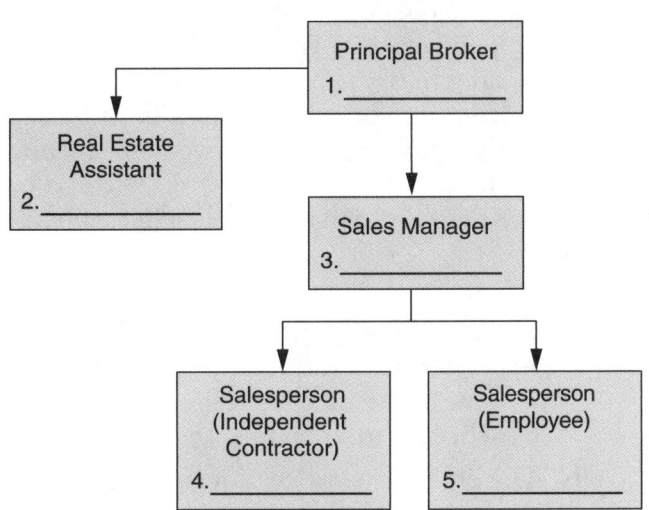

Open Door Realty

Principal Broker
1._____

Real Estate Assistant
2._____

Sales Manager
3._____

Salesperson (Independent Contractor)
4._____

Salesperson (Employee)
5._____

Ron: "I have a real estate license, but my job is limited to marketing and office management activities."

Joyce: "I'm a licensed real estate salesperson. I set my own hours and pay my own taxes."

Elaine: "I am a broker licensed to buy, sell, exchange, or lease real property for a fee. I am responsible for the trust account."

Sandra: "I am licensed to perform real estate activities on behalf of a broker. I have health insurance and a retirement plan."

Dora: "Although I don't have a real estate license, I work closely with the licensees to ensure that the office runs smoothly and transactions go to closing."

MULTIPLE CHOICE   *Circle a, b, c, or d.*

1. Why have real estate license laws been put into effect?

   a. To protect licensees from lawsuits

   b. To protect the public and establish standards of professionalism

   c. To prevent licensees from engaging in profit-making activities

   d. To establish maximum levels of competency and a moral marketplace

2. In real estate, a salesperson is always a(n)

   a. independent contractor.

   b. employee of a licensed broker.

   c. licensee who performs real estate activities on behalf of a broker.

   d. combination office manager, marketer, and organizer with a fundamental understanding of the real estate industry, who may or may not be licensed.

3. All of the following are the indicators of independent contractor status used by the Internal Revenue Service *EXCEPT*

   a. a current real estate license.

   b. specific hours stated in a written agreement.

   c. a written agreement that specifies that the individual will not be treated as an employee for tax purposes.

   d. 90% or more of the individual's income is based on sales production rather than hours worked.

4. The broker who owns Happy Homes Realty does not permit his salespeople to charge less than an 8 percent commission in any transaction. After reading a newspaper article about Happy Homes' policies, the broker of Open Door Homefinders decides to adopt the 8 percent minimum, too. Based on these facts, which of the following statements is *TRUE*?

   a. Happy Homes policy is price-fixing and violates the antitrust law.

   b. Although Happy Homes' original policy was legal, Open Door's adoption of the minimum commission may constitute an antitrust violation if both brokers are in the same real estate market.

   c. Both brokers engaged in illegal price-fixing.

   d. Neither broker has committed an antitrust violation.

5. A real estate broker had a listing agreement with a seller that specified a 6 percent commission. The broker showed the home to a prospective buyer. The next day, the buyer called the seller directly and offered to buy the house for 5 percent less than the asking price. The seller agreed to the price and informed the broker in writing that no further brokerage services would be required. The sale went to closing six weeks later. Based on these facts, which of the following statements is *TRUE*?

   a. While the broker was the procuring cause of the sale, the seller properly canceled the contract; without a valid employment agreement in force at the time of closing, the broker is not entitled to a commission.

   b. The broker is entitled to a partial commission, and the buyer is obligated to pay it.

   c. Under the facts as stated, the broker is not the procuring cause of this sale but is still entitled to a commission.

   d. The broker was the procuring cause of the sale and is entitled to the full 6% commission.

MULTIPLE CHOICE   *(continued)*

6. A qualified buyer makes a written offer on a property on March 6 by filling out and signing a sales agreement. Later that day, the seller accepts and signs the agreement, keeping one copy. The broker gives a copy of the signed agreement to the buyer on March 8. The seller's deed is delivered on May 1. The deed is recorded on May 7, and the buyer takes possession on May 15. When is the broker's commission payable if this is a *usual* transaction?

   a. March 8   c. May 7
   b. May 1   d. May 15

7. All of the following are violations of the federal antitrust laws *EXCEPT*

   a. group boycotting.
   b. allocation of customers.
   c. commission splitting.
   d. tie-in agreements.

8. All of the following are ways for the broker to charge for services *EXCEPT*

   a. standard community rate.
   b. flat fees.
   c. hourly rate.
   d. commission based on a percentage of the selling price.

9. What is the main value of a multiple-listing service (MLS)?

   a. Agents do not have to work so hard to locate properties.
   b. It slows down selling activities.
   c. An MLS provides very little cooperation among brokers.
   d. It exposes the property to a greater number of prospective buyers.

10. After license laws are enacted by the legislature, who is responsible for rules and regulations?

    a. Small committee that reports to the legislature
    b. Local REALTOR® association
    c. Licensing authority (division, commission, etc.)
    d. Brokers and salespeople appointed by the governor

11. When communicating with clients or consumers with e-mail, all of the following are examples of professional e-mail etiquette *EXCEPT*

    a. using spell-check.
    b. providing useful information in the subject line.
    c. avoiding sending large attachments.
    d. responding to e-mails within one week.

12. Although state laws vary regarding Internet advertising, which of the following is a typical element of state policy or law?

    a. E-mail sent by a licensee needs to include the licensee's name, office address, broker affiliation, and phone number.
    b. Ads must avoid misleading the potential client or customer.
    c. Real estate professionals are required to disclose only their status as agents or brokers on the home page of a Web site with ads.
    d. It is acceptable for only the salesperson's name (without the broker's name) to be shown in an ad.

13. The broker may still be entitled to a commission in which of the following situations where a pending property sale did *NOT* close?

    a. The buyer wanted to add the kitchen appliances to the sale but the seller refused.
    b. The buyer decided not to buy the property.
    c. The seller changed his or her mind and decided not to sell.
    d. Financing fell through for the buyer.

MULTIPLE CHOICE   *(continued)*

14. An arrangement to sell one product only if the buyer purchases another product as well is called a(n)

    a. tie-in agreement.

    b. fee-for-services.

    c. buydown provision.

    d. allocation of customers.

15. An agreement that a listing broker offers no services other than placing a listing in the MLS is called a(n)

    a. exclusive-brokerage agreement.

    b. full-service listing agreement.

    c. limited-service listing agreement.

    d. dual agency.

16. Even if a consumer has requested placement on the National Do-Not-Call Registry, a real estate professional may call the consumer up to _____ after the consumer's last purchase.

    a. 3 months   c. 12 months

    b. 6 months   d. 18 months

17. The current policy that the National Association of REALTORS® has adopted that allows all MLS members to have equal rights to display MLS data is called the

    a. virtual office Web site.

    b. Internet Listing Display Policy.

    c. Internet Data Exchange.

    d. Open Listing Data Service.

18. An important purpose of the "E-Sign" Act is to

    a. make contracts formed using e-mail have the same legal standing as those on paper.

    b. require stringent security measures for e-mail communication.

    c. prevent notarization of electronically transmitted agreements.

    d. require nonrepudiation of electronic signatures.

19. What is the compensation plan called if a salesperson's commission split increases depending on whether the salesperson achieves higher production goals?

    a. Procuring cause commission

    b. Cooperating broker commission

    c. Graduated commission split

    d. 100% commission plan

20. What is the practice called when a consumer selects specific services to use and only pays the licensee for those services?

    a. Unbundling services

    b. Tie-in agreement

    c. Discounted services

    d. Allocation of markets

MATH PRACTICE   *Circle a, b, c, or d.*

1. Julie listed and sold her property for $325,000. She agreed to pay the listing broker a 7 percent commission. The listing broker offered a listing 40/60 selling split to any cooperating broker who sold the property. How much did Julie have to pay in commission fees?
   a. $9,100
   b. $13,650
   c. $22,750
   d. Not enough information provided

2. The salesperson's agreement with the broker was a 40/60 split with the broker keeping 40 percent of the commission. The seller was charged 5.5 percent. How much did the salesperson receive if she listed and sold a house for $279,500?
   a. $6,150.20   c. $15,372.50
   b. $7,686.25   d. None of the above

3. The broker listed Stephanie's home for $425,000 with a 4 percent commission plus $3,000 for advertising costs. The buyer offered $380,000 and after several counteroffers, finally agreed to $400,000. What was the total cost to the seller?
   a. $16,000   c. $19,000
   b. $18,000   d. $20,000

4. Salespeople in PQR Realty are compensated based on the following formula: 35 percent of the commission earned on any sale, less a $200 per transaction desk rental. Salespeople are responsible for paying 75 percent of all marketing and sales expenses for any property they list, and a $75 per transaction fee to cover the monthly expenses of advertising and marketing PQR's services. If a salesperson sold a house for $500,000, with a 6 percent commission, how much would he or she be paid if the sale incurred $800 in marketing and advertising costs?
   a. $9,625   c. $10,225
   b. $9,700   d. $10,500

5. At Sure Sale Realty, salespeople pay a monthly desk rent of 15 percent of their monthly income. In May, one salesperson receives 5 percent on a $560,000 sale, 6 percent on a $348,000 sale, and 6.75 percent on an $89,500 sale. The only other salesperson at Sure Sale who received a commission in May got 6 percent on a $410,000 sale. How much did Sure Sale receive in May?
   a. $4,289.25   c. $12,251.53
   b. $7,095.97   d. $14,945

STATE LICENSE REQUIREMENTS

Fill in the license requirements in the table below based on your state's license laws, rules, and regulations.

Requirements	Sales License	Broker License
Age		
Education		
Experience		
Bond		
Credit Report		
Recommendations		
Photograph		
Fingerprints		
Continuing Education		
Licensure Period		
Expiration Date		

ANSWER KEY

Key Term Matching

1. c 2. n 3. h 4. f 5. k 6. o 7. e 8. i
9. g 10. d 11. l 12. j 13. m 14. a 15. b

True or False

1. **False.** All 50 states somehow regulate the activities of real estate brokers and salespeople.

2. **False.** The purpose of the real estate license laws is to regulate the real estate industry and protect the rights of purchasers, sellers, tenants, and owners.

3. **False.** A real estate *broker* is licensed to buy, sell, exchange, or lease real property for others, and to charge a fee for those services.

4. **True**

5. **True**

6. **True**

7. **False.** A broker is considered the *procuring* cause of a sale if he or she started an uninterrupted chain of events that resulted in the sale.

8. **True**

9. **False.** *Price-fixing* is the practice of competitors setting prices for products or services.

10. **True**

Who's Who

1.	Principal Broker	Elaine
2.	Real Estate Assistant	Dora
3.	Sales Manager	Ron
4.	Salesperson (Independent Contractor)	Joyce
5.	Salesperson (Employee)	Sandra

Multiple Choice

1. **b.** Choice a is incorrect because licensees will face lawsuits if they ignore the laws. Choice c is not correct because licensees engage in profit-making activities. Choice d is incorrect; minimum levels of competency are established.

2. **c.** While the salesperson may be treated as an independent contractor for income tax purposes, the salesperson must still work directly under the broker's name. Choice d is the definition of a *personal assistant*.

3. **b.** Choices a, c, and d are IRS requirements. Number of hours may not be specified.

4. **d.** Because the Open Door broker learned about Happy Homes' policies from a public source, that is, the newspaper, and without discussing the policy with Happy Homes, neither broker has committed an antitrust violation.

5. **d.** Obviously, the broker introduced a ready, willing, and able buyer to the seller prior to the seller's cancellation of the listing agreement and thus is entitled to the commission.

6. **b.** Although the commission was earned when the buyer was notified of the seller's acceptance (March 8), the commission is typically paid at the time the deed is delivered.

7. **c.** It is legal for agents to share and split commissions. Price fixing, allocation of customers, and group boycotting are illegal under the antitrust laws.

8. **a.** Under antitrust laws, brokers may not get together and agree to charge the same rates to customers. Brokers may charge for services using a flat fee, an hourly rate, or a commission based on a percentage of the selling price.

9. **d.** The MLS exposes the property to many different agents, encouraging cooperation among brokers and expediting sales.

10. **c.** Rules and regulations are written and adopted by the licensing authorities in each state. They have the same force as the law but are easier to change because they do not have to go through legislature.

11. **d.** Respond promptly to e-mails. A week is too long.

12. b. A phone number is not usually required in an e-mail, but the other elements are. Status as a broker or agent should be disclosed on every page of a Web site with ads. Both the salesperson's name and the broker's name should be shown in ads.

13. c. If the sale is not completed due to the seller's default (deciding not to sell), then the broker is generally due a commission. For Choices a, b, and d, the buyer was no longer a ready, willing, and able buyer prepared to buy on the seller's terms.

14. a. *Fee-for-services* refers to splitting apart the collection of services that a broker offers. A *buy-down provision* is a financing option. *Allocation of customers* refers to dividing a market and refraining from competing.

15. c. An exclusive-brokerage agreement sets out a minimum level of services that a consumer should expect from a licensee. Dual agency means that the licensee represents both the seller and buyer.

16. d. However, if the consumer specifically asks the company not to call, then the company must stop calling.

17. b. The virtual office Web site (VOW) and Internet Data Exchange (IDX) are older programs that are scheduled for replacement by July 1, 2006.

18. a. The "E-Sign" Act diminishes legal barriers in electronic contracting but does not set out required security measures. Notarization is allowed, and consumers cannot repudiate an electronic signature.

19. c. A 100 percent commission plan provides for a salesperson to pay a monthly service charge to the broker so that the salesperson can keep 100 percent of the commissions earned.

20. a. With discounted services, the consumer receives the full package of services but pays a discounted price. Allocation of markets involves an agreement between brokers to divide their markets and stop competition.

Math Practice

1. c. What the brokers agree to regarding splitting the commission is not relevant to the total cost to the seller. Julie paid $22,750 in commission fees: $325,000 × 7% = $22,750.

2. d. None of the above. The salesperson received $9,223.50: $279,500 × 5.5% × 60% = $9,223.50.

3. c. The seller's total cost is $19,000: $400,000 × 4% + $3,000 = $19,000.

4. a. The salesperson is paid $9,625: $500,000 × 6% = $30,000 × 35% = $10,500 − $200 − $75 − $600 ($800 × 75%) = $9,625.

5. a. In May, Sure Sale received $11,928.19:

$560,000 × 5% = $28,000

$348,000 × 6% = $20,880

$89,500 × 6.75% = $6,041.25

$410,000 × 6% = $24,600

$28,000 + $20,880 + $6,041.25 + $24,600 = $79,521.25 × 15% = $11,928.19

State License Requirements

Each state will have different answers. Students should work together when possible.

6

Listing Agreements and Buyer Representation

BEFORE YOU START...

After completing Chapter 6 of the textbook, you should be able to answer the following "learning assessment" questions. If you are able to answer these questions, then you are ready to move ahead with this chapter of the *Study Guide!* If, however, you are having some difficulty answering any of these learning assessment questions, we advise you to reread key sections of the textbook before attempting to answer the questions in this chapter of the *Study Guide*.

■ Can you describe the different types of listing agreements and buyer representation contracts?

■ Are you able to name the ways a listing agreement can be terminated and discuss each situation?

■ How would you use a competitive market analysis (CMA) or appraisal to help the seller set the listing price?

■ Do you know the types of information needed for a listing agreement?

■ What are the major provisions of a typical exclusive listing agreement?

MATCHING   *Write the letter of the matching term on the appropriate line.*

a. CMA

b. *option listing*

c. *exclusive-agency listing*

d. *exclusive buyer agency*

e. *exclusive-right-to-sell listing*

f. *listing agreement*

g. MLS

h. *net listing*

i. *open buyer agency*

j. *open listing*

1. _____ An employment contract for a broker's services

2. _____ A listing agreement under which the seller must pay the broker a commission regardless of who sells the property

3. _____ A listing agreement with a single broker, under which the seller retains the right to sell the property independently without being obligated to pay a commission

4. _____ A listing agreement in which the seller may employ multiple brokers, retains the right to market the property independently, and is obligated to compensate only the broker who produces a buyer, if any

5. _____ Marketing organization whose broker members make their own exclusive listings available to other brokers

6. _____ A listing agreement in which the seller receives a specific dollar amount from the sales price, and the selling broker retains the balance as his or her compensation

7. _____ A comparison of the sales prices of similar properties

8. _____ A contract between a buyer and a buyer's broker that permits the buyer to enter into an unlimited number of similar agreements

9. _____ A contract between a buyer and a buyer's broker in which the agent is entitled to compensation even if the buyer finds a suitable property independently

10. _____ A listing agreement in which the broker has the right to purchase the listed property

TRUE OR FALSE   *Circle the correct answer.*

1. T F Under a typical net listing, the broker's commission is based on a percentage of the seller's net from the transaction.

2. T F A *listing agreement* is a contract for the sale of real estate.

3. T F The parties to a listing agreement are a broker and a seller.

4. T F The salesperson sets the listing price for a property by using a competitive market analysis.

5. T F A listing agreement in which the seller retains the right to employ any number of brokers as agents is referred to as a *multiple listing*.

6. T F In an exclusive-agency listing, one broker is authorized to act as the exclusive agent of the principal, who retains the right to sell the property without obligation to the broker.

7. T F In buyer agency, the source of compensation is the major factor that determines the relationship.

TRUE OR FALSE   *(continued)*

8. T   F   In an exclusive-right-to-sell listing, the seller must pay the broker's commission even if the seller finds a buyer without the broker's assistance.

9. T   F   In an exclusive buyer agency agreement, the broker is entitled to payment only if he or she locates the property that the buyer ultimately purchases.

10. T   F   Because a listing agreement is a personal service contract between a broker and seller, the broker may transfer the listing to another broker with or without the seller's consent.

11. T   F   Verbal agreement by the seller is adequate for a broker to list the property in a MLS.

12. T   F   An option listing guarantees that the broker will purchase the property within a certain period of time.

13. T   F   A broker protection clause in a listing contract provides for payment of a commission to the listing broker if the owner sells the property within a certain number of days after the listing expires and to a broker-introduced buyer.

14. T   F   The seller disclosures of property conditions usually cover structural, mechanical, and other conditions that the buyer needs to know to make an informed decision.

15. T   F   Many states allow for a home warranty program to be provided in a listing contract or offer to purchase.

LISTING CONTRACTS

Label each of the three diagrams below to indicate the type of listing contract it represents.

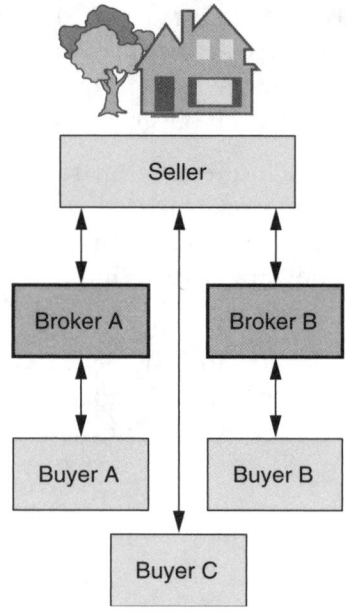

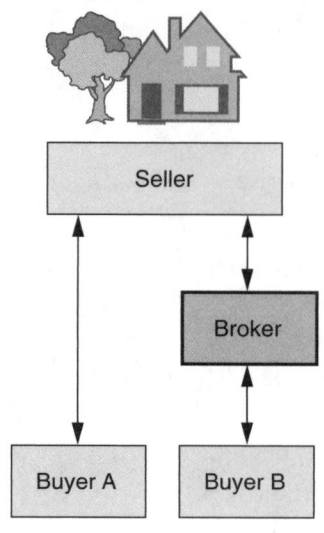

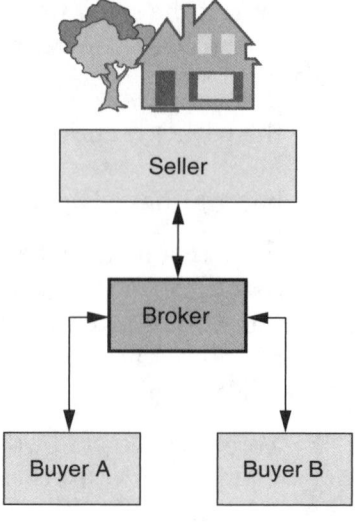

Seller retains any number of brokers; seller does not pay a commission to broker if seller finds the buyer.

Broker is the exclusive agent of the buyer; seller does not pay a commission to broker if seller finds the buyer.

One broker is the seller's only agent; seller pays broker a commission no matter who sells the property.

1. _____

2. _____

3. _____

MULTIPLE CHOICE   *Circle a, b, c, or d.*

1. In a typical buyer agency agreement, the buyer is the

   a. principal.   c. agent.

   b. customer.   d. employee.

2. The owner listed her home for sale with a broker. When the owner sold the home herself, she didn't owe anyone a commission. Based on these facts, what type of listing did the broker and the owner most likely sign?

   a. Exclusive-right-to-sell listing

   b. Net listing

   c. Multiple listing

   d. Open listing

3. All of the following information is generally included in a listing agreement *EXCEPT*

   a. lot size.

   b. termination clause.

   c. client's specific requirements for a suitable property to buy.

   d. property condition disclosures.

MULTIPLE CHOICE *(continued)*

4. On January 10, a salesperson met with a seller and described the advantages of listing the seller's property with his broker's office. On January 15, the seller agreed to the listing: The salesperson and the seller signed the agreement. On January 18, the broker signed the listing agreement as required by the office policy. On January 20, the salesperson posted a For Sale sign in front of the house. When did the listing agreement become effective?

   a. January 10   **c.** January 18

   b. January 15   **d.** January 20

5. The listed price of a property is always

   a. negotiable.

   b. a function of market value.

   c. the seller's decision.

   d. determined by a CMA.

6. What is a listing agreement?

   a. Contract between buyer and seller

   b. Contract to purchase real property

   c. Employment agreement between broker and salesperson

   d. Employment contract between seller and broker

7. Who are the parties to a listing agreement?

   a. Buyer and seller

   b. Seller and broker

   c. Seller and salesperson

   d. Buyer and salesperson

8. There are five different brokerage signs in the front yard. Evidently, the seller has signed a(n)

   a. exclusive-agency listing.

   b. exclusive-right-to-sell listing.

   c. net listing.

   d. open listing.

9. The broker has just explained the value of signing an exclusive-agency listing with a broker who is a member of the multiple-listing service. The broker is trying to overcome the misconceptions of the seller who asked about a(n)

   a. open listing.

   b. option listing.

   c. exclusive-right-to-sell listing.

   d. net listing.

10. What kind of listing agreement is illegal in most states because of the potential for conflict of interest between a broker's fiduciary responsibility to the seller and the broker's profit motive?

   a. Open listing

   b. Net listing

   c. Exclusive-right-to-sell

   d. Exclusive-agency listing

11. The buyer hired a broker to help locate a suitable property. However, on the way home from work, the buyer went by an open house, fell in love with it, and promptly signed a purchase agreement. The buyer was still obligated to pay the broker a commission because the original agreement was a(n)

   a. exclusive buyer agency agreement.

   b. exclusive-agency buyer agency agreement.

   c. net agency agreement.

   d. open buyer agency agreement.

12. Buyer agents may be compensated in any of the following ways *EXCEPT*

   a. flat fee for service.

   b. percentage of selling price.

   c. hourly rate.

   d. percentage of list price.

MULTIPLE CHOICE   *(continued)*

13. The buyer's agent must obtain information from the buyer. All of the following would be useful to the buyer's agent *EXCEPT*

    a. financial information.

    b. specific requirements for suitable property.

    c. how soon the buyer has to move.

    d. the cost of the buyer's previous home.

14. Any of the following will terminate a listing agreement *EXCEPT*

    a. performance.

    b. expiration.

    c. an offer to purchase.

    d. abandonment by broker.

15. Broker John is retiring and wants to sell his listings to another broker. How can he do this?

    a. Broker John must sign over the listings to the new broker.

    b. The new broker has to sign an acceptance agreement.

    c. Each salesperson must sign over his or her listing to the new broker.

    d. The sellers must agree to a new listing with the new broker.

16. In which of the following types of listing agreements is the broker appointed as the seller's only agent?

    a. Exclusive-right-to-sell and exclusive-agency listings

    b. Open listing

    c. Net listing

    d. Option listing

17. In most states, a broker's license can be suspended or revoked if he or she

    a. breaches the terms of the listing agreement.

    b. cancels the listing agreement without cause.

    c. takes a listing that does not include a date on which the listing expires.

    d. does not include an automatic extension clause in the listing agreement.

18. Why should a broker consider rejecting a listing if the seller wants to set a price that is too high based on local market values?

    a. Too many buyers will be attracted to the property.

    b. The broker will have a difficult time selling the property within the listing period.

    c. The broker will have low marketing costs.

    d. Buyers will have too easy a time getting a loan.

19. All of the following are information needed for the listing agreement *EXCEPT* the

    a. dimensions of the lot.

    b. possibility of seller financing.

    c. age of the seller.

    d. most recent property taxes.

20. An example of personal property that a seller may leave with the property and, therefore, *MUST* identify on the listing agreement is

    a. a built-in dishwasher.

    b. the door key.

    c. stacked firewood.

    d. a ceiling light fixture.

MATH PRACTICE   *Circle a, b, c, or d.*

1. The brokerage charged the seller $1,000 as an advertising fee and 4 percent of the selling price. The house was listed for $439,500 and sold for $429,350. What was the total amount the seller paid the brokerage?
   a. $15,174
   b. $15,580
   c. $16,580
   d. None of the above

2. The seller agreed to a 5 percent commission on a sale price of $175,000. The brokerage split with salespeople is 30/70, with 30 percent remaining with the company. How much is the salesperson's share if the salesperson both lists and sells the property?
   a. $2,625
   b. $6,125
   c. $8,750
   d. None of the above

3. It is the broker's office policy that salespeople keep 60 percent of the firm's share of any commission earned from any property they list. The salesperson listed a property that was later sold by a cooperating broker for $285,000. If the two brokers agree to split the 6.5 percent commission equally, what will the salesperson receive?
   a. $5,557.50
   b. $6,092.00
   c. $7,235.25
   d. $7,654.00

4. The commission on the sale of 119 South Wright was $16,500, based on a 7.5 percent commission rate. What was the final selling price of 119 South Wright?
   a. $127,000
   b. $145,000
   c. $199,000
   d. $220,000

5. The broker listed a home for $360,000 under a 90-day exclusive-right-to-sell listing agreement with a 6 percent commission. The next week, the broker began advertising the home in a local paper and showed the property to two prospective buyers. Later that week, the seller announced that he had decided to sell his home to a relative for $340,000. The seller is liable to the broker for
   a. $1,200.
   b. $20,400.
   c. $21,600.
   d. none of the above.

LISTING WORKSHEET

Fill in the practice listing worksheet below using the floor plan of John and Martha Rambler's property (128 Winding Way) shown on the opposite page. The scale is 1 inch = 12 feet (approximate dimensions are acceptable). The property is a 20-year-old, stuccoed, ranch-style house with terra cotta roof and no basement. Last year's taxes were $1,875. The original carpeting throughout is quite worn, but the tile baths are in excellent condition. A security system and TV cabling were installed in 2000. The kitchen was remodeled in 2003 with new dishwasher, range, refrigerator, compactor, disposal, and vinyl floor covering.

Property Address: _____   Lot Size: _____

Owners: _____   Taxes: _____

Style _____	**Utilities:**	Softener _____	Sunroom _____
Sq. Ft. _____	Electric _____	Sewer _____	Pool _____
Bedrooms _____	Heat _____	**Exterior:**	Shed _____
Age _____	A/C _____	Roof _____	Fence _____
# Stories _____	Humidifier _____	Siding _____	Landscaping _____
Basement _____	Air Filter _____	Deck _____	Other _____
Garage _____	Water _____	Patio _____	_____

Rooms	Level	Size	Floor Cover	Features	Comments
Living Room		×			
Dining Room		×			
Family Room		×			
Kitchen		×			
Rec. Room		×			
Master BR		×			
Bedroom 1		×			
Bedroom 2		×			
Bedroom 3		×			
Bath (full)		×			
Bath (¾)		×			
Bath (½)		×			
Other (Den)		×			
Utility Room		×			

John and Martha Rambler

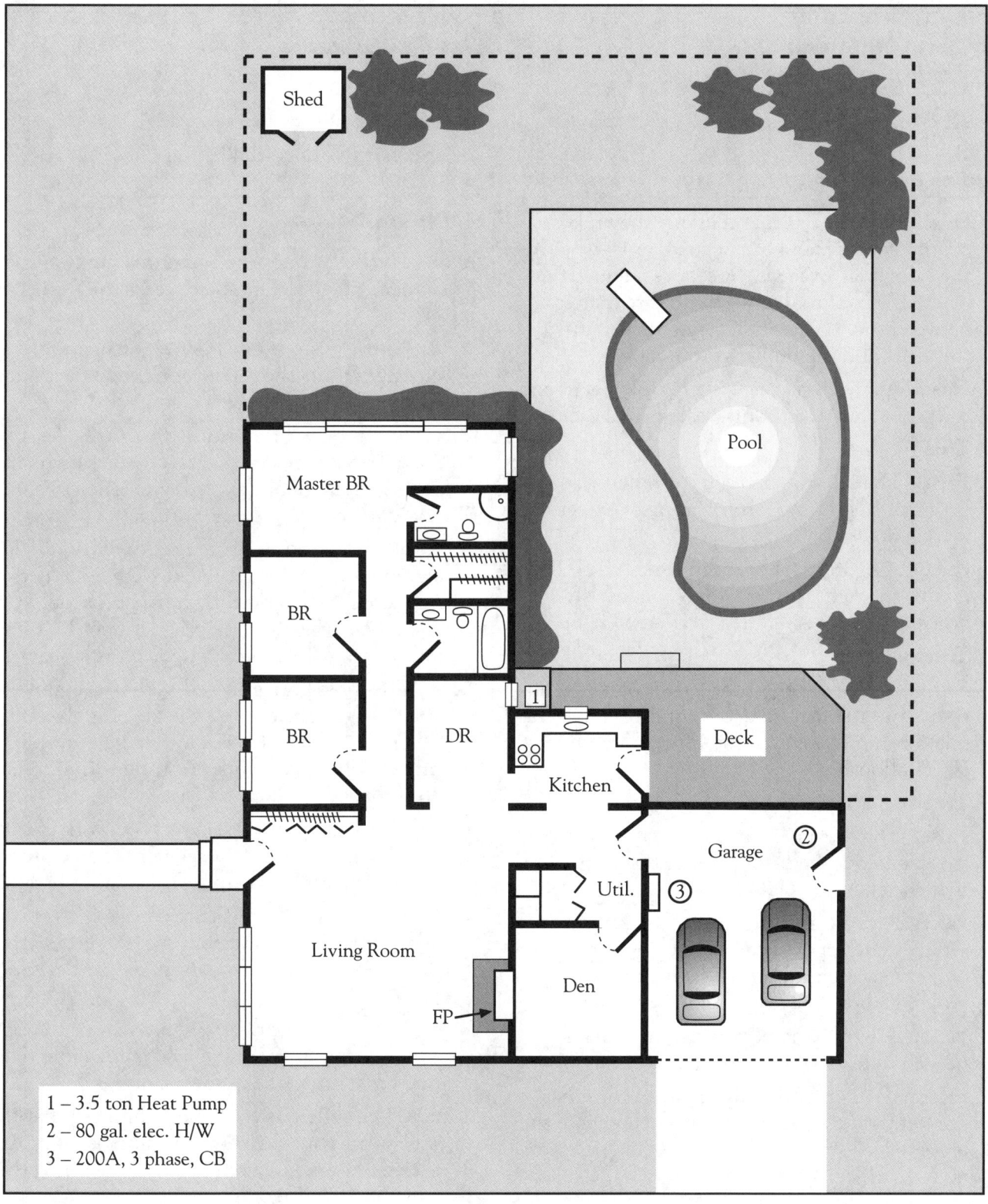

Shed

Pool

Master BR

BR

BR

DR

Kitchen

Deck

[1]

Garage

[2]

Util.

[3]

Living Room

Den

FP

1 – 3.5 ton Heat Pump
2 – 80 gal. elec. H/W
3 – 200A, 3 phase, CB

ANSWER KEY

Key Term Matching

1. f **2.** e **3.** c **4.** j **5.** g **6.** h **7.** a **8.** i
9. d **10.** b

True or False

1. **False.** Under a typical *net listing*, the broker's commission is based on the amount by which the sales price exceeds the seller's required net. There is a potential for a conflict of interest between the broker's fiduciary responsibility to the seller and the broker's profit motive.

2. **False.** A *listing agreement* is an employment contract, not a contract for the sale of real estate.

3. **True**

4. **False.** The salesperson *helps* the seller set the listing price for a property by using a competitive market analysis.

5. **False.** A listing agreement in which the seller retains the right to employ any number of brokers as agent is referred to as an *open listing*.

6. **True**

7. **False.** In buyer agency, the source of compensation is not the major factor that determines the relationship. Who does the hiring determines the relationship.

8. **True**

9. **False.** The broker is entitled to payment regardless of whether he or she locates the property that the client purchases.

10. **False.** Because a listing agreement is a personal service contract between a broker and seller, the broker may *not* transfer the listing to another broker without the seller's written consent.

11. **False.** A written agreement by the seller is needed to list the property on an MLS.

12. **False.** With an option listing, the broker has the right but not the obligation to purchase the property.

13. **True**

14. **True**

15. **True**

Listing Contracts

1. open listing
2. exclusive-agency listing
3. exclusive-right-to-sell listing

Multiple Choice

1. **a.** The buyer hires the agent in a buyer agency agreement; therefore the buyer is the principal-client.

2. **d.** Of the answers given, only the open listing clearly permits the seller to sell the house and not be obligated to pay a commission.

3. **c.** When taking the listing from the seller, the agent is not concerned at the moment what the seller's future housing needs are. Choices a, b, and d are relevant to the listing.

4. **c.** Some brokers delegate the responsibility for signing the listing agreement to the salesperson, but because this company has a policy of having the broker sign the listing, it does not become effective until the broker signs it on January 18.

5. **c.** The asking price as well as the acceptance of the final offer price from the buyer is always the seller's decision. This is another example of the broker being a special agent (one with limited authority).

6. **d.** The broker can *subcontract* the work to salespeople, but the listing agreement is an employment contract between the seller and the broker.

7. **b.** The seller and broker are parties to the listing agreement. Listings remain the property of the broker even if the salesperson leaves the company.

8. **d.** In an open listing, the seller retains the right to sell the property and may employ more than one broker to perform agency duties.

9. **a.** Often sellers are confused, thinking that the only way to find buyers from a number of brokers is to enter into an open listing. Explaining the advantages of the multiple-listing service can overcome the misconception.

10. b. If taking a net listing, the broker may not tell the seller the true value of the property in order to receive a higher commission. This is why net listings are generally illegal.

11. a. The exclusive buyer agency agreement is the counterpart to the exclusive-right-to-sell listing agreement. Even if the buyer finds the property on his or her own, the buyer is responsible for paying the brokerage fee.

12. d. Commissions are never calculated on the listing price, only on the selling price.

13. d. What the buyer paid for his or her current home is not relevant to the purchase of a new property.

14. c. Because an offer to purchase may not be accepted, it would not terminate the listing agreement.

15. d. Because the listing agreement is a contract for the personal services of the original broker, the sellers have the right to cancel their listing agreement and not go to the new broker.

16. a. Open, net, and option listings do not specifically exclude other brokers from acting as the seller's agent.

17. c. If the broker breaches the listing contract or cancels it without cause, he or she may be liable for damages but it is not usually grounds for suspension or revocation of the license. Courts have frowned on the use of automatic extension clauses, and these clauses are even illegal in some states.

18. b. Unrealistic prices make a property hard to sell. The broker can waste money on marketing, and few buyers will be interested. Even if a buyer makes an offer, he or she would have problems getting financing for an overpriced property.

19. c. Information needed for the listing agreement includes lot size, possibility of seller financing, and the property taxes. The age of the seller is not needed.

20. c. Firewood is not attached to the real property and is considered personal property. All the other items, even the door key, are normally considered to be part of the real property.

Math Practice

1. d. The seller paid the brokerage none of the above: The sales price is $429,350 \times 4\%$ + $1,000 = $18,174 (none of the above).

2. b. The salesperson's share is $6,125: $175,000 \times 5\% \times 70\% = $6,125.

3. a. The salesperson receives $5,557.50: $285,000 \times 6.5\% \times 50\% \times 60\% = $5,557.50.

4. d. The selling price was $220,000: $16,500 \times 7.5\% = $220,000

5. b. The seller is liable to the broker for $20,400: $340,000 \times 6\% = $20,400. Because the seller had signed an exclusive-right-to-sell listing agreement, the seller is responsible for paying a commission no matter who finds the buyer.

LISTING WORKSHEET

The answers below were derived from the floor plan and information included in the narrative. The room dimensions are approximate and were determined by measuring the floor plan with a ruler. Keep in mind that garages are not considered living space, thus are not included in the house square footage. The lot size was measured as 84' × 102' (8,820 sq. ft.) and converted to acres (8,820 × 43,560 = 0.20 acres). The electrical and heating system specifications presume some familiarity with these technical aspects of the floor plan.

Property Address: *128 Winding Way*

Owners: *John and Martha Rambler*

Lot Size: *1/5 acre*

Taxes: *$1,875*

Style *Ranch*	**Utilities:**	Softener *??*	Sunroom *none*
Sq. Ft. *1,374 ±*	Electric *200 amp. 3 phase cir brkr*	Sewer *??*	Pool *yes*
Bedrooms *3*	Heat *3.5 ton heat pump*	**Exterior:**	Shed *yes*
Age *20*	A/C *3.5 ton heat pump*	Roof *terra cotta*	Fence *yes*
# Stories *1*	Humidifier *??*	Siding *stucco*	Landscaping *yes*
Basement *none*	Air Filter *??*	Deck *yes – 12×16 + 4×9*	Other
Garage *2-car attached*	Water *80 gal. elec. h/w*	Patio *yes – around pool*	

Rooms	Level	Size	Floor Cover	Features	Comments
Living Room	1	23 × 21	carpet	fireplace, closet	carpet worn
Dining Room	1	8 × 11	carpet		
Family Room	–	–	–		
Kitchen	1	7 × 11	vinyl	modernized 2002	
Rec. Room	–	–	–		
Master BR	1	11 × 22L	carpet	walk-in closet	
Bedroom 1	1	10 × 11	carpet		
Bedroom 2	1	10 × 11	carpet		
Bedroom 3	–	–	–		
Bath (full)	1	6 × 8	tile		
Bath (¾)	1	5 × 8	tile		
Bath (½)	1	–	–		
Other (Den)	1	11 × 11	carpet		
Utility Room	1	5 × 11	??	has washer & dryer	

Interests in Real Estate

BEFORE YOU START...

After completing Chapter 7 of the textbook, you should be able to answer the following "learning assessment" questions. If you are able to answer these questions, then you are ready to move ahead with this chapter of the *Study Guide!* If, however, you are having some difficulty answering any of these learning assessment questions, we advise you to reread key sections of the textbook before attempting to answer the questions in this chapter of the *Study Guide*.

■ Can you describe the four government powers that affect the ownership of real estate?

■ What are the two types of estates in land?

■ Can you define and give examples of fee simple estates: fee simple absolute, fee simple defeasible, fee simple with a special limitation (determinable fee), and fee simple subject to a condition subsequent?

■ What is a life estate and how is it different from a conventional life estate and a legal life estate? Can you give examples of each?

■ What is the difference between remainder and reversionary interests?

■ Are you able to describe the general provisions of homestead laws?

■ What does the term *encumbrance* mean and cite at least five examples?

■ How are the terms *lien* and *deed restriction* different and what are examples of each?

■ Are you able to define and give examples of an appurtenant easement, easement in gross, party wall easement, easement by necessity, easement by prescription, and easement by condemnation, including the creation and termination of each?

■ What is the effect of a *license* on real property?

■ Do you know what an *encroachment* is and can you give examples?

■ Can you explain and give examples of riparian water rights, littoral water rights, and the doctrine of prior appropriation?

MATCHING A   *Write the letter of the matching term on the appropriate line.*

a. *condemnation*

b. *defeasible fee*

c. *eminent domain*

d. *escheat*

e. *estate in land*

f. *fee simple absolute*

g. *freehold estates*

h. *leasehold estates*

i. *police power*

j. *taxation*

1. _____ A state's ability to enact legislation to preserve order, protect the public health and safety, and promote the general welfare

2. _____ The right of a government to acquire privately owned real estate for public use

3. _____ The process by which the government exercises its right of eminent domain

4. _____ A charge imposed on real estate to raise funding for government services

5. _____ The automatic transfer of real property to the state when the owner dies without heirs or a will

6. _____ The degree, quantity, nature, and extent of an owner's interest in real property

7. _____ A class of estates in land that lasts for an indeterminable period of time

8. _____ A class of estates in land that lasts for a fixed period of time (or at will or sufferance)

9. _____ The highest interest in real estate recognized by law

10. _____ An estate qualified by some action or activity that must or must not be performed

---

TRUE OR FALSE   *Circle the correct answer.*

1. T F A state's power to enact legislation that preserves order, protects the public health and safety, and promotes the general welfare is referred to as its *police power*.

2. T F The four governmental powers that affect real estate are taxation, eminent domain, escheat, and police.

3. T F The process by which the government exercises its right to acquire privately owned real estate for public use through either judicial or administrative proceedings is called *condemnation*.

4. T F The purpose of *escheat* is to expand governmental property holdings.

5. T F A *freehold estate* is the highest interest in real estate recognized by law.

TRUE OR FALSE   *(continued)*

6. T   F   *Riparian rights* are common-law rights granted to owners of land that lie along the course of a river, stream, or similar body of water.

7. T   F   If the grantor is silent about what happens to property after a life estate ends, the grantor has a *remainder interest* in the property.

8. T   F   A *homestead* is a legal life estate in real estate occupied as a family home.

9. T   F   An *appurtenant* easement is said to run with the land and transfers with the deed of the servient tenement.

10. T   F   An easement that arises when an owner sells property that has no access to a street or public way except across the seller's remaining land is an *easement by prescription*.

11. T   F   The concept of *tacking* provides that successive periods of continuous occupation by different parties may be combined to reach the required total number of years necessary to establish a class for an easement in gross.

12. T   F   A license may be terminated or canceled by the person who granted it, and a license ends on the death of either party or the sale of the affected property by the licensor.

13. T   F   A *conventional life estate* may be created either by deed during the owner's life or after the owner's death by will.

14. T   F   Riparian and littoral rights are personal rights under the common law; they belong to the landowner and do not run with the land.

15. T   F   To secure water rights in a state in which the doctrine of prior appropriation is in effect, landowners must demonstrate that they plan a beneficial use for the water.

FILL-IN-THE-BLANK   *Select the word or words that best complete the following statements:*

accretion

appurtenant

avulsion

by condemnation

by necessity

by prescription

conventional life estate

freehold estate

future interest

in gross

legal life estate

public use

special limitation

1. Due to a court decision in 2005, many states are drafting legislation to establish a narrow meaning to the term _____ in eminent domain proceedings to stop condemnations justified solely for economic reasons.

2. A type of life estate established by state law rather than voluntarily by an owner is a(n) _____.

3. A fee simple determinable is qualified by a(n) _____ that ends the estate automatically on the current owner's failure to comply with this element.

4. A life estate is a type of _____ that is limited in duration to the life of the owner or some other specified person or persons.

5. The right of re-entry may never take effect. Therefore, this right is considered to be a(n) _____.

6. A railroad right of way is an example of an easement _____ _____.

7. The type of easement gained for a public purpose through the right of eminent domain is called an easement _____.

8. When a mudslide into the ocean removes several feet of land from Joe's property, the process is called _____.

9. When a claimant has used another person's land for a certain period of time defined by state law, he or she can claim an easement _____ _____.

10. When two properties share a party wall that straddles the boundary line between the two lots, each lot owner owns the half of the wall on his or her lot and has a(n) _____ easement in the other half of the wall.

COMPOUND INTERESTS IN SPINDLEY ACRES

Based on the narrative below, enter the name of each player in the Spindley Acres scenario into the appropriate box. Also label his or her interest in the estate and how it is conveyed from one to another.

Ben conveys a life estate in Spindley Acres to Carol, with a remainder to Bob, "so long as Spindley Acres continues to be a working farm." If it ceases to be a farm, the property will go back to Ben (or his estate).

Meanwhile, Carol conveys a life estate in Spindley Acres to Sally "for as long as my Cousin Tom shall live." When Tom dies, the estate will return to Carol for the remainder of her life.

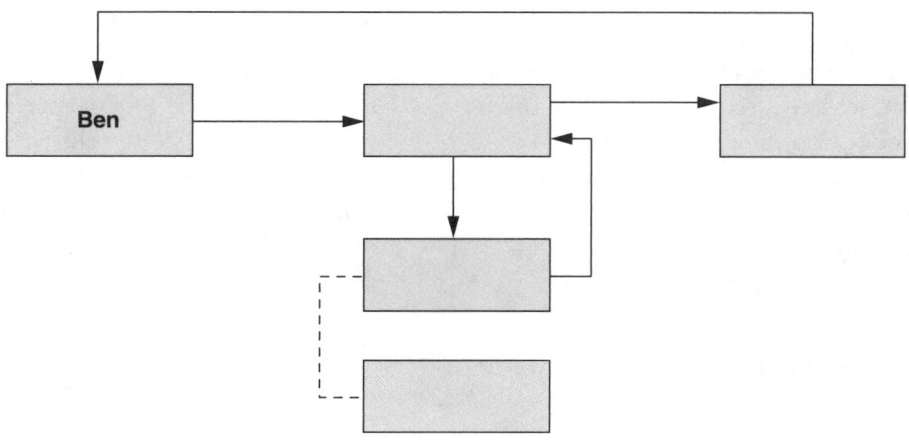

MULTIPLE CHOICE   *Circle a, b, c, or d.*

1. An elderly man left the family home to his second wife with the provision that when she dies, the home goes to a son by his first wife. The second wife owns a bundle of rights; however, she does not own the right to

   a. will the property.

   b. sell the property.

   c. lease the property.

   d. decorate the property.

2. Every workday for the past 20 years, Michelle has parked her car in a specific place in the nearby parking garage. Today she receives a notice that the garage will be replaced by an office building. Can they do this to her after all the years she parked there?

   a. No, because she has been parking there for more than 20 years, she has an easement by prescription.

   b. No, since she paid regularly on time.

   c. Yes, because she only had a license.

   d. Yes, because she has nothing in writing.

MULTIPLE CHOICE   *(continued)*

3. Fred conveyed a one-acre parcel of land to the Wee Fry Preschool. In the deed, Fred stated that the property was to be used only as a playground; Fred reserved a right of re-entry. What kind of estate has Fred granted?

   a. Leasehold

   b. Fee simple subject to a condition subsequent

   c. Fee simple absolute

   d. Freehold

4. Trent owns a farm that lies long the edge of the Brackish River, which is too shallow to be navigable. If Trent does not live in a jurisdiction that recognizes the doctrine of prior appropriation, how much (if any) of the river does Trent own?

   a. Trent owns the land to the edge of the river; the land under the river is owned by the state.

   b. Trent owns the land to the mean high water mark, and a right to apply for a water use permit.

   c. Trent owns the land up to the water's edge and the right to use the water.

   d. Trent owns the land under the river to the exact center of the waterway, and the right to use the water.

5. Over the past 15 years, the Brackish River has been slowly depositing soil along its eastern bank. As a result, the river is some 12 feet narrower than it used to be, and Rambling Acres, the property on the east side of the river, is now 12 feet larger than it used to be. This scenario is an example of which of the following processes?

   a. Reliction   c. Alluvion

   b. Erosion   d. Accretion

6. If the government acquires privately owned real estate through a condemnation suit, it is exercising its power of

   a. escheat.   c. eminent domain.

   b. reverter.   d. defeasance.

7. Larry owned two acres. Larry sold one acre to Brittany and reserved an easement appurtenant for entrance and exit over Brittany's acre to reach the public road. Brittany's land is

   a. capable of being cleared of the easement if Brittany sells to a third party.

   b. called the servient tenement.

   c. called the dominant tenement.

   d. subject to an easement in gross.

8. Nate owns a large undeveloped parcel of land on the side of a hill. The property borders a road on the lower edge. Nate sells the lower portion of the property to Stephanie, and she builds a home on it. Several years later, Nate sells the upper portion of the property to Sean. Sean's property does not border the road. For Sean to gain access to the road, Sean must claim by implication of law an easement

   a. by necessity.   c. by prescription.

   b. in gross.   d. by restriction.

9. If the dominant estate merges with the servient estate, which of the following is *TRUE*?

   a. The easement remains in effect for the entire parcel.

   b. The easement is suspended but cannot be terminated.

   c. The easement is terminated.

   d. The new owner must bring a suit seeking severance of the easement from the combined properties.

10. In the state of New Freedonia, the homestead exemption is $15,000. Four years ago, George, a resident of New Freedonia, purchased a home for $58,000. George then fell on hard times. At a court-ordered sale, George's property is purchased for $60,000. If George has an outstanding mortgage balance of $35,000 and other debts amounting to $24,360, how much is protected by the homestead exemption?

    a. $640   c. $15,000

    b. $2,140   d. $16,500

MULTIPLE CHOICE (continued)

11. In some states, a husband cannot sell his property unless his wife also signs the deed. His wife's interest is called
    a. common law rights.
    b. homestead rights.
    c. curtesy rights.
    d. dower rights.

12. The state's authority to enact legislation to protect the public is passed through to municipalities and counties through
    a. police power.   c. licensing laws.
    b. enabling acts.   d. processing papers.

13. The state requires enough land to build a four-lane highway. In order for the state to acquire the needed land, the state must do all of the following EXCEPT
    a. demonstrate that this is for the public good.
    b. pay a fair and just compensation to the owner.
    c. allow the property owner the right to appeal any decision.
    d. reimburse the property owner for the amount that the property owner paid for the land.

14. A 100-year old woman died in a nursing home. She had outlived all of her relatives and had not written a will. What happens to her $250,000 estate?
    a. It escheats to the state.
    b. The nursing home gets to keep it.
    c. It will be split between the nursing home and the county.
    d. It can be paid over to her church.

15. Which of the following is a claim, charge, or liability that attaches to real estate?
    a. Lien
    b. Easement
    c. Deed restriction
    d. Encumbrance

16. Which of the following MUST exist for an appurtenant easement to exist?
    a. Two adjacent parcels, different owners
    b. Two adjacent parcels, one owner
    c. Landlocked property that requires passage to the street
    d. Long-time unauthorized usage

17. What are deed restrictions?
    a. Public land restrictions
    b. Illegal land restrictions
    c. Private agreements affecting the use of the land
    d. Informal agreements between neighbors

18. The electric company has the right to string its wires over 50 parcels of land. What right does the electric company have?
    a. Appurtenant easement
    b. Easement by necessity
    c. Easement by prescription
    d. Easement in gross

19. For as long as anyone can remember, neighbor families have used a foot path to get to the river. Recently, the current owner erected a fence across the path. Which of the following easements may require that he take down the fence?
    a. Easement by necessity
    b. Easement by prescription
    c. Easement in gross
    d. Appurtenant easement

20. The rights of property owners of land next to large bodies of water, such as the ocean or the Great Lakes, are called
    a. riparian rights.
    b. littoral rights.
    c. prior appropriation.
    d. reversionary rights.

MATCHING B *Write the letter of the matching term on the appropriate line.*

a. *deed restriction*

b. *prior appropriation*

c. *encroachment*

d. *encumbrance*

e. *homestead*

f. *easement*

g. *life estate per autrie vie*

h. *lien*

i. *right of re-entry*

j. *remainderman*

1. _____ The owner's right to retake possession of property through legal action if a limiting condition is broken

2. _____ An estate based on the lifetime of a person other than the life tenant

3. _____ The person to whom property passes when a life estate ends

4. _____ A legal life estate in which an individual's primary residence is protected, in whole or in part, against certain creditors

5. _____ Any claim, charge, or liability that attaches to real estate

6. _____ A charge against property that provides security for a debt or obligation of the property owner

7. _____ A private agreement that affects the use of land

8. _____ The right to use another's land for a particular purpose

9. _____ All or part of a structure that extends beyond the land of its owner or beyond legal building lines

10. _____ The doctrine that the right to use any water, with the exception of limited domestic uses, is held and controlled by the state

ANSWER KEY

Key Term (Matching (A)

1. i **2.** c **3.** a **4.** j **5.** d **6.** e **7.** g **8.** h
9. f **10.** b

True or False

1. True
2. True
3. True
4. **False.** The purpose of *escheat* is to prevent property from being ownerless or abandoned.
5. **False.** A *fee simple absolute estate* is the highest interest in real estate recognized by law.
6. True
7. **False.** If the grantor is silent about what happens to property after a life estate ends, the grantor has a *reversionary* interest in the property.
8. True
9. **False.** An *appurtenant easement* is said to run with the land and transfers with the deed of the *dominant* tenement.
10. **False.** An easement that arises when an owner sells property that has no access to a street or public way except across the seller's remaining land is an *easement by necessity*.
11. **False.** The concept of *tacking* provides that successive periods of continuous occupation by different parties may be combined to reach the required total number of years necessary to establish a claim for an *easement by prescription*.
12. True
13. True
14. **False.** Riparian and littoral rights are attached to the land.
15. True

Fill-in-the-Blank

1. Due to a court decision in 2005, many states are drafting legislation to establish a narrow meaning to the term *public use* in eminent domain proceedings to stop condemnations justified solely for economic reasons.
2. A type of life estate established by state law rather than voluntarily by an owner is a *legal life estate*.
3. A fee simple determinable is qualified by a *special limitation* that ends the estate automatically on the current owner's failure to comply with this element.
4. A life estate is a type of *freehold estate* that is limited in duration to the life of the owner or some other specified person or persons.
5. The right of re-entry may never take effect. Therefore, this right is considered to be a *future interest*.
6. A railroad right of way is an example of an *easement in gross*.
7. The type of easement gained for a public purpose through the right of eminent domain is called an easement *by condemnation*.
8. When a mudslide into the ocean removes several feet of land from Joe's property, the process is called *avulsion*.
9. When a claimant has used another person's land for a certain period of time defined by state law, he or she can claim an easement *by prescription*.
10. When two properties share a party wall that straddles the boundary line between the two lots, each lot owner owns the half of the wall on his or her lot and has an *appurtenant* easement in the other half of the wall.

COMPOUND INTERESTS IN SPINDLEY ACRES

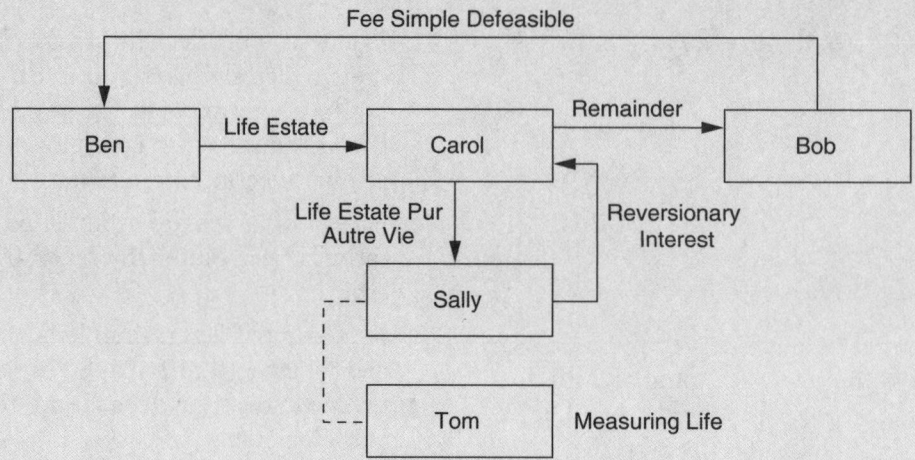

Multiple Choice

1. a. The second wife owns a life estate, and she has the entire bundle of rights except the right to will the property.

2. c. A license is a personal right to enter the property for a specific purpose. There is no *build-up* of rights.

3. b. Fred has granted a fee simple subject to a condition subsequent. If, at some point in the future, the land is not used as a playground, Fred or his heirs may exercise the right of re-entry by retaking physical possession of the land.

4. d. Unless otherwise stipulated by state rules or a deed, the owner of property along a river has the right to use the water and owns the land under the water to the center of the stream.

5. d. Accretion is the increase in the land resulting from the deposit of soil by the water action. The new deposits may be referred to as alluvion. Reliction is the resulting land when water dries up, and erosion is the slow washing away of land by natural forces.

6. c. The right of the state to acquire private property for public use is *eminent domain*. The court action is called *condemnation*. Property *escheats* back to the state when it becomes ownerless, that is, the owner dies leaving no heirs and no will.

7. b. Larry's parcel is the dominant tenement and benefits from the easement. The easement runs over Brittany's property, the servient tenement.

8. a. An *easement by necessity* is created by court order in order to permit legal access to Sean's property.

9. c. *Merger*, that is, one owner with two lots, terminates the easement.

10. c. The homestead exemption is $15,000. So, when the property is sold for $60,000, the mortgage of $35,000 is paid, $15,000 is reserved, leaving $10,000 for the rest of the creditors who will be paid on priority—first recorded, first paid—until the money runs out.

11. d. A wife's interest in her deceased husband's property is *dower*; a husband's interest is *curtesy*; protection for some part of the family home is referred to as *homestead rights*.

12. b. The state passes police power to local counties and municipalities through enabling acts. Licensing laws are an example of police power.

13. d. To acquire private property through eminent domain, the state must prove that the purchase is for public good, pay a fair price, and allow the property owner full rights to appeal. The price may or may not reflect what the owner had actually paid for the property.

14. a. Because the woman died without a will and there are no heirs, essentially, the $250,000 is ownerless. It reverts to the state.

15. d. Encumbrances include liens, easements, and deed restrictions.

16. a. An easement appurtenant must have two owners and two parcels of land. A landlocked parcel would require an easement by necessity; long-time unauthorized usage would lead to an easement by prescription.

17. c. *Deed restrictions* are private agreements written into the deed and are privately enforced. Examples of public restrictions include zoning and building codes.

18. d. Commercial easements are called easements in gross. There are only servient tenements, no dominant tenement.

19. b. Long-time unauthorized usage may create legal rights leading to an easement by prescription. An easement in gross is a personal right, often used by utility companies. An easement by necessity could be imposed by court order in order to provide access to a landlocked property.

20. b. Property owners along large bodies of water have littoral rights; riparian rights are those found along rivers and streams. The doctrine of prior appropriation refers to the state controlling the right to water from the river, rather than the adjacent property owner.

Key Term Matching (B)

1. i **2.** g **3.** j **4.** e **5.** d **6.** h **7.** a **8.** f **9.** c **10.** b

8

Forms of Real Estate Ownership

BEFORE YOU START...

After completing Chapter 8 of the textbook, you should be able to answer the following "learning assessment" questions. If you are able to answer these questions, then you are ready to move ahead with this chapter of the *Study Guide!* If, however, you are having some difficulty answering any of these learning assessment questions, we advise you to reread key sections of the textbook before attempting to answer the questions in this chapter of the *Study Guide*.

- Can you define the following: *ownership in severalty, tenancy in common, joint tenancy, tenancy by the entirety,* and *community property?*

- Do you know how different types of co-ownership can be created and terminated?

- Can you explain how a *living trust* is different from a *testamentary trust?*

- How would you explain the concept of a *land trust?*

- Are you able to list the ownership types under which business organizations can own real estate?

- Can you describe the differences between a *cooperative* and a *condominium?*

- What is *time-sharing?*

MATCHING A   *Write the letter of the matching term on the appropriate line.*

a. *tenancy in common*

b. *joint tenancy*

c. *partition*

d. *partnership*

e. *proprietary lease*

f. *severalty*

g. *tenancy by the entirety*

h. *board of directors*

i. *trust*

j. *testamentary trust*

1. _____ Ownership of real estate by one individual

2. _____ A form of property ownership in which owners hold undivided fractional interests that are inheritable by their heirs

3. _____ A form of ownership in which multiple owners hold property with a right of survivorship

4. _____ A legal method for dissolving a co-ownership

5. _____ A special form of co-ownership for married couples

6. _____ A device by which one person transfers ownership of property to someone else to hold or manage for the benefit of a third party

7. _____ A form of trust established by will after the owner's death

8. _____ An association of two or more persons who carry on a business for profit as co-owners

9. _____ The evidence of possession in a cooperative

10. _____ The governing body of a cooperative

TRUE OR FALSE   *Circle the correct answer.*

1. T F There are three basic ways in which a fee simple estate may be held: in severalty, in co-ownership, and in trust.

2. T F The term *severalty* means that there is only one owner of a single property.

3. T F In a tenancy in common, property is owned by two or more owners with the right of survivorship.

4. T F The ownership of an undivided fractional interest in a property is characteristic of a *tenancy in common.*

5. T F A joint tenancy continues indefinitely, until there is only one remaining owner, who then holds title in entirety.

6. T F When title to a single parcel of real estate is held by two or more individuals, the parties may be referred to as *concurrent owners.*

7. T F The four unities characteristic of a tenancy in common are possession, interest, title, and time.

8. T F A joint tenant may freely convey his or her interest in the jointly held property to a new owner, who becomes a joint tenant.

9. T F Co-tenants may terminate their co-ownership by asking a court to partition the property.

10. T F In a tenancy by the entirety neither spouse can convey a half-interest to a third party and neither spouse may take court action to partition or divide the property.

11. T F A tenancy by the entirety may be terminated only by divorce or death.

12. T F In a community property state, *community property* includes all property, both real and personal, acquired by either party prior to or during the marriage.

TRUE OR FALSE *(continued)*

13. T F The person who creates a trust is referred to as the *trustor*.

14. T F In a general partnership, the death of one of the partners does not affect the organization's continuity.

15. T F When a corporation buys real property, the stockholders have a direct ownership interest in the real estate that is proportional to their stock interest.

16. T F A *syndicate* is a form of partnership in which two or more people or firms carry out a single business project, with no intention of establishing an ongoing or permanent relationship.

17. T F Condominium owners hold their own units in fee simple and the common elements under proprietary leases.

18. T F The management and operation of a cooperative are determined by the bylaws of the corporation that owns the property.

19. T F Ownership of a cooperative interest is personal property.

20. T F A time-share estate is the right to use the property for a certain period of time.

21. T F An advantage of an S corporation is a more favorable tax treatment than that which applies to corporations.

22. T F A syndicate is a type of legal entity that is separate from a partnership or corporation.

23. T F An owner can transfer or sell a condominium unit to anyone, unless the condominium association provides for a right of first refusal.

24. T F A major advantage of living trusts is that they reduce the time and costs of probate.

25. T F A real estate investment trust is a type of housing connected by common walls.

TYPES OF OWNERSHIP

Check the characteristics that apply to ownership for each type of property.

Condominium
- ❏ corporate ownership
- ❏ undivided interest in common elements
- ❏ occupancy and use for limited periods
- ❏ proprietary lease
- ❏ fee simple ownership of units

Cooperative
- ❏ corporate ownership
- ❏ undivided interest in common elements
- ❏ occupancy and use for limited periods
- ❏ proprietary lease
- ❏ fee simple ownership of units

Time-Share
- ❏ corporate ownership
- ❏ undivided interest in common elements
- ❏ occupancy and use for limited periods
- ❏ proprietary lease
- ❏ fee simple ownership of units

MATCHING B   *Write the letter of the matching term on the appropriate line.*

a. *assessments*

b. *condo fee*

c. *condominium*

d. *corporation*

e. *general partnership*

f. *joint venture*

g. *limited liability company*

h. *separate property*

i. *time-share estate*

j. *time-share use*

1. ____ A business organization in which all members participate in the operation and management of the business and share full liability for business losses and obligations

2. ____ A business organization that is a legal entity managed and operated by a board of directors

3. ____ A business organization in which two or more people or firms carry out a single business project

4. ____ A business organization that combines the tax advantages of limited partnerships and limited liability of corporations

5. ____ In a community property state, real or personal property that was owned solely by either spouse prior to marriage or acquired by inheritance or gift during the marriage

6. ____ A form of property ownership in which each owner holds an undivided interest in certain common elements in addition to holding his or her own property in fee simple

7. ____ Special payments required of condominium unit owners to address specific expenses

8. ____ Recurring fees required of condominium unit owners to cover basic maintenance and operations

9. ____ A fee simple interest in a property that entitles the owner to use the facility for a certain period of time

10. ____ A contract right under which a developer retains ownership of property and the purchaser receives the right to occupy and use the facilities for a certain period

MULTIPLE CHOICE   *Circle a, b, c, or d.*

1. Which of the following may never take title as a joint tenancy with right of survivorship?
   a. Wife and husband
   b. Two female business partners
   c. Two brothers in partnership
   d. A corporation

2. When two or more individuals decide to buy a property together, it results in a
   a. cooperation.
   b. co-ownership.
   c. community effort.
   d. joint venture.

3. Three brothers bought a farm together. The deed listed only each of their names. What form of ownership are they presumed to have taken?
   a. Tenancy by the entireties
   b. Joint tenancy with right of survivorship
   c. Tenancy in common
   d. In severalty

MULTIPLE CHOICE   *(continued)*

4. What form of ownership is employed when one person transfers ownership to someone else to hold and manage for a third person?

   a. Joint venture   c. Trust

   b. Joint tenancy   d. Severalty

5. A man with two sons and a woman with two daughters are getting married and buying a house together. They ask the real estate licensee for advice on how to take title. What advice should the licensee offer?

   a. Tenants in common, so that each one-half in interest would go to the appropriate children

   b. Joint tenancy to protect, so that if one dies, the other gets the house

   c. Suggest that they consult with the employing broker

   d. Suggest that they consult with an attorney

6. The will provided that the local banker take care of the deceased person's estate until the children turned age 25. What kind of trust is this?

   a. Testamentary trust

   b. Living trust

   c. Land trust

   d. Trust deed

7. What kind of ownership do the horizontal property acts regulate?

   a. Cooperatives

   b. Condominiums

   c. Time-sharing

   d. Planned unit development

8. Shareholders in a cooperative receive a share of stock that is connected to the

   a. common elements.

   b. trust deed.

   c. proprietary lease.

   d. corporate deed.

9. Membership camping is similar to

   a. cooperative ownership.

   b. condominium ownership.

   c. planned use development.

   d. time-share use.

10. In a large high-rise condominium, each unit is owned by individual owners. The elevators, parking garage, and swimming pool are referred to as

    a. community property.

    b. separate property.

    c. common elements.

    d. proprietary elements.

11. Paula and Ali own an apartment building together as joint tenants. They share equally in the expenses and profits. One day, Paula decides to end the relationship. If Paula sells her interest to Kurt by signing and delivering a deed, which of the following statements is *TRUE?*

    a. Kurt will become a joint tenant with Ali.

    b. Kurt and Ali will be tenants in common.

    c. Kurt will be a tenant in common with Ali and a joint tenant with Paula.

    d. The conveyance will be invalid: Paula and Ali will remain joint tenants.

12. In February, Geoff conveyed an undivided one-half interest in Sunny Orchard to Tara. In March, Geoff conveyed the remaining one-half interest to Rob. The deed to Rob included the following statement: "Rob is to be a joint tenant with Tara." Both deeds were recorded. Based on these facts, which of the following statements is *TRUE?*

    a. Tara and Rob hold title to Sunny Orchard as joint tenants under the terms of the two conveyances from Geoff.

    b. Tara and Rob own Sunny Orchard by partition.

    c. Tara and Rob are tenants in common.

    d. Rob owns Sunny Orchard as a joint tenant; Tara owns Sunny Orchard as a tenant in common.

MULTIPLE CHOICE   *(continued)*

13. Ellen, Kayla, and Jon own a large parcel of unde-
    veloped land in joint tenancy. Ellen wants to
    build a shopping center on the property, while
    Kayla and Jon want to use it as an organic farm.
    Ellen tries to buy the other tenants' interests,
    but they refuse to sell. Which of the following is
    Ellen's *BEST* option?

    a. File a suit for partition
    b. Begin building a shopping center on one-
       third of the property
    c. Wait for Kayla and Jon to die
    d. File a suit to quiet title

14. Arnie owns a cottage in the Walden Acres
    community on the shore of Loon Lake. Arnie's
    ownership of the cottage is in fee simple. Arnie
    also owns an undivided percentage interest in a
    parking lot, a golf course, and a swimming pool,
    all located in the Walden Acres development.
    Based on these facts alone, Arnie's ownership
    is probably *BEST* described as a

    a. time-share estate.
    b. time-share use.
    c. condominium.
    d. cooperative.

15. Mike, Rebecca, and Noah agree to purchase
    and operate Rickety Tower as a permanent
    investment. Mike and Rebecca each contribute
    $50,000. Noah contributes $30,000 and agrees
    to run the day-to-day operations of the business,
    which they call "Rickety Tower Joint Venture
    Partners." Neither Mike nor Rebecca has any
    right to participate in the operation of the
    venture. Based on these facts, what type of
    business organization have Mike, Rebecca, and
    Noah established?

    a. Joint venture
    b. Limited partnership
    c. General partnership
    d. Limited liability company

16. Based on the facts in the previous question, if
    Rickety Tower collapses, resulting in injury and
    property damage worth $275,000, what will be
    Mike's liability?

    a. None   c. $91,667
    b. $50,000   d. $100,000

17. All of the following are unities required for a
    joint tenancy *EXCEPT* unity of

    a. title.   c. time.
    b. ownership.   d. possession.

18. All of the following are characteristics of a ten-
    ancy by the entirety *EXCEPT*

    a. title may be conveyed only by a deed signed
       by both parties.
    b. the surviving spouse automatically becomes
       sole owner of the property upon the death of
       the other spouse.
    c. each spouse owns an equal, undivided interest
       in the property as a single, indivisible unit.
    d. the surviving spouse automatically owns
       one-half of the property acquired during the
       marriage.

19. Neal creates a trust to pay for Melanie's real
    estate education. The trust is operated by Olga,
    who makes payments on Melanie's behalf
    directly to The Real Estate School. Based on
    these facts, which of the following statements
    BEST characterizes the relationships among
    these parties?

    a. Olga is the trustor, Melanie is the beneficiary,
       and Neal is the trustee.
    b. Neal is the trustor, the Real Estate School is
       the beneficiary, and Olga is the trustee.
    c. Neal is the trustor, Melanie is the beneficiary,
       and Olga is the trustee.
    d. Neal is the trustor, Melanie is the beneficiary,
       Olga is the trustee, and The Real Estate
       School is the fiduciary.

MULTIPLE CHOICE *(continued)*

20. XYZ is a legal entity, created by charter under the laws of the state of East Carolina. XYZ is managed and operated by a board and is permitted to buy and sell real estate. When one of its directors dies, XYZ continues to operate. Because of its structure, XYZ's income is subject to double taxation. XYZ is best described as a(n)

a. partnership.

b. S corporation.

c. corporation.

d. limited liability company.

21. What is one reason that brokers and salespersons should understand the fundamental types of property ownership?

a. So they will know who must sign various documents

b. To explain the legal implications of various ownerships to sellers

c. To advise buyers on how to set up the property ownership

d. So they can help clients locate property with the appropriate ownership

22. When a corporation takes ownership of property, it is considered to be ownership in

a. joint tenancy.

b. tenancy in common.

c. partnership.

d. severalty.

23. If Scott wants to create a joint tenancy between himself and Marshall, many states require that Scott first convey the property to a nominee or

a. grantor. c. remainderman.

b. beneficiary. d. straw man.

24. In a tenancy in common, if the fractions of ownership are *NOT* stated in the deed, how are they determined?

a. The tenants need a judicial decision to determine the fractional shares.

b. The tenants are presumed to hold equal shares.

c. The tenants settle the issue through binding arbitration.

d. The tenants must terminate the tenancy in common through partition.

25. In the case of land trusts, the beneficiary is usually also the

a. trustor. c. fiduciary.

b. trustee d. attorney in fact.

ANSWER KEY

Key Term Matching (A)

1. f **2.** a **3.** b **4.** c **5.** g **6.** i **7.** j **8.** d
9. e **10.** h

True of False

1. True

2. True

3. **False.** In a *joint tenancy*, property is owned by two or more owners with the right of survivorship.

4. True

5. **False.** A joint tenancy continues indefinitely, until there is only one remaining owner, who then holds title in *severalty*.

6. True

7. **False.** The four unities characteristic of a *joint tenancy* are possession, interest, title, and time.

8. **False.** A joint tenant may freely convey his or her interest in the jointly held property to a new owner, but doing so will destroy the unities of time and title and the new owner *cannot* become a joint tenant.

9. True

10. True

11. **False.** A tenancy *by the entirety* may be terminated by divorce, agreement, court order, or the death of one of the parties.

12. **False.** In a community property state, *community property* includes all property, both real and personal, acquired by either party only during the marriage, except by gift or inheritance.

13. True

14. **False.** A general partnership must be dissolved and reorganized if one partner dies.

15. **False.** When a corporation buys real property, the stockholders own the corporation that owns the real estate. Therefore their ownership of the real property is *indirect*.

16. **False.** A *joint venture* is a form of partnership in which two or more people or firms carry out a single business project, with no intention of establishing an ongoing or permanent relationship.

17. **False.** Condominium owners hold their own units in fee simple and the common elements as *tenants in common*.

18. True

19. True

20. True

21. True

22. **False.** A *syndicate* is two or more people or firms joined together to make and operate a real estate investment. It is not a separate legal entity and can be organized into a co-ownership, partnership, trust, or corporation.

23. True

24. True

25. **False.** A *town house* is a type of housing connected by common walls and is usually located on a small lot.

Types of Ownership

Condominium
- ✓ undivided interest in common elements
- ✓ fee simple ownership of units

Cooperative
- ✓ corporate ownership
- ✓ proprietary lease

Time-Share
- ✓ undivided interest in common elements
- ✓ occupancy and use for limited periods
- ✓ fee simple ownership of units

Key Term Matching (B)

1. e **2.** d **3.** f **4.** g **5.** h **6.** c **7.** a **8.** b
9. i **10.** j

Multiple Choice

1. **d.** Because a corporation continues indefinitely until terminated by legal action, a corporation may never take title as a joint tenant. It would never die.

2. **b.** When two or more people buy property together, it is called *co-ownership*. A *joint venture* is a form of partnership in which two or more people carry out a single business project with no intention of establishing an ongoing relationship.

3. **c.** The brothers are presumed to be tenants in common because they did not indicate "as joint tenants with right of survivorship." Joint tenancy requires extra wording; it is sometimes called the "poor man's will." Severalty ownership indicates one owner.

4. **c.** Severalty indicates one owner. A joint venture is a form of partnership. Joint tenancy is a form of ownership whereby, as joint owners die, the surviving owners acquire the deceased tenant's interest.

5. **d.** The only possible answer here is to refer the couple to an attorney. Real estate licensees and their brokers are not permitted to give legal advice.

6. **a.** A testamentary trust is established by will after the trustor's death. A living trust is established during the trustor's lifetime. Real estate is the only asset in a land trust. Trust deed is another name for a deed of trust, a financing instrument.

7. **b.** Condominiums are regulated by the horizontal property acts enacted in most states.

8. **c.** Common elements refer to the property owned jointly by condominium owners. The proprietary lease is part of the cooperative stock and gives the owner the right to a specific apartment.

9. **d.** The owner of membership camping purchases the right to use the developer's facilities; the owner may not be limited to a specific time as in the case of a typical time-share arrangement.

10. **c.** The property that condominium owners own together is referred to as common elements. Community property is a system of property ownership based on the theory that each spouse has an equal interest in property acquired during the marriage, making a distinction from property acquired before marriage, that is, separate property.

11. **b.** A co-owner can sell what he or she owns. However, once the unities of time, title, and interest are destroyed, as they are when Paula sells her interest to Kurt, there can no longer be a joint tenancy.

12. **c.** Because there are two deeds, made at different times, the four unities of joint tenancy have not been met. Therefore, Tara and Rob are tenants in common.

13. **a.** When co-owners cannot come to an agreement, they must file for partition in court. The property will not physically be divided; rather, one or more will be given the opportunity to buy the others out. If this is not possible, then the property will be sold, and the money will be divided appropriately.

14. **c.** It appears that Arnie has condominium ownership because he owns the cottage as well as the interest in the common elements. Cooperative ownership is ruled out because he does not have a proprietary lease. It is not a time-share because he clearly owns more than the right to use at specific times.

15. **b.** A limited partnership limits the participation of the silent partners as well as limiting their liability. A general partnership would require that all are equally involved in running the operation and all are exposed to liability.

16. **b.** Mike is a limited partner and is limited in liability to the $50,000 amount of his investment.

17. **b.** There is no such thing as unity of ownership. The missing unity is that of interest.

18. **d.** Choices a, b, and c are all true statements about tenancy by the entirety. Choice d is a summary of community property.

19. c. Neal is the owner-trustor; Melanie is the beneficiary; Olga is the person who manages the trust, that is, the trustee.

20. c. Both the S corporation and the corporation would not be affected if one of the directors dies. The tip-off to this answer is *double taxation*. The S corporation was created to avoid the double taxation imposed on a corporation.

21. a. Brokers and salespersons must be careful not to give clients legal advice, such as what types of ownership to select.

22. d. Corporations are artificial persons and therefore hold ownership in severalty.

23. d. After conveying the property to the straw man, the nominee conveys it back to Scott and Marshall. A grantor sets up a trust with a trustee and beneficiary.

24. b. If there are two tenants, each owns an undivided half interest. Tenancy in common only needs to be terminated through partition if the parties do not voluntarily agree to its termination.

25. a. The beneficiary retains management and control of the real property and has the right of possession and the right to any income.

9

Legal Descriptions

BEFORE YOU START...

After completing Chapter 9 of the textbook, you should be able to answer the following "learning assessment" questions. If you are able to answer these questions, then you are ready to move ahead with this chapter of the *Study Guide!* If, however, you are having some difficulty answering any of these learning assessment questions, we advise you to reread key sections of the textbook before attempting to answer the questions in this chapter of the *Study Guide*.

■ Do you know the importance of an accurate legal description?

■ Are you able to describe the three methods of legally describing real estate?

■ Can you apply legal descriptions of property to specific problems?

■ Are you able to describe how elevations are measured, including their measurements in the legal description of a condominium?

■ How do you distinguish various units of land measurement?

MATCHING   *Write the letter of the matching term on the appropriate line.*

a. *metes-and-bounds*

b. *rectangular survey system*

c. *correction lines*

d. *monuments*

e. *lot-and-block*

f. *benchmarks*

g. *datum*

h. POB

i. *township lines*

j. *ranges*

1. _____ The type of legal description that relies on a property's physical features to determine and to describe the boundaries and measurements of the parcel

2. _____ The designated starting point for a metes-and-bounds description

3. _____ Fixed objects used to identify significant points of measurement in a metes-and-bounds description

4. _____ A land description system based on principal meridians and base lines

5. _____ Lines running six miles apart and parallel to the base line

6. _____ Strips of land running parallel to the meridian

7. _____ A device to compensate for inaccurate measurements and the shape of the earth

8. _____ A system of description that uses numbers referred to in a plat map

9. _____ A point, line, or surface from which elevations are measured

10. _____ Permanent reference markers, usually found on embossed brass markers set in concrete or asphalt

TRUE OR FALSE   *Circle the correct answer.*

1. T F The metes-and-bounds description was established by Congress in 1785.

2. T F In the metes-and-bounds system, a monument may be either a natural object or a human-made marker.

3. T F With the use of new technology, such as global positioning systems, the metes-and-bounds system is the most accurate method.

4. T F For a parcel described under the lot-and-block system, the lot refers to the numerical designation of the any particular parcel.

5. T F A government check is the area bounded by two guide township lines and two correction lines.

6. T F Areas smaller than full quarter-sections were numbered and designated as correction lots.

7. T F Principal meridians run east and west.

8. T F Township lines and base lines are parallel.

9. T F Ranges are strips of land six miles wide that run parallel to the base line.

10. T F When the horizontal township lines and the vertical range lines intersect, they form township squares.

11. T F Every township contains 36 sections of 640 acres each.

12. T F A datum is a permanent reference point, usually found on an embossed brass marker set into a solid concrete or asphalt base.

TRUE OR FALSE *(continued)*

13. T F Section 6 is always in the northeast or upper left-hand corner.

14. T F Air lots are composed of the airspace within specific boundaries located over a parcel of land.

15. T F When preparing a plat map of a new condominium, the surveyor shows the elevations of floor and ceiling surfaces.

MULTIPLE CHOICE *Circle a, b, c, or d.*

1. All of the following are used to express a legal description *EXCEPT*
   a. lot-and-block.
   b. metes-and-bounds.
   c. rectangular survey system.
   d. benchmarks.

2. Air lots, condominium descriptions, and other vertical measurements may be computed from the U.S. Geological Survey
   a. datum.
   b. benchmark.
   c. principal meridian.
   d. base line.

3. Kyle sells six acres of prime undeveloped property to Lars for $2.25 per square foot. How much did Lars pay?
   a. $466,560
   b. $588,060
   c. $612,360
   d. $733,860

4. Which township section number is directly north of Section 7?
   a. Section 1
   b. Section 6
   c. Section 5
   d. Section 8

5. Which of the following *MOST* accurately describes a quarter-section?
   a. ¼ mile by ¼ mile
   b. ½ mile by ½ mile
   c. ½ mile by 1 mile
   d. ⅛ mile by ⅛ mile

6. A farmer is willing to pay $1,200 per acre. He is planning to buy the SE ¼ of the SE ¼ of the SE ¼ of Section 11. How much will he pay for the land?
   a. $3,000
   b. $6,000
   c. $12,000
   d. $24,000

7. Years ago, a farm was typically a quarter section. How many acres is that?
   a. 20 acres
   b. 80 acres
   c. 160 acres
   d. 320 acres

8. How many acres are contained in a parcel described as follows: The NE ¼ of the NW ¼; the N ¼ of the NW ¼, NE ¼, Section 10?
   a. 40 acres
   b. 60 acres
   c. 70 acres
   d. 74 acres

9. Undersized or oversized sections are classified as
   a. school sections.
   b. government sections.
   c. range sections.
   d. fractional sections.

10. Metes-and-bounds descriptions may be required in rectangular survey system descriptions in all of the following situations *EXCEPT*
    a. when a tract is too large to be described by quarter sections.
    b. when describing an irregular tract.
    c. when a tract is too small to be described by quarter-sections.
    d. when a tract does not follow the lot or block lines of a recorded subdivision or section.

MULTIPLE CHOICE *(continued)*

11. What is the square footage for the following property described by the metes-and-bounds method?

    Beginning at a point on the southerly side of Smith Street, 200 feet easterly from the corner formed by the intersection of the southerly side of Smith Street and the easterly side of Johnson Street; then East 200 feet; then South 100 feet; then West 200 feet; then North 100 feet to the POB.

    a. 5,000 square feet   c. 15,000 square feet
    b. 10,000 square feet   d. 20,000 square feet

12. The end of a metes-and-bounds land description is always a

    a. monument.   c. point of beginning.
    b. benchmark.   d. base line.

13. The lot-and-block system starts with the preparation of a(n)

    a. subdivision plat.   c. survey.
    b. range map.   d. air lot.

Refer to the plat on the next page for Question 14 through Question 20.

14. Which lot in Block A has the MOST frontage on Jasmine Lane?

    a. 1   c. 7
    b. 2   d. 11

15. How many lots have easements?

    a. 1   c. 4
    b. 3   d. 6

16. Which road or roads run east and west?

    a. Wolf and Jasmine
    b. Carney and Goodrich
    c. Wolf only
    d. Goodrich only

17. Which lot has the LEAST street exposure?

    a. Lot 3, Block A   c. Lot 9, Block A
    b. Lot 15, Block B   d. Lot 10, Block B

18. Beginning at the intersection of the West line of Carney Street and the North line of Wolf Road, running west 140 feet, then North 120 feet, then North 50 degrees East 120 feet, then following the southeasterly curvature of the South line of Jasmine Lane for 100 feet, then South 120 feet to POB.

    To which lot does this description refer?

    a. Lot 15, Block B
    b. Lot 8, Block A
    c. Lot 7, 8, and 9, Block A
    d. Lot 8 and 9, Block A

19. If lot 13 and lot 14, Block A were combined into one parcel, how many square feet would it contain?

    a. 1,020   c. 22,800
    b. 19,800   d. 21,600

20. If Brian is willing to pay $2 per square foot for lot 13, Block A, how much would he pay for the land?

    a. $10,000   c. $16,000
    b. $12,000   d. $24,000

MULTIPLE CHOICE *(continued)*

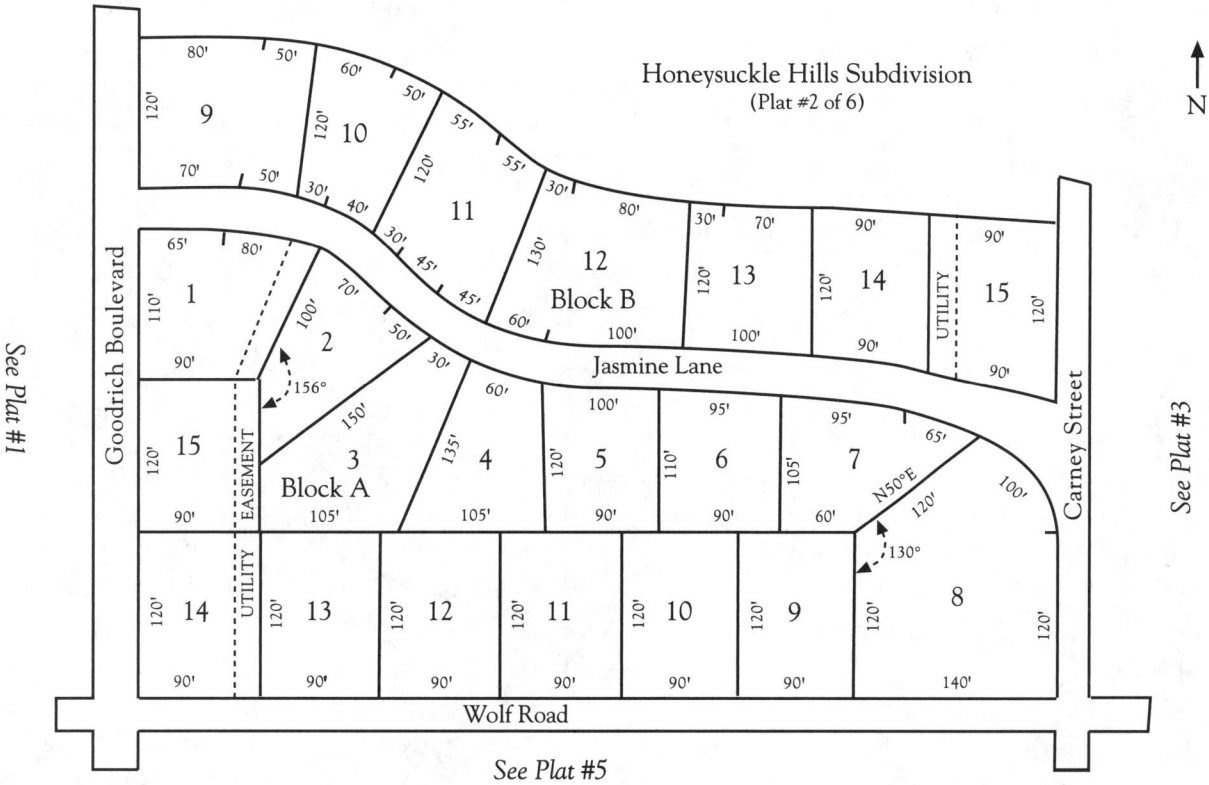

ANSWER KEY

Key Term Matching

1. a   **2.** h   **3.** d   **4.** b   **5.** i   **6.** j   **7.** c   **8.** e
9. g   **10.** f

True or False

1. False. The *rectangular survey system* was established by Congress in 1785.

2. True

3. True

4. True

5. False. A government check is the area bounded by two guide *meridians* and two correction lines.

6. False. Areas smaller than full quarter-sections were numbered and designated as government lots.

7. False. A principal meridian runs *north and south*.

8. True

9. False. Range lines are strips of land six miles wide that run parallel to the *principal meridian*.

10. True

11. True

12. False. A *benchmark* is a permanent reference point that is usually found on an embossed brass marker set into a solid concrete or asphalt base and used for marking datums.

13. False. Section 6 is always in the *northwest* or upper left-hand corner.

14. True

15. True

Multiple Choice

1. d. A *benchmark* is a permanent reference point used as a reference for marking datums.

2. a. The U.S. Geological Survey *datum* is defined as the mean sea level at New York Harbor. A surveyor uses the datum to determine the height of a structure or to establish the grade of a street.

3. b. Lars paid $588,060: $43,560 × 6 = 261,360 square feet × $2.25 = $588,060

4. b. A township is numbered in an "s" fashion: 1 through 6, right to left and 7 to 12, left to right. Section 7 is directly south of section 6.

5. b. A *section* is one square mile.

6. c. The farmer paid $12,000: ¼ × 640 = 160 × ¼ = 40 × ¼ = 10 acres × $1,200 = $12,000.

7. c. A quarter of 640 acres is 160 acres.

8. b. There are two parcels in this description denoted by the semicolon (;). The first: ¼ of 640 = 160; ¼ of 160 = 40. The second; ¼ of 640 = 160 × ¼ = 40 × ½ = 20. 20 + 40 = 60.

9. d. By law, section number 16 was set aside for school purposes. It was a standard size section.

10. a. Large size is not a difficulty when using the rectangular survey system.

11. d. The property is 200 × 100 = 20,000 square feet.

12. c. A metes-and-bounds description must always begin and end at the point of beginning, thus *encircling* the described property.

13. a. The legal description must be determined before a survey can be prepared. An air lot refers to air above land.

14. c. In Block A, Lot 7 with 160 feet has the longest frontage.

15. c. Four lots have easements: Lots, 1, 14, and 15, Block A. Lot 15, Block B.

16. a. Wolf and Jasmine roads run east and west.

17. a. Lot 3, Block A with 30 feet has the least street exposure.

18. b. The description refers to Lot 8, Block A.

19. d. The combined parcel would have 21,600 square feet: 120 × 90 = 10,800 × 2 = 21,600.

20. d. Brian would pay $24,000: 100 × 120 = 12,000 square feet × $2 = $24,000.

10

Real Estate Taxes and Other Liens

BEFORE YOU START...

After completing Chapter 10 of the textbook, you should be able to answer the following "learning assessment" questions. If you are able to answer these questions, then you are ready to move ahead with this chapter of the *Study Guide!* If, however, you are having some difficulty answering any of these learning assessment questions, we advise you to reread key sections of the textbook before attempting to answer the questions in this chapter of the *Study Guide*.

- Can you define the term *lien* and give examples of the following types of liens: voluntary, involuntary, statutory, equitable, general, and specific?

- Are you able to distinguish between general real estate taxes (ad valorem taxes) and special assessments?

- How are assessments and the amount of real estate taxes determined in your area?

- Do you know the procedures for the enforcement of tax liens?

- Are you aware of the general requirements for filing a mechanic's lien?

- Can you describe a judgment lien and its effect on title?

- Do you know the other types of liens discussed in the textbook and their effects on title?

MATCHING A   *Write the letter of the matching term on the appropriate line.*

a. *ad valorem*

b. *equitable lien*

c. *subordination*

d. *involuntary lien*

e. *lien*

f. *priority*

g. *specific lien*

h. *general lien*

i. *taxes*

j. *voluntary lien*

1. ____ A charge or claim against a person's property, to enforce the payment of money

2. ____ A lien that is created intentionally by the property owner's action

3. ____ A lien created by law

4. ____ A lien that arises out of common law

5. ____ A lien that affects all the real and personal property owned by a debtor

6. ____ A lien that is secured by and only affects certain property

7. ____ The order in which claims against property will be satisfied

8. ____ A written agreement between lienholders to change the priority of a lien

9. ____ Charges imposed by state and local governments to fund their functions and services

10. ____ A general recurring real estate tax

TRUE OR FALSE   *Circle the correct answer.*

1. T F A voluntary lien may be classified as either statutory or equitable.

2. T F A charge or claim against a person's property by a creditor, made to enforce the payment of money, is referred to as a *lien*.

3. T F All encumbrances are liens.

4. T F Both federal estate taxes and state inheritance taxes are general, statutory, and involuntary liens.

5. T F Taking out a mortgage loan is an example of the creation of an equitable lien.

6. T F A lien attaches to real property at the time the lien is filed.

7. T F A special assessment is always a specific, statutory, and involuntary lien.

8. T F A court's decree that establishes the amount owed by a debtor is enforced by a judgment directing the sheriff to seize and sell the debtor's property.

9. T F Mechanics' liens never take priority over tax or special assessment liens.

10. T F *Ad valorem* taxes apply to the difference between the assessed value of a property and the value added by resale or improvement.

11. T F All liens are encumbrances.

12. T F The presence of a lien on real property does not prevent the owner from conveying title to another party.

13. T F A taxing body determines the appropriate tax rate by dividing the total monies needed for the coming fiscal year by the total assessments of all real estate located within the taxing body's jurisdiction.

14. T F A delinquent taxpayer may redeem property at any time prior to a tax sale by exercising his or her statutory right of redemption.

15. T F A mechanic's lien is a specific, involuntary lien.

MATCHING B   *Write the letter of the matching term on the appropriate line.*

a. *assessment*	**1.** ____ The official process of valuing real estate for tax purposes
b. *money judgment*	**2.** ____ A device to achieve uniformity in statewide assessments
c. *equalization factor*	**3.** ____ 1/1,000 of a dollar, or $0.001
d. *equitable right of redemption*	**4.** ____ The right of a delinquent taxpayer to recover property before a tax sale
e. *lis pendens*	**5.** ____ The right of a delinquent taxpayer to recover property after a tax sale
f. *attachment*	**6.** ____ Taxes levied on specific properties that benefit from public improvement
g. *mechanic's lien*	**7.** ____ A specific, involuntary lien that gives security to persons or companies who perform labor or furnish material to improve real property
h. *mill*	**8.** ____ A court decree that establishes the amount owed by a debtor and provides for money to be awarded
i. *special assessments*	**9.** ____ A notice of a possible future lien based on a lawsuit
j. *statutory right of redemption*	**10.** ____ A writ that permits a court to retain custody of a debtor's property until the creditor's lawsuit is concluded

LIEN CHARACTERISTICS

Identify the characteristics of liens by placing check marks in the appropriate columns.

Type of Lien	General	Specific	Voluntary	Involuntary	Equitable	Statutory
Mechanic's Lien						
Special Assessment						
Mortgage						
Bail Bond						
Municipal Utility Lien						
Federal Estate Tax Lien						
Corporate Franchise Tax						
State Inheritance Tax						
Judgment						
Real Property Tax						

FILL-IN-THE-BLANK *Select the word or words that best complete the following statements:*

assessed value

certificate of sale

golf course

hospital

*Local Improvement
District (LID)*

mechanic's lien

prorated share

satisfaction of judgment

subordination agreement

tax levy

tax lien

title search

writ of attachment

1. To reveal any recorded liens, a property buyer should require a(n) _____ before closing the real estate transaction.

2. A county assessor usually bases a property's _____ on the sale prices of comparable properties.

3. Usually a vote of the taxing district's governing body is needed to impose a(n) _____.

4. In many states, when a purchaser at a tax sale receives the _____ _____, he or she gains the right to take possession of the property.

5. When new streetlights were installed on Maple Avenue, the homeowners were charged a special assessment that was a(n) _____ of the total amount of the assessment.

6. The priority of a(n) _____ may be established as of the date construction began or materials were first furnished.

7. A court order against the property of another person that directs the sheriff to take control of a property is called a(n) _____.

8. When real property is sold to pay off a debt, the debtor should get a legal document known as a(n) _____.

9. An example of a property that is exempt from taxation is a(n) _____ _____.

10. When an improvement project will be on a large scale, such as sewer construction, a(n) _____ may be created.

MULTIPLE CHOICE *Circle a, b, c, or d.*

1. Generally, in a court-ordered sale, which of the following is paid first?
   a. First mortgage
   b. Mechanics' liens
   c. Child support liens
   d. Real estate taxes

2. Which of the following is an example of a specific lien?
   a. Decedent's debts
   b. Internal Revenue Service liens
   c. Mortgage lien
   d. Corporate franchise liens

3. The millage breakout for ad valorem taxes are: library: .5; school: 1; school debt service: .5; community college: 1; vocational school: .5; and all others: 5. If the property is assessed at $165,000, how much is the tax bill?
   a. $1,200.25
   b. $1,402.50
   c. $1,405.75
   d. $1,800.50

4. All of the following are liens against real property EXCEPT
   a. a mortgage.
   b. real estate taxes.
   c. lis pendens.
   d. home improvement loan of a deceased property owner.

MULTIPLE CHOICE *(continued)*

5. Which of the following characteristics apply to a real estate tax lien?

   a. Specific, involuntary lien

   b. Specific, voluntary lien

   c. General, involuntary lien

   d. General, voluntary lien

6. Which of the following may be either an involuntary or voluntary lien on real property?

   a. Mortgage loan

   b. Real estate tax

   c. Special assessment

   d. Mechanic's lien

7. Which of the following would permit a law enforcement officer to seize a debtor's property?

   a. Lis pendens

   b. Satisfaction of judgment

   c. Writ of execution

   d. Writ of attachment

8. If the property owners in a neighborhood petition the city for new sidewalks and paved alleys, which of the following *BEST* describes the character of the lien that may result if the city agrees to the improvements?

   a. General, statutory, and voluntary

   b. Specific, equitable, and involuntary

   c. Specific, statutory, and voluntary

   d. General, equitable, and involuntary

9. Which of the following is a general, statutory, and involuntary lien on both real and personal property?

   a. Federal tax lien

   b. Mechanic's lien

   c. Special assessment

   d. Consumer loan lien

10. The owner stopped making mortgage payments to Marke Mortgage in June. In February, the owner contracted with Bill to have his billiard room converted into a sauna and never paid for the work. The owner is two years delinquent in property taxes to Ventnor County and owes more than $30,000 on a custom luxury automobile purchased from Don's Cars in January. The state gives mechanics' liens priority.

    If all these creditors obtain judgments against the owner in November, what will be the priority of their liens (first to last)?

    a. Don's Cars → Bill → Marke Mortgage → Ventnor

    b. Ventnor → Marke Mortgage → Bill → Don's Cars

    c. Bill → Ventnor → Don's Cars → Marke Mortgage

    d. Ventnor → Bill → Marke Mortgage → Don's Cars

11. A town wants to construct new concrete curbs in a residential neighborhood. How will the town most likely raise the money necessary for the improvement?

    a. Ad valorem tax

    b. Special assessment

    c. Equalized assessment

    d. Utility lien

12. All of the following liens must be recorded to be effective *EXCEPT*

    a. money judgment.

    b. mechanic's lien.

    c. real estate tax lien.

    d. voluntary lien.

MULTIPLE CHOICE *(continued)*

13. The market value of an undeveloped parcel is $40,000. Its assessed value is 40 percent of market value, and properties in its county are subject to an equalization factor of 1.50. If the tax rate is $4 per $100, what is the amount of the tax owed on the property?

    a. $480   **c.** $1,080

    b. $960   **d.** $1,800

14. To establish a potential claim against the property and to establish priority, one needs to file a(n)

    a. lis pendens.   **c.** general lien.

    b. attachment.   **d.** specific lien.

15. Soo Lan was considering having a new garage built. Soo Lan talked about the project with several contractors, including Yanni. In April, while Soo Lan was on vacation, Yanni began building the garage according to Soo Lan's specifications. Work was complete by the end of May. In June, Soo Lan returned from vacation and refused to pay for the garage. Yanni decides to file a mechanic's lien in July. Is Yanni entitled to a lien?

    a. Yes, because the garage was constructed according to Soo Lan's specifications.

    b. Yes, because the garage is not a part of an owner-occupied residence.

    c. No, because notice of the lien should have been filed in May, when the work was completed.

    d. No, because there was no express or implied contract between Soo Lan and Yanni.

ANSWER KEY

Key Term Matching (A)

1. e **2.** j **3.** d **4.** b **5.** h **6.** g **7.** f **8.** c
9. i **10.** a

True or False

1. **False.** An *involuntary* lien may be classified as either statutory or equitable.

2. **True**

3. **False.** Not all encumbrances are liens. Others are easements and encroachments.

4. **True**

5. **False.** Taking out a mortgage loan is an example of the creation of a *voluntary* lien.

6. **True**

7. **False.** A special assessment is always a specific and statutory lien, but it may be *either involuntary or voluntary*, depending on the nature of the improvement being funded.

8. **False.** A court's decree that establishes the amount owed by a debtor is enforced by a *writ of execution* directing the sheriff to seize and sell the debtor's property.

9. **True**

10. **False.** *Ad valorem* taxes are based on the value of the property being taxed.

11. **True**

12. **True**

13. **True**

14. **False.** A delinquent taxpayer may redeem property any time prior to a tax sale by exercising his or her *equitable* right of redemption.

15. **True**

Key Term Matching (B)

1. a **2.** c **3.** h **4.** d **5.** j **6.** i **7.** g **8.** b
9. e **10.** f

Fill-in-the-Blank

1. To reveal any recorded liens, a property buyer should require a *title search* before closing the real estate transaction.

2. A county assessor usually bases a property's *assessed value* on the sales prices of comparable properties.

3. Usually a vote of the taxing district's governing body is needed to impose a *tax levy*.

4. In many states, when a purchaser at a tax sale receives the *certificate of sale*, he or she gains the right to take possession of the property.

5. When new streetlights were installed on Maple Avenue, the homeowners were charged a special assessment that was a *prorated share* of the total amount of the assessment.

6. The priority of a *mechanic's lien* may be established as of the date construction began or materials were first furnished.

7. A court order against the property of another person that directs the sheriff to take control of a property is called a *writ of attachment*.

8. When real property is sold to pay off a debt, the debtor should get a legal document known as a *satisfaction of judgment*.

9. An example of a property that is exempt from taxation is a *hospital*.

10. When an improvement project will be on a large scale, such as sewer construction, a *Local Improvement District (LID)* may be created.

Multiple Choice

1. **d.** Real estate taxes do not have to be recorded to be effective, and they take precedence over all other liens.

2. **c.** A mortgage lien is a specific, voluntary lien.

3. **b.** The tax bill is $1402.50:
.5 + 1 + .5 + 1 + .5 + 5 = 8.5 mills or $.0085
$165,000 × .0085 = $1,402.50.

4. **c.** A lis pendens is only the notice of a possible future lien. However, if it becomes a lien, the priority is established by the date and time that the lis pendens was originally filed.

5. **a.** A real estate tax is levied on an individual property; few would argue that individuals choose to have the tax levied, hence, an involuntary lien.

6. **c.** If property owners request that the city or county make an improvement and agree to a special assessment, it is considered voluntary. In other situations, the property owners may fight the proposed improvement, and the special assessment is therefore involuntary.

7. **c.** A *writ of execution* directs the sheriff to seize and sell as much of the debtor's property as necessary to pay both the debt and the expenses of the sale.

8. **c.** Because the property owners have petitioned the city to make the improvements, the lien is voluntary. Because it will be levied on only the properties that receive the benefit, it is specific. It is created by statute.

9. **a.** An Internal Revenue Service lien is a general lien against the person, that is, against the real and personal property owned by the delinquent taxpayer.

10. **d.** The priority is taxes, mechanic's lien, first mortgage, and then personal property. Although the mortgage was filed first, property taxes always have first priority, and the state has given second priority to mechanic's liens. The personal property lien is last in priority.

11. **b.** The town will levy a specific lien against the benefiting properties to pay for the new concrete curbs.

12. **c.** Ad valorem real estate tax liens do not have to be recorded to be effective, and they always take precedence over all other liens. This is why many lenders collect $\frac{1}{12}$ of the taxes each month, so that the lender can pay the taxes when due. Unpaid taxes take priority over mortgage liens.

13. **b.** The tax owned on the property is $960: $40,000 × 40% × 1.5 ÷ 100 × 4 = $960.

14. **a.** A *lis pendens* is a notice of a possible future lien. If it becomes an actual lien, the effective date of the lien is the date and time that the lis pendens was filed.

15. **d.** Because the contractor, Yanni, was in no way given authority to act, Yanni has no right to file a mechanic's lien.

LIEN CHARACTERISTICS

Type of Lien	General	Specific	Voluntary	Involuntary	Equitable	Statutory
Mechanic's Lien		✓		✓		✓
Special Assessment		✓	✓	✓		✓
Mortgage		✓	✓		✓	
Bail Bond		✓	✓			✓
Municipal Utility Lien		✓		✓	✓	
Federal Estate Tax Lien	✓			✓		✓
Corporate Franchise Tax	✓			✓		✓
State Inheritance Tax	✓			✓		✓
Judgment	✓			✓	✓	
Real Property Tax		✓		✓		✓

11

Real Estate Contracts

BEFORE YOU START...

After completing Chapter 11 of the textbook, you should be able to answer the following "learning assessment" questions. If you are able to answer these questions, then you are ready to move ahead with this chapter of the *Study Guide!* If, however, you are having some difficulty answering any of these learning assessment questions, we advise you to reread key sections of the textbook before attempting to answer the questions in this chapter of the *Study Guide.*

- Can you describe an *express contract* (written and oral) and an *implied contract?*

- Do you know the differences between a *bilateral contract* and a *unilateral contract?*

- How are an *executed contract* and an *executory contract* different?

- What do the legal effects of *void, voidable,* and *unenforceable* contracts mean to you?

- Can you outline the essential elements of a valid contract?

- What does the phrase *time is of the essence* mean as it pertains to the performance of a contract?

- Are you able to distinguish between the *assignment* and the *novation* of a contract?

- Can you describe the ways a contract can be discharged?

- Do you know the rights of the seller and the buyer in the event of a default by either one of the parties?

■ Can you distinguish between listing agreements, sales contracts, option agreements, and land contracts?

■ Are you able to list the information required for a sales contract?

MATCHING A   *Write the letter of the matching term on the appropriate line.*

a. *bilateral contract*

b. *consideration*

c. *contract*

d. *executed contract*

e. *executory contract*

f. *express contract*

g. *implied contract*

h. *mutual assent*

i. *offeree*

j. *unilateral contract*

1. _____ A voluntary, legally enforceable promise between legally competent parties to perform (or refrain from performing) some legal act

2. _____ A contract in which the parties show their intentions in words

3. _____ A contract established by the acts and conduct of the parties

4. _____ A contract in which both parties promise to perform some act

5. _____ A one-sided agreement

6. _____ A contract that has been completely performed

7. _____ The status of a real estate sales contract prior to closing

8. _____ The person who accepts the offer in a contract

9. _____ Complete agreement about the purpose and terms of a contract

10. _____ Something of legal value offered by one party and accepted by another as an inducement to act or refrain from acting

TRUE OR FALSE   *Circle the correct answer.*

1. T F An agreement to be bound by most of the terms proposed in an offer constitutes *acceptance.*

2. T F All contracts must be in writing to be enforceable.

3. T F A listing agreement is the same as a contract for the sale of real estate.

4. T F *Consideration* is something of legal value offered by one party and accepted by the other as an inducement to act.

5. T F In an implied contract, the actual agreement between the parties is inferred from general or vague statements in the written agreement itself.

6. T F The difference between a bilateral and a unilateral contract is the number of parties involved.

7. T F A sales contract is an executory contract from the time it is signed until closing; at closing, it becomes an executed contract.

8. T F A contract that may be rescinded or disaffirmed by one or both of the parties based on some legal principle is void, even though it may appear on the surface to be valid.

9. T F The person who makes an offer is the *offeree;* the person who accepts or rejects the offer is the *offeror.*

10. T F A contract entered into by a mentally ill person is voidable during the illness and for some time after the individual is cured.

11. T F An oral agreement for the sale of real estate is unenforceable.

TRUE OR FALSE   *(continued)*

12. T F Under a *land contract*, the buyer obtains both possession and title to the property by agreeing to make regular monthly payments to the seller over a number of years.

13. T F *Assignment* is the substitution of a new contract in place of the original one, while *novation* is a transfer of rights or duties under a contract.

14. T F An offer or counteroffer may be revoked at any time prior to its acceptance.

15. T F An *option contract* is an agreement by which the optionee gives the optionor the right to buy or lease property at a fixed price within a specific period of time.

16. T F *Commingling* occurs when a broker mixes his or her personal funds with a buyer's earnest money deposit.

17. T F The interest held by a buyer during the time between the signing of a sales contract and the transfer of title is known as *equitable title*.

18. T F An example of an addendum to a real estate sales contract is an attached page that describes a detailed provision that the purchase is contingent on the sale of the buyer's current home within 90 days.

19. T F An option agreement is a unilateral contract.

20. T F A contract entered into by a minor is void.

MULTIPLE CHOICE   *Circle a, b, c, or d.*

1. Which of the following is an example of a unilateral contract?
   a. Lease
   b. Agreement of sale
   c. Option
   d. Listing agreement

2. Sally Seller accepted all of the terms that Betty Buyer offered, making only one small change in the amount of the earnest money. At the moment, these agreements constitute a(n)
   a. offer.
   b. counteroffer.
   c. acceptance.
   d. rejection.

3. Betty Buyer changed her mind about buying a particular lot. She called her agent and said, "Withdraw my offer." Her action is called a
   a. counteroffer.
   b. rejection.
   c. breach of contract.
   d. revocation.

4. A real estate broker announces to the salespeople in her office that she will pay a $1,000 bonus to the top-selling salesperson each quarter. This contract is a(n)
   a. implied bilateral contract.
   b. express unilateral contract.
   c. implied unilateral contract.
   d. express bilateral contract.

5. Courtney makes an offer on a house, and Anya, the seller, accepts. What is the current status of this relationship?
   a. Courtney and Anya do not have a valid contract until Anya delivers title at closing.
   b. Courtney and Anya have an express, bilateral executed contract.
   c. Courtney and Anya have an express, bilateral executory contract.
   d. Courtney and Anya have an implied, unilateral executory contract.

MULTIPLE CHOICE   *(continued)*

6. Will offers to buy Harshad's house for the full $215,000 asking price. The offer contains the following clause: "Possession of the premises on August 1." Harshad is delighted to accept Will's offer and signs the contract. First, however, Harshad crosses out "August 1" and replaces it with "August 3," because Harshad won't be back from vacation on the first of the month. Harshad then begins scheduling movers. What is the status of this agreement?

   a. Because Harshad changed the date of possession rather than the amount, Will and Harshad have a valid contract.

   b. Harshad has accepted Will's offer. Because the reason for the change was out of Harshad's control, the change is of no legal effect once he signed the contract.

   c. Harshad has rejected Will's offer and made a counteroffer, which Will is free to accept or reject.

   d. While Harshad technically rejected Will's offer, Harshad's behavior in scheduling movers creates an implied contract between the parties.

7. A contract that is entered into by a person who is under the age of contractual capacity is

   a. unenforceable.   c. voidable.

   b. void.   d. valid.

8. Tilda is buying Howard's house and wants to take over Howard's mortgage. The lender releases Howard from the obligation, substituting Tilda as the party liable for the debt. This new agreement is called a(n)

   a. assignment.   c. conversion.

   b. novation.   d. consideration.

9. Quentin, a buyer, and Bob, a seller, enter into a sales contract for the sale of Bob's home. Bob changes his mind at the last minute, and Quentin suffers a financial loss of $1,500 and must rent a home to live in. Unless the contract provides otherwise, all of the following are legal actions that are likely to succeed *EXCEPT*

   a. Quentin may sue Bob for specific performance, forcing the sale of the farm to Quentin.

   b. Quentin may sue Bob for damages to recover the $1,500 loss.

   c. Bob is not liable because Quentin should not have incurred the $1,500 cost before the sale.

   d. Quentin may sue Bob for the rent he paid.

10. On March 7, Nora and Larry execute a contract for the purchase of Nora's property. Closing is set for June 10. On April 15, the property is struck by lightning and virtually destroyed by the resulting fire. If the Uniform Vendor and Purchaser Risk Act has been adopted by the state in which the property is located, which party bears liability for the loss?

    a. Under the Act, Nora and Larry share the loss equally.

    b. Under the Act, Nora bears the loss alone.

    c. The Act does not apply. Larry bears the loss alone, by virtue of his equitable title.

    d. Under the Act, neither Nora nor Larry bears the loss. A state fund covers the loss.

11. Roberto is trying to sell Dreadful Manor but is having difficulty finding a buyer. Harriet wants to buy Dreadful Manor but isn't sure whether or not she will be transferred out of the country by her employer. Roberto agrees to accept a $500 payment from Harriet, in return for which Dreadful Manor will be taken off the market for three months. Harriet may purchase Dreadful Manor for a certain price any time during that period. This is a(n)

    a. unenforceable contract.

    b. land contract.

    c. sales contract.

    d. option contract.

MULTIPLE CHOICE *(continued)*

12. All the following are essential to a valid real estate sales contract *EXCEPT*

   a. an adequate description of the property.

   b. consideration.

   c. an earnest money deposit, held in an escrow account.

   d. legally competent parties.

13. A 14-year-old comes into a brokerage office and says, "I want to make an offer on the Walnut Street property. Here is a certified check for 10 percent of the asking price. Please help me with the paperwork." Why should the broker be concerned?

   a. Because one of the parties is a minor, the contract is illegal.

   b. The earnest money deposit must be at least 20 percent of the asking price when a minor is involved in the transaction.

   c. The sales contract may be disaffirmed by the minor.

   d. The sales contract will be void because the minor's age is a matter of public record.

14. In case the buyer decides not to buy for no legal reason, the contract may provide that the earnest money is there as

   a. actual damages.

   b. nominal damages.

   c. punitive damages.

   d. liquidated damages.

15. The buyer and seller agreed to a closing date of September 7, *time is of the essence*. Which of the following is the closest meaning of the phrase?

   a. It would be very nice if both parties can have their affairs together to close on that date.

   b. If closing is not held on September 7, there is an automatic extension built in.

   c. Closing must be on or before September 7.

   d. If either party gives notice, the date can be moved back.

16. A promise made by one party, requesting something in exchange for that promise is called a(n)

   a. offer.   **c.** consideration.

   b. acceptance.   **d.** rescission.

17. If Alex threatens Brian to get him to sign a contract to sell property for a low price, the contract is voidable because it violates the doctrine of

   a. reality of consent.

   b. legally competent parties.

   c. consideration.

   d. offer and acceptance.

18. If a contract seems on the surface to be valid but neither party can sue the other to force performance, the contract is said to be

   a. voided.   **c.** rescinded.

   b. breached.   **d.** unenforceable.

19. What is minimum consideration in a valid contract?

   a. One dollar

   b. Any item that can be appraised with a market value

   c. Specified goods or services

   d. Anything the parties agree is "good and valuable"

20. If a contract does *NOT* contain a time or date for performance, when should the act be done?

   a. Immediately, if that is possible

   b. Within one week

   c. Within two weeks

   d. Within one month

21. If Brock allows Ann to back out of a contract, returns the earnest money to Ann, and both are back to the positions they held before the contract, the contract has been

   a. cancelled.   **c.** assigned.

   b. rescinded.   **d.** executed.

MULTIPLE CHOICE *(continued)*

22. When is an offer considered to be accepted?
    a. When the broker notifies the buyer that the seller has accepted the offer
    b. When the buyer gives a signed receipt to the broker to show the buyer has received the acceptance.
    c. The moment the seller accepts the buyer's offer.
    d. One business day after the offer is accepted and signed by the seller.

23. Additional conditions that must be satisfied before a sales contract is fully enforceable are called
    a. binders.
    b. amendments.
    c. addendums.
    d. contingencies.

24. The amount of the earnest money in a sales contract should accomplish what purpose?
    a. Cover any expenses the buyer might incur if the seller defaults.
    b. Discourage the buyer from walking away from the agreement.
    c. Pay the broker's commission.
    d. Pay for any required inspections.

25. The purchaser's right to inspect the property shortly before closing the sale is called the
    a. walk-through.
    b. open house.
    c. title search.
    d. subordination agreement.

MATCHING B   *Write the letter of the matching term on the appropriate line.*

a. *void*

b. *assignment*

c. *breach*

d. *contingencies*

e. *earnest money*

f. *land contract*

g. *liquidated damages*

h. *equitable title*

i. *listing agreement*

j. *novation*

1. _____ A contract that is without legal force or effect because it lacks one or more essential elements

2. _____ The transfer of rights or duties under a contract

3. _____ The substitution of a new contract to replace an earlier one

4. _____ A violation of any of the terms or conditions of a contract without legal excuse

5. _____ An employment contract between a broker and a seller

6. _____ A deposit customarily made by a prospective purchaser when making an offer

7. _____ The interest held by a buyer prior to delivery and acceptance of the deed

8. _____ An amount of money that the parties agree will be the complete compensation available in the event of a breach

9. _____ Additional conditions that must be satisfied before a property sales contract is fully enforceable

10. _____ A contract under which the seller retains legal title to property and the buyer only obtains possession until the terms of the contract have been satisfied

SALES CONTRACT

The document on page 98 is the first page of a standard real estate sales contract. Fill it in using information from the narrative below.

You are the buyer. The date is today. The property is 1105 Azalea Street in Poleduck County, City of Pleasant Valley, Virginia 98765. The lot dimensions are 70 feet by 160 feet. The sellers are Paul and Polly Purveyor, who currently live in the house being sold.

The buyer is particularly insistent that the kitchen appliances (a stove, dishwasher, and refrigerator) convey with the property, and that an outdoor gas cooker and swing set stay as well. The earnest money deposit is 15 percent of the purchase price of $317,500, paid by check, with an additional 10 percent of the balance due in one business week.

The closing will take place exactly 64 days from today at the office of the buyer's attorney, R. Tassel. The financing will be by conventional, fixed-rate mortgage, in the amount of the balance due. The buyer will not accept an interest rate greater than 7.5 percent. The commitment date is two weeks from today. The listing broker is F. J. Broker.

SAMPLE RESIDENTIAL SALES CONTRACT

Agreement for Sale of Real Estate

BUYER(S): _____

Address: _____

City: _____ State: ___ Zip _____ agrees to purchase, and

SELLER(S): _____

Address: _____

City: _____ State: ___ Zip _____ agrees to sell to Buyer(s)

at the Price of : _____ Dollars ($_____)

the Property commonly described as _____

(City of _____, County of _____ State of _____)

1. PROPERTY DESCRIPTION: "the Property," a complete legal description of which may be attached to this contract by either party. The Property has approximate lot dimensions of _____, together with all existing improvements and fixtures, if any, to be transferred to the Buyer(s) by Bill of Sale at the time of closing, including (but not limited to): hot water heater, furnace, plumbing and electrical fixtures, sump pumps, central heating and cooling systems, fixed floor coverings, built-in kitchen appliances and cabinets, storm and screen windows and doors, window treatment hardware, shelving systems, all planted vegetation, garage door openers and car units, and the following items of personal property:

2. EARNEST MONEY: Buyer has paid $_____ by check by note (*delete one*), and will pay within _____ days the further sum of $_____, as earnest money to be applied against the purchase price. The earnest money shall be held by the Listing Broker for the mutual benefit of the parties. The balance of the purchase price, $_____, shall be paid in full at closing.

3. CLOSING DATE: The closing date shall be _____,20__, at _____.

4. POSSESSION: Possession shall be at closing.

5. COMMISSION: Seller(s) agree that _____, Listing Broker, brought about this sale and agrees to pay a Broker's commission as agreed in the listing agreement.

6. FINANCING: This contract is subject to the condition that Buyer(s) shall, by _____, 20__, obtain a written commitment for a loan secured by a mortgage or deed of trust on the Property in the amount of $_____. Financing shall be secured in the form of a mortgage of the following type: (delete those items that do not apply); Conventional (fixed or adjustable rate); FHA mortgage; VA mortgage; assumption of existing mortgage; financing by Seller(s).

ANSWER KEY

Key Term Matching (A)

1. c   **2.** f   **3.** g   **4.** a   **5.** j   **6.** d   **7.** e   **8.** i
9. h   **10.** b

True or False

1. **False.**   An agreement to be bound by *all* of the terms proposed in an offer constitutes *acceptance*.

2. **False.**   While a contract may be written or oral, only certain types of contracts must be in writing to be enforceable.

3. **False.**   A listing agreement is *an employment contract* between a broker and a seller.

4. **True**

5. **False.**   In an implied contract, the actual agreement between the parties is *demonstrated by their acts and conduct*.

6. **False.**   The difference between a bilateral and a unilateral contract is the presence or absence of the exchange of mutual promises.

7. **True**

8. **False.**   A contract that may be rescinded or disaffirmed by one or both of the parties based on some legal principle is *voidable*, even though it may appear on the surface to be valid.

9. **False.**   The person who makes an offer is the *offeror*; the person who accepts or rejects the offer is the *offeree*.

10. **True**

11. **True**

12. **False.**   Under a *land contract*, the buyer obtains possession but the seller retains legal title until the terms of the contract have been satisfied.

13. **False.**   *Novation* is the substitution of a new contract in place of the original one, while *assignment* is a transfer of rights or duties under a contract.

14. **True**

15. **False.**   An *option contract* is an agreement by which the *optionor* gives the *optionee* the right to buy or lease property at a fixed price within a specific period of time.

16. **True**

17. **True**

18. **True**

19. **True**

20. **False.**   A contract entered into by a minor is *voidable*.

Multiple Choice

1. **c.**   The optionor-owner of the property must sell at the agreed upon price only if the optionee decides to buy. Only one party is obligated to perform.

2. **b.**   Even changing one "small" term constitutes a rejection and a new counteroffer that the other party is not under obligation to accept.

3. **d.**   The buyer may revoke her offer anytime until she is notified that the seller has accepted the offer.

4. **b.**   This is an *express contract* because the broker clearly stated her intentions in words to the salespeople. It is a *unilateral contract* because she is obligated to keep her promise, but the salespeople are not obligated to perform.

5. **c.**   Because the seller has promised to sell and the buyer has promised to buy, it is clearly a *bilateral contract*. It is *express* because they announced their intentions in writing. The contract is *executory* because the sale has not yet closed.

6. **c.**   Even changing the smallest of terms, for whatever reason, constitutes a rejection and counteroffer that the other party is not under obligation to accept.

7. **c.**   The underage party may void the contract, but the older party who entered into the contract with the minor cannot.

8. **b.**   Substituting a new contract where the intent is to discharge the old obligation is known as *novation*. In this situation, it is also called *release of liability*.

9. **c.** In this case, Bob breached the contract without legal excuse. Quentin is likely to be successful if he sues Bob for specific performance, for the $1,500 loss, and for the cost of rent as a hardship; however, many contracts limit the remedies available to parties,

10. **b.** In states that have adopted the Uniform Vendor and Purchaser Act, the seller remains responsible for the property until the day of closing.

11. **d.** Harriet has the right to buy at an agreed on price within a certain time frame, but she doesn't have to. Roberto will have to sell to Harriet within that time frame whether or not he receives a higher offer from another prospect.

12. **c.** Earnest money is an option to a contract, not a requirement. It is available for liquidated damages. The *consideration* is the exchange of promises, that is, the seller promises marketable title and the buyer promises a certain amount of money.

13. **c.** A minor may void the contract citing, "I am underage." A minor's guardian may purchase for the minor.

14. **d.** Liquidated damages limit the compensation available to the injured party should a breach of contract occur.

15. **c.** *Time is of the essence* requires that the contract be completed during that time frame or the party who fails to perform on time is liable for breach of contract.

16. **a.** An offer must be made before it can be accepted. Consideration is something of legal value. Rescission refers to cancellation of a contract.

17. **a.** The contract would have an offer and acceptance (even if obtained under duress); there is no indication that Alex or Brian are not competent to enter into the contract; and there is consideration (even if the price is low). Reality of consent is being violated because of the duress.

18. **d.** The example is an oral contract for the sale of real estate. It is *unenforceable* because the statute of frauds requires real estate contracts to be in writing.

19. **d.** It is up to the parties to agree that the consideration is "good and valuable." The courts don't look into whether the consideration is adequate.

20. **a.** Unless the parties agree otherwise, the act should be done immediately. However, courts have sometimes declared contracts invalid if they did not contain a time or date for performance.

21. **b.** Cancellation terminates a contract without a return to the original position. An executed contract is one in which all parties have fulfilled their promises.

22. **a.** Buyer notification is the key. It is not an accepted offer until the buyer is notified, and there is no lag time after that point.

23. **d.** A *binder* is a short version of a sales contract that is used until a more complete version is drawn up by a lawyer. *Amendments* are changes to the existing content of a contract. A *contingency* might be spelled out in an addendum, but other provisions also may be contained in addendums.

24. **b.** The amount should be sufficient that the seller feels reassured that the buyer is committed to the purchase. Earnest money is paid by the buyer so it can't compensate the buyer for expenses. Earnest money is not used to pay for inspections or the broker's commission.

25. **a.** The title search establishes the property ownership and encumbrances. A subordination agreement is an agreement between lienholders to change the order of priority of liens.

Key Term Matching (B)

1. a   2. b   3. j   4. c   5. i   6. e   7. h   8. g
9. d   10. f

SALES CONTRACT

Agreement for Sale of Real Estate

BUYER(S): _Student's Name_

   Address: _Student's Address_

   City: _____ State: ___ Zip _____ agrees to purchase, and

SELLER(S): _Paul and Polly Purveyor (h/w)_

   Address: _1105 Azalea St._

   City: _Pleasant Valley_ State: _VA_ Zip _98765_ agrees to sell to Buyer(s)

at the Price of : _Three Hundred Seventeen Thousand Five Hundred_ Dollars ($ _317,500_)

the Property commonly described as _1105 Azalea St._

(City of _Pleasant Valley_ , County of _Poleduck_ State of _Virginia_)

1. PROPERTY DESCRIPTION: "the Property," a complete legal description of which may be attached to this contract by either party. The Property has approximate lot dimensions of _70' by 160'_ , together with all existing improvements and fixtures, if any, to be transferred to the Buyer(s) by Bill of Sale at the time of closing, including (but not limited to): hot water heater, furnace, plumbing and electrical fixtures, sump pumps, central heating and cooling systems, fixed floor coverings, built-in kitchen appliances and cabinets, storm and screen windows and doors, window treatment hardware, shelving systems, all planted vegetation, garage door openers and car units, and the following items of personal property:

     Kitchen stove, dishwasher, refrigerator, outdoor gas cooker and swing set

2. EARNEST MONEY: Buyer has paid $ _47,625.00_ by check ~~by note~~ (delete one), and will pay within _5_ days the further sum of $ _26,987.50_ , as earnest money to be applied against the purchase price. The earnest money shall be held by the Listing Broker for the mutual benefit of the parties. The balance of the purchase price, $ _242,887.50_ , shall be paid in full at closing.

3. CLOSING DATE: The closing date shall be _today + 64 days_ ,20_ , at _Law Office of R. Tassel_ .

4. POSSESSION: Possession shall be at closing.

5. COMMISSION: Seller(s) agree that _F. J. Broker_ , Listing Broker, brought about this sale and agrees to pay a Broker's commission as agreed in the listing agreement.

6. FINANCING: This contract is subject to the condition that Buyer(s) shall, by _today + 2 wks_ ,20 _ , obtain a written commitment for a loan secured by a mortgage or deed of trust on the Property in the amount of $ _____ . Financing shall be secured in the form of a mortgage of the following type: (delete those items that do not apply); Conventional (fixed ~~or adjustable~~ rate); ~~FHA mortgage; VA mortgage; assumption of existing mortgage; financing by Seller(s)~~ .*Not to exceed 7.5%.*

12

Transfer of Title

BEFORE YOU START...

After completing Chapter 12 of the textbook, you should be able to answer the following "learning assessment" questions. If you are able to answer these questions, then you are ready to move ahead with this chapter of the *Study Guide*! If, however, you are having some difficulty answering any of these learning assessment questions, we advise you to reread key sections of the textbook before attempting to answer the questions in this chapter of the *Study Guide*.

- Do you know the two meanings of *title* as it pertains to real estate?

- Can you explain *voluntary alienation* and list the ways property is transferred by this method?

- What are the basic requirements for a valid deed?

- Can you describe the basic rules affecting corporate deeds?

- What are the important elements of the types of deeds listed in the text?

- Can you describe transfer taxes and are they applicable in your area?

- What does the term *involuntary alienation* mean, and what are the ways property is transferred by this method?

- Do you know the ways in which a deceased person's property is transferred?

MATCHING A   *Write the letter of the matching term on the appropriate line.*

a. *acknowledgment*

b. *deed*

c. *deed in trust*

d. *grantee*

e. *quiet enjoyment*

f. *grantor*

g. *granting clause*

h. *seisin*

i. *title*

j. *voluntary alienation*

1. _____ The right to and evidence of ownership of land

2. _____ The transfer of title by gift or sale

3. _____ A written instrument by which an owner intentionally conveys the right, title, or interest in a parcel of real estate to someone else

4. _____ The person who transfers title

5. _____ The person who acquires title by gift or sale

6. _____ A statement of the intention to convey property by deed

7. _____ A formal declaration, made before a notary public, that the person who is signing the deed is doing so voluntarily and that his or her signature is genuine

8. _____ A covenant in a deed that warrants the grantor is the owner of the property and has the right to convey it

9. _____ A guarantee in a deed that the grantee's title will be good against any third party who might bring legal action to establish superior title

10. _____ A conveyance by deed from a trustor to a trustee for the benefit of a beneficiary

---

TRUE OR FALSE   *Circle the correct answer.*

1. T F A *title* to real estate is a printed document signed by the secretary of state.

2. T F A *deed* is the written instrument by which an owner of real estate intentionally conveys the right, title, or interest in a parcel to someone else.

3. T F To be valid, a deed must include a recital of consideration, an identifiable grantee, and a recital of exceptions and reservations.

4. T F A title is considered transferred when the deed is actually signed and acknowledged by the grantor.

5. T F To be valid, a deed must be signed by both the grantor and the grantee.

6. T F In a special warranty deed, the covenant of seisin warrants that the grantor's title will be good against third parties.

7. T F In a general warranty deed, the covenant of further assurance represents a promise by the grantor that he or she will obtain and deliver any instrument needed to ensure good title.

8. T F A bargain and sale deed does not contain any express warranties against encumbrances.

9. T F If a trustee wanted to convey real estate back to the trustor, he or she would use a trustee's deed.

10. T F In a deed executed due to a court order, the full amount of consideration is stated in the deed.

11. T F Adverse possession is an example of involuntary alienation of property.

TRUE OR FALSE *(continued)*

12. T F When a property owner dies, his or her heirs by descent or by will may immediately take possession of any real estate.

13. T F While a deed must be delivered during the grantor's lifetime, a will takes effect only after the owner's death.

14. T F A person who receives real property through a testamentary transfer is referred to as the *devisee*.

15. T F Real property of an owner who dies intestate is distributed according to the laws of the state in which the owner resided at the time of his or her death.

16. T F The type of ownership under which the grantees to a deed will receive the property is stated in the deed.

17. T F Encumbrances that run with the land, such as an easement, are stated in the sale disclosures rather than the deed.

18. T F One of the functions of probate is to determine the precise assets of the deceased person.

19. T F Many states have laws establishing a transfer tax that must be paid on conveyances of real estate.

20. T F When an estate is probated, the court usually selects the executor to distribute the assets to the heirs.

MULTIPLE CHOICE *Circle a, b, c, or d.*

1. The grantor is conveying an interest that is less than fee simple absolute. This explanation of the extent of ownership will be found in the
  a. seisin clause.
  b. granting clause.
  c. habendum clause.
  d. exceptions and reservations.

2. Fiona conveys Happy Acres to Rena by a written document that contains five covenants protecting Rena's title. What is Fiona's role in this transaction?
  a. Grantee
  b. Grantor
  c. Devisor
  d. Devisee

3. The verification that the grantor's signature is both genuine and voluntary is a(n)
  a. judgment.
  b. attachment.
  c. consideration.
  d. acknowledgment.

4. Which of the following is an example of involuntary alienation?
  a. Sale
  b. Gift
  c. Escheat
  d. Will

5. In most states, an attorney in fact is allowed to sign a deed for a
  a. beneficiary.
  b. grantor.
  c. grantee.
  d. lender.

6. The transfer of any interest in a parcel of real estate is typically in a document called the
  a. title.
  b. deed.
  c. attachment.
  d. mortgage.

7. All of the following are necessary to a valid deed *EXCEPT*
  a. recital of consideration.
  b. words of conveyance.
  c. grantee's signature.
  d. delivery.

MULTIPLE CHOICE (continued)

8. "I do hereby convey to my nearest relative all my interest in the property known as 123 Main Street, Elkhorn, West Dakota, to have and to hold, in consideration of receipt of the amount of $10 and other good and valuable consideration." When signed, this document is a(n)

   a. valid conveyance by deed.

   b. invalid conveyance by deed, because the property conveyed is inadequately described.

   c. invalid conveyance by deed, because there is no recital of exceptions and reservations.

   d. invalid conveyance by deed, because the grantee is inadequately identified.

9. The type of deed that imposes the least liability on the grantor is a

   a. special warranty deed.

   b. bargain and sale deed.

   c. quitclaim deed.

   d. general warranty deed.

10. Title is *NOT* considered transferred until the deed is

   a. signed by the grantor.

   b. delivered to and accepted by the grantee.

   c. delivered to the grantee.

   d. released from escrow.

11. Which of the following is a guarantee that the grantor has the right to convey the property?

   a. Covenant against encumbrances

   b. Covenant of seisin

   c. Covenant of further assurance

   d. Covenant of quiet enjoyment

12. A bargain and sale deed contains how many express warranties?

   a. 0   **c.** 3

   b. 2   **d.** 5

13. Which type of deed is used by a grantor whose interest in the real estate may be unknown?

   a. Bargain-and-sale deed

   b. Special warranty deed

   c. General warranty deed

   d. Quitclaim deed

14. Under the law of the state of North Michigan, one-half of an intestate decedent's property goes to his or her spouse, one-fourth is divided equally among his or her children, and one-fourth goes to the state. If there is no spouse, the children divide three-fourths equally. Cathy, a citizen of North Michigan, dies intestate, survived by an ex-spouse and seven adult children. If Cathy's estate is $865,550, how much will each child receive under North Michigan law?

   a. $0   **c.** $61,825.25

   b. $92,737.50   **d.** $123,650.00

15. In East Carolina, the transfer tax is $1.20 for each $300 (or fraction of $300) of the sales price of any parcel of real estate. If a seller's property sold for $250,000, what will be the amount of the transfer tax due?

   a. $97.00   **c.** $1,000.80

   b. $999.99   **d.** $1,250.50

16. In front of witnesses, Carrie says to Ron, "I never made a will, but I want you to have The Quarteracre Farm when I die." If Ron becomes the owner of The Quarteracre Farm, it is because the state recognizes what kind of will?

   a. Holographic   **c.** Nuncupative

   b. Testamentary   **d.** Probated

MULTIPLE CHOICE (continued)

17. Terry inherited Stately Manor from his uncle in 1995. Terry has never visited Stately Manor or taken any responsibility for it. In 1998, without Terry's knowledge, Lou moved into the empty house. Between 1998 and 2004, Lou repaired and maintained Stately Manor as if it were her own home. She invited neighbors to attend holiday parties on the grounds. In 2004, Lou moved out of Stately Manor, and her son moved in. If the applicable period for adverse possession is 15 years, when can Lou's son claim title?

    a. Lou's son can claim title by adverse possession in the year 2019.

    b. Lou's son cannot claim title, because Lou failed to satisfy the requirements for adverse possession.

    c. Lou's son can claim title by adverse possession on the 15th anniversary of the date when Lou moved into Stately Manor.

    d. Lou's son cannot claim title, because Terry is the true legal owner of Stately Manor.

18. In one state, the transfer tax is $0.80 per $500 or fraction thereof. There is no tax charged on the first $500 of the price. What tax must the seller pay if the property sells for $329,650?

    a. $525.60   c. $527.20

    b. $526.40   d. $528.00

19. A modification to the original will is called a(n)

    a. addendum.   c. probate.

    b. amendment.   d. codicil.

20. All of the following are reasons for probate EXCEPT to

    a. ensure that the heirs do not fight among themselves.

    b. confirm that the will is valid.

    c. determine the exact assets of the deceased person.

    d. identify which persons get any of the estate.

21. When a corporation transfers ownership of property, the deed must be signed by a(n)

    a. authorized officer.   c. broker.

    b. shareholder.   d. grantee.

22. The granting clause in a special warranty deed generally contains the words

    a. "grantor conveys and warrants."

    b. "grantor grants, bargains, and sells."

    c. "grantor remises, releases and quitclaims."

    d. "grantor remises, releases, alienates, and conveys."

23. What is the MOST common use of a quitclaim deed?

    a. To transfer property between a trustee and anyone other than the trustor.

    b. To transfer property between members of a family.

    c. To transfer property according to a court order.

    d. To transfer property from a trustor to a trustee.

24. If a person dies intestate, the estate passes to the deceased person's heirs according to the

    a. deceased person's will.

    b. judgment of the executor.

    c. federal escheat laws.

    d. state's statute of descent and distribution.

25. What limits are set by the covenants in a general warranty deed?

    a. None

    b. The covenants are limited to matters that occurred during the time the grantor owned the property.

    c. The covenants are limited to the matters that occurred within the last 10 years.

    d. The covenants are limited to the matters that occurred before the grantor owned the property.

DEED CHARACTERISTIC

Identify the characteristics of deeds by placing check marks in the appropriate columns.

Characteristics	Types of Deeds			
	General Warranty	Special Warranty	Bargain and Sale	Quitclaim
Covenant of Warranty Forever				
Covenant of Further Assurance				
Covenant of Quiet Enjoyment				
Covenant Against Encumbrances				
Covenant of Seisin				
Express Warranties				
Implied Warranties				
Delivery and Acceptance				
Legal Description				
Habendum Clause				
Granting Clause				
Identifiable Grantee				
Signature of Grantor				
Consideration				
Grantor of Sound Mind				
Grantor of Lawful Age				

MATCHING B   *Write the letter of the matching term on the appropriate line.*

a. *reconveyance deed*

b. *devise*

c. *involuntary alienation*

d. *probate*

e. *quitclaim*

f. *special warranty*

g. *bargain and sale*

h. *testate*

i. *testator*

j. *trustee's deed*

1. _____   A type of deed that warrants only that the grantor deed received title and that the property has not been encumbered during the grantor's ownership

2. _____   A deed that contains no express warranties against encumbrances but that implies that the grantor holds title and possession of the property

3. _____   A deed that contains no covenants, warranties, or implications and that provides the least protection of any deed

4. _____   A conveyance by deed from a trustee to anyone other than the trustor

5. _____   A conveyance by deed from a trustee to the trustor

6. _____   The transfer of title without the owner's consent

7. _____   Having prepared a will indicating how property is to be disposed of after death

8. _____   The gift of real property by will

9. _____   The person who makes a will

10. _____   A formal judicial process to confirm a will's validity and to see that assets are distributed correctly

ANSWER KEY

Key Term Matching (A)

1. i **2.** j **3.** b **4.** f **5.** d **6.** g **7.** a **8.** h
9. e **10.** c

18. True
19. True
20. False. The executor is usually named in the will.

True or False

1. False. A title to real estate is not an actual printed document.

2. True

3. False. To be valid, a deed must include a recital of consideration and an identifiable grantee; a deed *may* contain a recital of exceptions and reservations.

4. False. A title is considered transferred when the deed is actually *delivered to the grantee by the grantor*.

5. False. To be valid, a deed must be signed by all grantors named in the deed.

6. False. In a *general warranty deed*, the covenant of seisin warrants that the grantor is the owner of the property and has the right to convey it.

7. True

8. True

9. False. If a trustee wanted to convey real estate back to the trustor, he or she would use a reconveyance deed.

10. True

11. True

12. False. When a property owner dies, his or her heirs by descent or will immediately take *title* to the property, but they may take possession *only after probate*.

13. True

14. True

15. False. Real property of an owner who dies intestate is distributed according to the laws of the state in which *the property is located*.

16. True

17. False. A deed must note any encumbrances that affect the title being conveyed.

Multiple Choice

1. c. The *habendum clause* is the *to have and to hold* clause that defines the extent of ownership that is being conveyed.

2. b. Because Fiona is conveying her interest, Fiona is the *grantor*. The person who receives the interest is the *grantee*.

3. d. The person who observes the signing and verifies its authenticity will often ask for a picture ID.

4. c. Dying may not be voluntary, but writing a will is. When a person dies intestate and leaves no heirs, his or her estate will *escheat* to the state.

5. b. Most states permit an attorney in fact to sign for a grantor on a deed. A grantee, for example, a lender, does not sign a deed.

6. b. A *deed* is the written document that transfers a real estate interest. Evidence of ownership (*title*) is written in the deed. An *attachment* is the process of taking a person's property into legal custody by a court order. A mortgage provides the security for a loan.

7. c. See #5 above. The grantee does not need to sign the deed because the grantee receives the property.

8. d. Although the property may be adequately described, the grantee is not sufficiently identified. There is no transfer.

9. c. A quitclaim deed offers little or no protection. It transfers an interest, if any.

10. b. The most complete answer is "delivered to and accepted by" the grantee during the grantor's lifetime.

11. **b.** The *covenant against encumbrances* is a warranty that the property is free from encumbrances, except as so noted. The grantor further assures that he or she will do what is needed to make the title good. *Quiet enjoyment* guarantees that the title will be good against third parties who might try to bring legal action to gain the property.

12. **a.** A bargain and sale deed contains no express warranties against encumbrances, but it does imply that the grantor holds title and possession of the property.

13. **d.** A quitclaim deed is used to clear up clouds on the title. The grantor *quits* his or her claim, if any.

14. **b.** The ex-spouse gets nothing. The state gets one-fourth; and three-fourths will be divided equally among the seven children: $865,550 ÷ 4 = $216,387.50 to the state. The remaining amount, $649,162.50, is divided seven ways, leaving $92,737.50 per child.

15. **c.** The transfer tax due is $1,000.80: $250,000 ÷ 300 = $833.3333 or $834 × $1.20 = $1,000.80

16. **c.** A holographic will is completely handwritten. A testamentary trust is established by will after the owner's death. *Probate* is the process of determining the validity of the will and distributing the assets of the estate.

17. **c.** Although the son has not occupied the property very long, he can *tack* his adverse possession to that of Lou's. Lou's occupancy was certainly *open and notorious*.

18. **c.** The seller must pay $1, 527.20: $329,650 − the free $500 ÷ $500 increments = $658.30 rounded UP to $659 × $.80 = $1,527.20.

19. **d.** Additional agreements attached to an agreement of sale are *addenda*; an *amendment* is a change to the existing content of a contract. *Probate* is the process of determining the validity of a will.

20. **a.** Hopefully, the probate process will not anger too many heirs, but keeping them happy is not the reason for probate.

21. **a.** Proper authority for the sale must be given by bylaws or a resolution passed by the board of directors. Shareholders are not necessarily officers, nor are brokers. A grantee does not sign a deed.

22. **d.** Choice a refers to a general warranty deed. Choice b refers to a bargain and sale deed. Choice c refers to a quitclaim deed.

23. **b.** Answer a refers to a trustee's deed. Answer c refers to a deed executed pursuant to court order. Answer d refers to a deed of trust.

24. **d.** A person who dies intestate does not have a will nor an executor named in a will. State escheat laws revert property ownership to the state if no heirs are determined by the statute of descent and distribution.

25. **a.** The grantor defends the title against the grantor and all those who previously held title.

Key Term Matching (B)

1. f **2.** g **3.** e **4.** j **5.** a **6.** c **7.** h **8.** b
9. i **10.** d

DEED CHARACTERISTICS

Characteristics	Types of Deeds			
	General Warranty	Special Warranty	Bargain and Sale	Quitclaim
Covenant of Warranty Forever	✓			
Covenant of Further Assurance	✓			
Covenant of Quiet Enjoyment	✓			
Covenant Against Encumbrances	✓	✓		
Covenant of Seisin	✓	✓		
Express Warranties	✓	✓		
Implied Warranties	✓	✓	✓	
Delivery and Acceptance	✓	✓	✓	✓
Legal Description	✓	✓	✓	✓
Habendum Clause	✓	✓	✓	✓
Granting Clause	✓	✓	✓	✓
Identifiable Grantee	✓	✓	✓	✓
Signature of Grantor	✓	✓	✓	✓
Consideration	✓	✓	✓	✓
Grantor of Sound Mind	✓	✓	✓	✓
Grantor of Lawful Age	✓	✓	✓	✓

Note: The check marks in the top two boxes of the **Special Warranty Deed** column show that its basic warranties are similar to the **General Warranty's** covenants of seisin and against encumbrances. Remember that a **Special Warranty Deed contains two warranties:** (1) that the grantor received title and (2) that the property was not encumbered during the time the grantor held it.

13

Title Records

BEFORE YOU START...

After completing Chapter 13 of the textbook, you should be able to answer the following "learning assessment" questions. If you are able to answer these questions, then you are ready to move ahead with this chapter of the *Study Guide!* If, however, you are having some difficulty answering any of these learning assessment questions, we advise you to reread key sections of the textbook before attempting to answer the questions in this chapter of the *Study Guide*.

■ Can you describe the differences among the following terms *constructive notice, actual notice,* and *inquiry notice?*

■ What does the term *chain of title* mean?

■ Can you describe a *title search?*

■ Are you able to define *abstract of title* and describe its purpose?

■ What is *marketable title?*

■ Can you explain the kinds of *evidence of title* that are used in your area and list advantages and disadvantages of each?

■ Do you know the different kinds of title insurance policies, and can you differentiate between owners' policies and mortgagee policies?

■ Are you able to explain the Uniform Commercial Code provisions for a *security agreement* and a *financing statement?*

MATCHING   *Write the letter of the matching term on the appropriate line.*

a. *abstractor*

b. *actual notice*

c. *chain of title*

d. *constructive notice*

e. *title insurance*

f. *recording*

g. *security agreement*

h. *priority*

i. *suit to quiet title*

j. *title search*

1. ____   The act of placing documents in the public record

2. ____   The legal presumption that information may be obtained through diligent inquiry

3. ____   A type of notice also known as *direct knowledge*

4. ____   The order of rights in time, such as who recorded first, which party was in possession first, etc.

5. ____   The record of a property's ownership

6. ____   A legal action to remove a cloud on the title and establish legal ownership

7. ____   An examination of all the public records to determine if any defects exist in a property's history of ownership

8. ____   The individual who prepares a summary report of the results of a title search

9. ____   A contract under which a policyholder is protected from losses arising from defects in title

10. ____   A document required by the UCC for a lender to create a lienable interest in personal property

TRUE OR FALSE   *Circle the correct answer.*

1. T F Any individual who is interested in a particular property may review the public records to learn about the documents, claims, and other issues that affect its ownership.

2. T F Any written document that affects any estate, right, title, or interest in land must be recorded in the county in which the property owner resides.

3. T F To be eligible for recording, a document pertaining to real estate must be drawn and executed in accordance with the requirements of the UCC.

4. T F *Constructive notice* means that information about a property is not only available but that someone has been given access to that information.

5. T F A search of the public records will disclose all liens that exist against a property.

6. T F The term *chain of title* refers to the record of a property's ownership.

7. T F In a typical title search, the chain of title is examined, beginning with the earliest records of ownership and proceeding forward up to the present owner.

8. T F A standard coverage title insurance policy protects a homeowner against rights of parties in possession and unrecorded liens.

TRUE OR FALSE   *(continued)*

9. T F One of the requirements of marketable title is that it could convince a reasonably well-informed and prudent purchaser, acting on business principles and with full knowledge of the significant facts, that the property could be resold or mortgaged at a later time.

10. T F A certificate of title is a guarantee of legal ownership.

FILL-IN-THE-BLANK   *Select the word or words that best complete the following statements:*

actual notice

attorney's opinion of title

constructive notice

exclusions

improperly delivered deeds

inquiry notice

marketable title

once, at closing

preliminary title search

rights of parties in possession

suit to quiet title

Torrens system

twice, at purchase and resale

1. To protect the buyer, in some states, a(n) _____ is conducted as soon as an offer to purchase has been accepted.

2. The type of notice that means the information is not only available but someone has been given the information and knows it is called _____.

3. If a title has no serious defects, does not expose a purchaser to litigation, or does not have a poor likelihood of resale, it is called _____.

4. Rather than a certificate of title, in some parts of the country, a(n) _____ is used as evidence of title.

5. The premium for a title insurance policy is paid _____.

6. Uninsurable losses, such as zoning ordinances, named in a title insurance policy, are called _____.

7. A type of notice that the law presumes a reasonable person would obtain by asking questions or research into a property is called _____.

8. The standard coverage title policy insures against hidden defects such as _____.

9. Registration in the _____ provides evidence of title without needing to make an additional search of public records.

10. The legal presumption that information about rights in a property may be obtained by a person through diligent questioning and research is called _____.

MULTIPLE CHOICE   *Circle a, b, c, or d.*

1. All of the following are acceptable evidence of an owner's title, *EXCEPT* a(n)

    a. abstract of title and attorney's opinion.

    b. recorded deed.

    c. title insurance policy.

    d. certificate of title.

2. Where is the deed recorded?

    a. City where owner lives

    b. County or, in some states, town where property is located

    c. State capital

    d. Largest city in the state

3. Five years ago, a lien was recorded against Newacre by Rabbit Construction Company. When the lien was recorded, Pete was the owner of Newacre and Chris was an active partner in Rabbit Construction. Newacre is in County 12, but the lien was recorded in County 21. Now, Chris is trying to buy Newacre from Pete. A title search in County 12 disclosed no liens against Newacre. Which of the following is *TRUE*?

    a. Chris has constructive notice of the lien but not actual notice, because of the mistake in recording.

    b. Chris has actual notice of the lien but not constructive notice, because of the mistake in recording.

    c. Chris has both actual and constructive notice of the lien, because of his association with Rabbit Construction and the recorded lien.

    d. Chris has no notice of the lien.

4. Nancy purchased Blue Acres from Mark. Shortly after closing, Nancy discovered that there were serious flaws in the title that made it unlikely that Blue Acres could be resold in the future. What can Nancy do now?

    a. Because the title was flawed, Nancy can legally void the sale, and Mark must return any consideration.

    b. Nancy has no recourse.

    c. Because Mark conveyed unmarketable title, Nancy is entitled to a new title report.

    d. Because Nancy has accepted the deed, Nancy's only recourse is to sue Mark under any covenants contained in the deed.

5. The reason that deeds and liens and other claims are recorded is to give

    a. constructive notice.

    b. actual notice.

    c. direct notice.

    d. nominal notice.

6. A history of all recorded liens and encumbrances is revealed in the

    a. title insurance policy.

    b. unrecorded documents.

    c. chain of title.

    d. abstract.

7. The person who prepares a certificate of title is the

    a. broker.   c. buyer.

    b. abstractor.   d. seller.

8. Which of the following would be covered in a standard title insurance policy?

    a. Defects discoverable by physical inspection

    b. Unrecorded liens

    c. Forged documents

    d. Easements and restrictive covenants

MULTIPLE CHOICE *(continued)*

9. A title insurance policy that protects the interests of a mortgagee is referred to as a(n)

   a. leasehold policy.

   b. lender's policy.

   c. certificate of sale policy.

   d. ALTA policy.

10. The Uniform Commercial Code applies to

   a. all real property transactions.

   b. sales and leases of commercial property.

   c. real property transactions involving a mortgage loan.

   d. personal property or fixtures used as security for a loan.

TRACING THE CHAIN OF TITLE

The abstract below illustrates the complete title record for Lot 27, Block 6 of Springfield Pines Subdivision. Mark the point at which the chain of title is broken.

Grantor	Grantee	By Instrument	Conveyance Date
Ferris-Bumper Builders, Inc.	Barton Doyle and Jane Doyle	Warranty Deed	January 19, 1909
Barton Doyle and Jane Doyle	Market Title & Trust Company	Trust Deed	January 20, 1909
Market Title & Trust Company	Barton Doyle and Jane Doyle	Reconveyance Deed	June 10, 1935
Barton Doyle and Jane Doyle	Anton Feldspar	Bargain and Sale Deed	March 7, 1940
Peter Parker and Mary Parker	Lamont Cranston and Gloria Reeve	Warranty Deed	November 16, 1958
Lamont Cranston and Gloria Reeve	Brookfield Bank and Trust Company	Mortgage	November 8, 1958
Lamont Cranston and Gloria Reeve	Gerald Carlos and Lydi Carlos	Warranty Deed	September 4, 1979
Brookfield Bank and Trust Co.	Lamont Cranston and Gloria Reeve	Release	May 2, 1995

ANSWER KEY

Key Term Matching

1. f **2.** d **3.** b **4.** h **5.** c **6.** i **7.** j **8.** a
9. e **10.** g

True or False

1. True

2. False. Any written document that affects any estate, right, title, or interest in land must be recorded in the county or, in some states, town in which the *property is located*.

3. False. To be eligible for recording, a document pertaining to real estate must be drawn and executed in accordance with the requirements of the *recording acts of the state in which the property is located*.

4. False. *Actual notice* means that not only is the information about property available, but someone has been given access to that information.

5. False. A search of the public records will disclose all *recorded* liens that exist against a property.

6. True

7. False. In a typical title search, the chain of title is examined beginning with the *present owner and tracing backwards to the earliest records of ownership or a definite period of years, depending on state statute*.

8. False. An *extended* coverage title insurance policy would protect a homeowner against rights of parties in possession and unrecorded liens.

9. True

10. False. A certificate of title is evidence but not a guarantee of ownership.

Fill-in-the-Blank

1. To protect the buyer, in some states, a *preliminary title search* is conducted as soon as an offer to purchase has been accepted.

2. The type of notice that means the information is not only available but someone has been given the information and knows it is called *actual notice*.

3. If a title has no serious defects, does not expose a purchaser to litigation, or has not a poor likelihood of resale, it is called *marketable title*.

4. Rather than a certificate of title, in some parts of the country, an *attorney's opinion of title* is used as evidence of title.

5. The premium for a title insurance policy is paid *once, at closing*.

6. Uninsurable losses, such as zoning ordinances, named in a title insurance policy are called *exclusions*.

7. A type of notice that the law presumes a reasonable person would obtain by asking questions or research into a property is called *inquiry notice*.

8. The standard coverage title policy insures against hidden defects such as *improperly delivered deeds*.

9. Registration in the *Torrens system* provides evidence of title without needing to make an additional search of public records.

10. The legal presumption that information about rights in a property may be obtained by a person through diligent questioning and research is called *constructive notice*.

Multiple Choice

1. b. A recorded deed is nothing more than just that. Choices a, c, and d are all verifications of thorough examinations of recorded documents that could affect the title.

2. b. Because land is immobile, it makes sense to record all information about title to the property in the county where it is located. Owners move around all the time and would be hard to find.

3. b. Because Chris was a partner, he knew that the lien was filed. Constructive notice is not given because the lien was not filed in the county where the property is located, the place where it would be expected to be.

4. d. This is an example of why professionals should look at the evidence of ownership before closing. There is more leverage to get problems corrected before closing than after closing.

5. a. The recorder's office is a central place to deposit and discover information. If it is recorded, then no one can say that he or she did not know. They would have known if they had researched the records.

6. d. The title insurance policy lists overage and exceptions to the policy. Unrecorded documents have not been examined. The chain of title traces ownership. The abstract is the most complete documentation of recorded liens and encumbrances.

7. b. The abstractor searches all the public records, then summarizes the various events that affected the title throughout its history.

8. c. Title insurance does not protect against claims of parties in possession because the grantee should have visited the property, nor does it cover unrecorded liens. Easements and restrictive covenants are found in the deed and should be known to the grantee.

9. b. The mortgagee is the lender. The mortgagee's policy is transferable.

10. d. The Uniform Commercial Code does not apply to real estate. The UCC governs the documents when personal property is used as security for a loan.

TRACING THE CHAIN OF TITLE

In November of 1958, Peter and Mary Parker conveyed title as grantors, but there is no indication that they ever received title as grantees from Anton Feldspar.

Grantor	Grantee	By Instrument	Conveyance Date
Ferris-Bumper Builders, Inc.	Barton Doyle and Jane Doyle	Warranty Deed	January 19, 1909
Barton Doyle and Jane Doyle	Market Title & Trust Company	Trust Deed	January 20, 1909
Market Title & Trust Company	Barton Doyle and Jane Doyle	Reconveyance Deed	June 10, 1935
Barton Doyle and Jane Doyle	Anton Feldspar	Bargain and Sale Deed	March 7, 1940
Peter Parker and Mary Parker	Lamont Cranston and Gloria Reeve	Warranty Deed	November 16, 1958
Lamont Cranston and Gloria Reeve	Brookfield Bank and Trust Company	Mortgage	November 8, 1958
Lamont Cranston and Gloria Reeve	Gerald Carlos and Lydi Carlos	Warranty Deed	September 4, 1979
Brookfield Bank and Trust Co.	Lamont Cranston and Gloria Reeve	Release	May 2, 1995

14

Real Estate Financing: Principles

BEFORE YOU START...

After completing Chapter 14 of the textbook, you should be able to answer the following "learning assessment" questions. If you are able to answer these questions, then you are ready to move ahead with this chapter of the *Study Guide!* If, however, you are having some difficulty answering any of these learning assessment questions, we advise you to reread key sections of the textbook before attempting to answer the questions in this chapter of the *Study Guide*.

■ Can you distinguish *title theory*, *lien theory*, and *intermediate theory* and identify which best describes your state's laws?

■ What is *hypothecation* and how does it relate to the collateral for a loan?

■ Do you know how a *mortgage* is different from a *deed of trust?*

■ Are you able to describe the provisions of a *note* and the requirements for a negotiable instrument?

■ What do the terms *interest* and *usury* mean?

■ Why do lenders charge *discount points?*

■ Why do you think lenders use prepayment clauses and penalties?

■ Do you know the various provisions found in a mortgage or a deed of trust, including those relating to default, assignment, release, foreclosure, redemption, and deficiency?

■ Can you explain the provisions of a land contract as a financing document?

■ Are you able to relate the procedures involved in a foreclosure?

MATCHING A   *Write the letter of the matching term on the appropriate line.*

a. *acceleration clause*

b. *hypothecation*

c. *discount points*

d. *execute*

e. *deed of trust*

f. *mortgagor*

g. *mortgagee*

h. *usury*

i. *interest*

j. *promissory note*

1. ____ The borrower in a mortgage loan clause

2. ____ The lender in a mortgage loan

3. ____ The act of signing a loan instrument

4. ____ A borrower's personal pledge to repay a debt according to agreed-on terms

5. ____ The pledging of a property as security for payment of a loan without actually surrendering the property itself

6. ____ A financing instrument that conveys bare legal title on behalf of a beneficiary but no right of possession

7. ____ A charge for the use of money

8. ____ The act of charging interest in excess of the maximum legal rate

9. ____ A charge imposed by lenders to adjust for the difference between a loan's interest rate and the yield an investor demands

10. ____ The part of a financing agreement that gives the lender the right to declare the entire debt due and payable immediately on default

TRUE OR FALSE   *Circle the correct answer.*

1. T F A mortgage is classified as an involuntary lien on real estate.

2. T F A *mortgage* is a two-party financing agreement in which a mortgagee pledges real property to the mortgagor as security for the debt.

3. T F In title theory states, the mortgagor actually gives legal title to the mortgagee, while retaining equitable title.

4. T F When a property is mortgaged, the owner must execute both a promissory note and a security instrument.

5. T F *Subordination* is the pledging of property as security for payment of a loan while retaining possession of the property.

6. T F In a typical deed of trust, the mortgagee is the beneficiary and the borrower is the trustor.

7. T F A point is 1 percent of the purchase price of the property being offered as security for the loan.

8. T F In the event of a borrower's default, a subordination clause makes foreclosure easier by giving a lender the right to declare the entire debt due and payable.

9. T F In most mortgage documents, the defeasance clause requires the mortgagee to execute a satisfaction when the note has been fully paid, returning to the mortgagor all interest in the real estate.

10. T F When a real estate loan secured by a deed of trust has been repaid in full, the beneficiary executes a discharge that releases the property back to the trustor.

11. T F A buyer who purchases real property and assumes the seller's debt becomes personally obligated for the repayment of the entire debt.

TRUE OR FALSE *(continued)*

12. T F A mortgage or deed of trust must be recorded in the recorder's office of the county in which the real estate is located.

13. T F In states that permit strict foreclosure, no sale of the property takes place.

14. T F The right of a defaulted borrower to redeem his or her real estate after default but before the foreclosure sale is known as the statutory right of redemption.

15. T F *Usury* is defined as the act of charging interest in excess of the maximum legal rate.

16. T F After the redemption period (if applicable), the successful bidder at a foreclosure sale receives a deed that conveys whatever title the borrower had and no warranties.

17. T F Lenders are allowed to charge prepayment penalties on mortgage loans insured or guaranteed by the federal government.

18. T F If the lender must obtain insurance on property because the borrower let it lapse, the lender can add the premium cost to the unpaid debt.

19. T F An assignment of mortgage occurs when the borrower pays off the loan.

20. T F When a mortgage lender finds that a borrower has not made necessary repairs to the property, the lender usually immediately proceeds to foreclosure.

MULTIPLE CHOICE *Circle a, b, c, or d.*

1. States that recognize the lender as the *owner* of the mortgaged property are known as
   a. intermediate states.
   b. recordation theory states.
   c. title theory states.
   d. lien theory states.

2. A document that indicates that a loan has been made is referred to as a
   a. promissory note.   c. deed of trust.
   b. mortgage deed.   d. satisfaction.

3. Renee defaults on her mortgage, and the lender forecloses. The lender's foreclosure suit is filed on March 15, and the sale is to be held on May 10. If Renee attempts to redeem the property on May 1, which of the following statements applies?
   a. Renee is exercising her statutory right of redemption.
   b. Renee is exercising her equitable right of redemption.
   c. Renee's attempt to redeem the property is too early; by statute, she must wait until after the sale.
   d. Renee cannot redeem the property after a foreclosure suit is filed.

MULTIPLE CHOICE   (continued)

4. A house is listed for $250,000. Ben buys it for $230,000, with a 20 percent down payment. Ben borrows the balance on a fixed-rate mortgage at 6 percent. The lender charges four points. If there are no other closing costs involved, how much money does Ben need at closing?

a. $7,360

b. $26,000

c. $46,000

d. $53,360

5. Tran is a real estate broker. One afternoon, a client calls Tran at home. The client is obviously upset: "My lender just told me that my note and mortgage is a negotiable instrument!" the client says, voice shaking. "What does that mean?" Which of the following would be Tran's *BEST* response?

a. "That's great! It means the lender is willing to negotiate on the interest rate."

b. "Oh no! That means the mortgage can't be assumed by the next person you sell to."

c. "Don't worry! That means the mortgage can be sold by the lender but you're not affected."

d. "Uh-oh! That means we have to go back to the sellers and ask them to pay the points."

6. A deed of trust involves all of the following terminology *EXCEPT*

a. lender.

b. borrower.

c. trustee.

d. mortgagor.

7. The state of West Oregon is a lien theory state. Nellie purchases Pineacre from Kent and gives him a mortgage as part of the purchase price. Therefore, Nellie is the borrower and Kent is the lender. All of the following statements are correct *EXCEPT*

a. Nellie retains equitable title to Pineacre.

b. if Nellie defaults on the loan, Kent must go through a formal foreclosure proceeding to recover the security.

c. Nellie has given legal title to Kent.

d. Kent has only a lien interest in Pineacre.

8. Where a trust deed is used, the lender is the

a. trustee.

b. beneficiary.

c. trustor.

d. maker.

9. The Mortgage Company charges borrowers a 1.5 percent loan origination fee. Sam buys a house for $210,000 and pays $50,000 in cash. Sam applies for a mortgage to cover the balance. What will the Mortgage Company charge as a fee if the asking price of the house was $235,000?

a. $2,400

b. $3,150

c. $3,525

d. $3,750

10. A mortgage document contains the following clause: "In the event of Borrower's default under the terms of this Agreement, Lender may declare the entire unpaid balance of the debt due and payable immediately." This clause is referred to as a(n)

a. hypothecation clause.

b. acceleration clause.

c. defeasance clause.

d. release clause.

11. This month, Handel made the last payment on a mortgage loan secured by Blackacre. Handel's lender must execute a

a. release deed.

b. promissory note.

c. possessory note.

d. satisfaction of mortgage.

MULTIPLE CHOICE *(continued)*

12. Ann took out a 30-year mortgage on Wetacre in 1992. On April 1, 2005, Ann's lender discovered that Wetacre lies in a flood hazard area as defined by the National Flood Insurance Reform Act of 1994. The lender informed Ann of the situation on April 15. Based on these facts, which of the following statements is correct?

a. The National Flood Insurance Reform Act of 1994 does not apply to Ann's property.

b. Ann has until May 15 to purchase flood insurance.

c. Ann has until May 30 to purchase flood insurance.

d. If Ann refuses to purchase flood insurance, the lender must do so, but the lender may not charge the cost of the additional insurance to Ann.

13. Dave purchases Potter's Field from Ella for $45,000 in cash and assumes Ella's outstanding mortgage balance of $98,500. The lender executes a release for Ella. Dave fails to make any mortgage payments, and the lender forecloses. At the foreclosure sale, Potter's Field is sold for $75,000. Based on these facts, who is liable and for what amount??

a. Ella is solely liable for $23,500.

b. Dave is solely liable for $23,500.

c. Dave and Ella are equally liable for $23,500.

d. Dave is solely liable for $30,000.

14. All of the following statements are characteristic of a typical land contract *EXCEPT*

a. at the end of the loan term, the seller will deliver clear title.

b. the buyer is granted equitable title and possession.

c. the vendee holds legal title during the contract term.

d. in the event of a default, the vendor may retain any money already paid.

15. The borrower defaulted on his mortgage loan, leaving an unpaid balance of $95,000. After receiving only $85,000 from the sale of the property, the lender filed for a

a. lis pendens.

b. release deed.

c. satisfaction piece.

d. deficiency judgment.

16. Barb was the owner of Hasty Manor. When Barb defaulted on her loan, the trustee immediately sold Hasty Manor to recover the debt. The trustee acted under the terms of the security instrument. Based on these facts, which of the following statements is *TRUE?*

a. The exercise of this power of sale clause is an example of strict foreclosure.

b. The trustee's sale of Hasty Manor was illegal, unless Barb's state permits such a so-called *friendly foreclosure*.

c. The exercise of this power of sale clause is an example of nonjudicial foreclosure.

d. Barb could have exercised her statutory right of redemption at any time prior to the trustee's sale of Hasty Manor.

17. The difference between the interest rate that the lender charges and what the investor demands is made up by charging

a. discount points.

b. loan origination fees.

c. satisfaction fees.

d. underwriting fees.

18. What is the term that refers to a lender charging an interest rate that is higher than that permitted by law?

a. Alienation   c. Hypothecation

b. Usury   d. Defeasance

MULTIPLE CHOICE   *(continued)*

19. Parties to lending agreements are referred to by different terms. Which of the following refers to the same party?

    a. Borrower = Beneficiary

    b. Borrower = Mortgagor

    c. Trustee = Borrower

    d. Trustor = Mortgagee

20. If the lender wants to call the entire note due and payable if the borrower stops making payments, the lender must include a(n)

    a. acceleration clause.

    b. defeasance clause.

    c. alienation clause.

    d. prepayment clause.

21. The type of mortgage law that is based on the principles of title theory but requires that the mortgagee foreclose to obtain legal title is

    a. lien theory.

    b. intermediate theory.

    c. subordination theory.

    d. assumption theory.

22. What is the purpose of usury laws?

    a. To maximize a lender's yield from real estate loans

    b. To set limits on the loan origination fees lenders can charge

    c. To protect consumers from lenders charging excessively high rates

    d. To set limits on discount points investors can demand from lenders

23. How does an acceleration clause help lenders?

    a. Without the acceleration clause, lenders would have to sue the borrower for every overdue payment.

    b. Lenders would rather foreclose on property than hold a long-term loan.

    c. It results in a deed in lieu of foreclosure rather than the default process.

    d. It sets out the provisions for the impound account.

24. After a foreclosure sale, what responsibility does the purchaser have for the mortgage and any junior liens?

    a. The purchaser pays off the mortgage after the sale, but the junior lienholders receive nothing.

    b. The mortgage holder receives funds from the sale, but the purchaser must pay off the junior lienholders to obtain title.

    c. The purchaser must pay off both the mortgage and junior lienholders after the sale.

    d. The purchaser has no responsibility because the purchaser receives the property title without the mortgage and junior liens.

25. What is a major disadvantage to lenders of accepting a deed in lieu of foreclosure?

    a. The lender takes the real estate subject to all junior liens.

    b. The lender gains rights to private mortgage insurance.

    c. The process is lengthy and involves a lawsuit.

    d. It is an adverse element in the borrower's credit history.

MATCHING B   *Write the letter of the matching term on the appropriate line.*

a. *alienation clause*

b. *deed in lieu of foreclosure*

c. *loan origination fee*

d. *deficiency judgment*

e. *equitable right of redemption*

f. *foreclosure*

g. *lien theory*

h. *defeasance clause*

i. *statutory right of redemption*

j. *subordination agreement*

k. *prepayment penalty*

l. *title theory*

m. *beneficiary*

n. *trustee*

o. *trustor*

1. _____ Percentage of loan amount charged to borrower for costs of generating loan

2. _____ The part of a financing agreement that requires the lender to execute a satisfaction or release when the note has been paid in full

3. _____ A provision in a financing agreement that permits the lender to declare the entire debt due immediately in the event the property is sold

4. _____ A device by which one lender agrees to change the priority of its loan relative to another lender

5. _____ A legal procedure in which property pledged as security is sold to satisfy the debt

6. _____ A document by which property is transferred to the lender by mutual agreement rather than by lawsuit

7. _____ A borrower's option of reinstating a defaulted debt prior to the foreclosure sale by paying the amount due

8. _____ A right established by state law that permits a defaulted borrower to recover property within a limited time after a foreclosure sale

9. _____ A procedure for obtaining the unpaid balance of a debt where the foreclosure sale does not generate sufficient funds

10. _____ Idea that a mortgage is purely a lien on real property

11. _____ Concept that the borrower actually gives legal title to the lender (or other party) and retains equitable title

12. _____ The borrower's legal status on a deed of trust

13. _____ Fee that borrower pays on any payment made ahead of schedule (if allowed)

14. _____ The lender's legal status on a deed of trust

15. _____ On a deed of trust, a third party who holds the deed as security for the loan

REDEMPTION RIGHTS TIMELINE

Write "Equitable" or "Statutory" in the appropriate "Right of Redemption" boxes below.

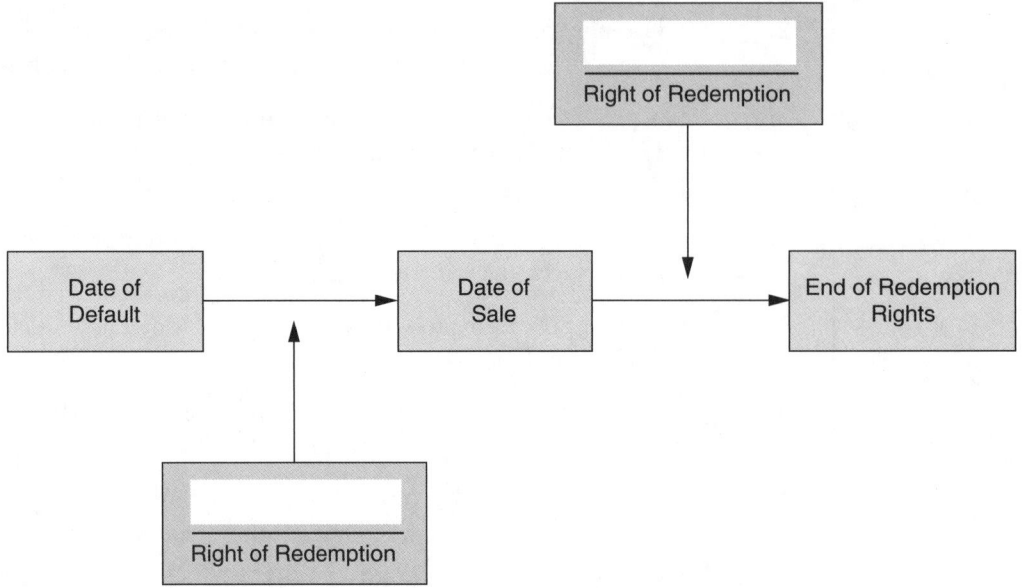

ANSWER KEY

Key Term Matching (A)

1. f **2.** g **3.** d **4.** j **5.** b **6.** e **7.** i **8.** h
9. c **10.** a

True or False

1. **False.** A mortgage is classified as a voluntary lien on real estate.

2. **False.** A *mortgage* is a two-party financing agreement in which a *mortgagor* pledges real property to the *mortgagee* as security for the debt.

3. **True**

4. **True**

5. **False.** *Hypothecation* is the pledging of property as security for payment of a loan while retaining possession of the property.

6. **True**

7. **False.** A *point* is 1 percent of the *amount being borrowed.*

8. **False.** In the event of a borrower's default, an *acceleration clause* makes foreclosure easier by giving a lender the right to declare the entire debt due and payable.

9. **True**

10. **False.** After a real estate loan, secured by a deed of trust, has been repaid in full, the *trustee* executes a release deed that releases the property back to the trustor.

11. **True**

12. **True**

13. **True**

14. **False.** The right of a defaulted borrower to redeem his or her real estate after default but before the foreclosure sale is known as the *equitable right of redemption.*

15. **True**

16. **True**

17. **False.** Mortgage lenders also cannot charge prepayment penalties on loans which have been sold to Fannie Mae or Freddie Mac.

18. **True**

19. **False.** An assignment of mortgage occurs when the lender sells the loan to an investor or other mortgage company.

20. **False.** The loan documents may provide for a grace period, such as 30 days, within which the borrower can meet the obligation and cure the default.

Multiple Choice

1. **c.** In lien theory states, a mortgage is simply a lien on the property whereas title theory states interpret a mortgage to mean that the lender is the owner of the mortgaged property.

2. **a.** The evidence that a loan has been made is found in the promissory note. A mortgage or deed of trust provides security for the loan. A satisfaction or release indicates that the loan has been repaid in full.

3. **b.** Renee has an equity interest in the property until the foreclosure sale is complete; thus she is exercising her equitable right of redemption. In some states, she may retain a statutory right of redemption for a period of time after the foreclosure sale.

4. **d.** Ben needs $53,360 at closing. Three steps: (1) Calculate down payment: $230,000 × 20% = $46,000. (2) Determine points charge: $230,000 × 80% × 4% = $7,360. (3) Total up: $46,000 + $7,360 = $53,360.

5. **c.** Negotiable instruments are transferable. A note and mortgage will often be sold on the secondary market.

6. **d.** A mortgagor is the borrower in a mortgage. In a deed of trust, the borrower is the trustor and the trustee holds naked title in trust for the beneficiary (lender).

7. **c.** In a lien theory state, a borrower who gives a mortgage, even in the seller financing situation described in this question, retains both equitable and legal title to the property serving as security.

8. **b.** The trustor (borrower) conveys naked or bare title to the trustee who holds it in trust for the beneficiary (lender).

9. a. Sam's loan origination fee is $2,400: $210,000 − $50,000 × 1.5% = $2,400. The asking price is not relevant to this problem.

10. b. *Hypothecation* is the act of offering the property as security without giving up possession. The *defeasance clause* in a mortgage defeats the granting clause. A *release* indicates that the loan has been repaid in full.

11. d. The *promissory note* shows that a loan was made. The *satisfaction* indicates that the loan was fully repaid. Satisfaction of mortgage is also sometimes called a *release*, but not a release deed.

12. c. If the lender discovers that a secured property is in a flood hazard area, the borrower must be notified. The borrower has 45 days to purchase flood insurance. If the borrower does not buy the insurance, the lender must purchase the insurance and charge back the cost of the insurance to the borrower.

13. b. Because the lender released the original borrower, the second borrower is fully responsible for the deficiency.

14. c. The *vendor* retains legal title during the contract term in this form of seller financing.

15. d. *Lis pendens* gives notice that the property is the subject of legal action. A *satisfaction* indicates that the loan was fully repaid. A *deficiency* results when the foreclosed property does not bring enough money to fully repay the loan.

16. c. Strict foreclosure does not involve a sale. Proper notice is given to the delinquent borrower who is given time to make the payments. If they are not made, the court awards the property to the lender. A nonjudicial foreclosure does not involve the courts.

17. a. Loan origination fees are charged to cover the cost of making the loan. The satisfaction indicates that the loan has been fully repaid.

18. b. *Hypothecation* is giving property as security without giving up possession.

19. b. The person who makes the payments to repay the loan is called the borrower. The person who gave the property as security is called the mortgagor. Both are the same person.

20. a. The acceleration clause permits the lender to declare the entire note due upon default by the borrower. The alienation clause is also known as the *due on sale* clause, permitting the lender to declare the entire note due if the property is sold and thus preventing a loan assumption.

21. b. Lien theory does not include principles of title theory.

22. c. Usury laws limit the interest rates lenders can charge so that consumers are protected from unscrupulous lenders.

23. a. A lender's purpose is to make long-term loans, not foreclose. The impound account is set up under a different provision of the loan.

24. d. The proceeds from the sale are used to pay off the mortgage and junior lienholders. If the proceeds are insufficient, these creditors can seek a deficiency judgment against the original owner for the remaining debt. The purchaser is not involved unless he or she is a mortgage or lienholder.

25. a. The lender loses rights to FHA or private mortgage insurance or VA guarantees. The process is called *friendly foreclosure* because a lawsuit is not involved. It is an adverse element for the borrower but that does not affect the lender.

Key Term Matching (B)

1. c **2.** h **3.** a **4.** j **5.** f **6.** b **7.** e **8.** i
9. d **10.** g **11.** l **12.** o **13.** k **14.** m **15.** n

REDEMPTION RIGHTS TIMELINE

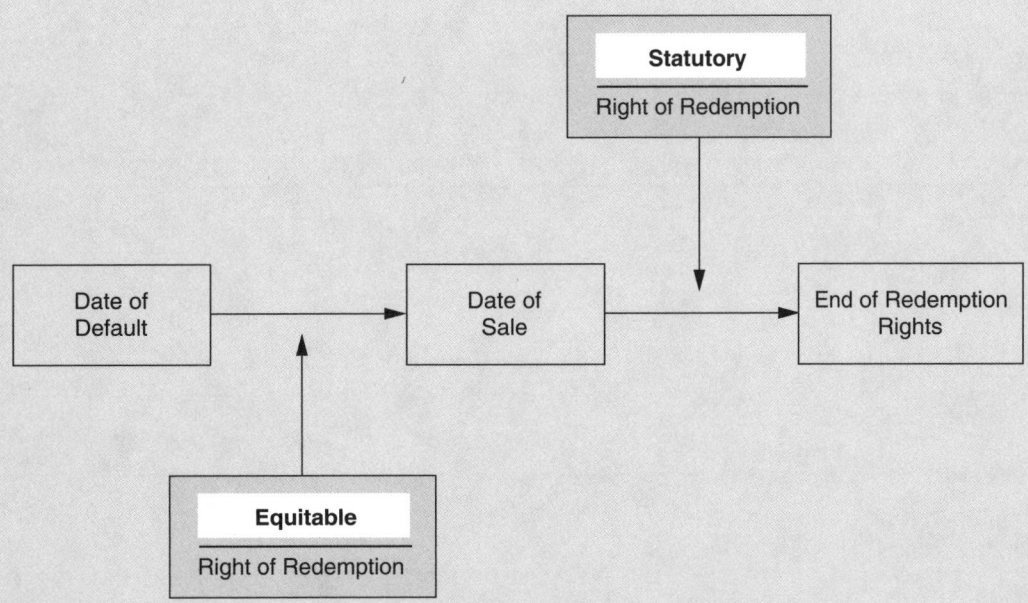

15

Real Estate Financing: Practice

BEFORE YOU START...

After completing Chapter 15 of the textbook, you should be able to answer the following "learning assessment" questions. If you are able to answer these questions, then you are ready to move ahead with this chapter of the *Study Guide!* If, however, you are having some difficulty answering any of these learning assessment questions, we advise you to reread key sections of the textbook before attempting to answer the questions in this chapter of the *Study Guide*.

- Do you know about *amortized loans*, including fully and partially amortized loans and level payment mortgage loans?

- What are key features of straight loans, interest-only loans, adjustable-rate mortgages (ARMs), balloon payment loans, growing-equity mortgages (GEMs), and reverse-annuity mortgages (RAMs)?

- Can you describe *conventional loans* and private mortgage insurance (PMI)?

- How would you describe government (FHA) *insured loans* and government *guaranteed (VA) loans?*

- Are you able to outline other financing techniques, including purchase-money mortgages, package loans, blanket loans, wraparound loans, open-end loans, construction loans, sales and leasebacks, buydowns, and home equity loans?

- Can you give examples of the various sources of financing in the primary mortgage market and their activities, including servicing loans?

■ What do you think is the government's role in mortgage lending, including the Federal Reserve, the secondary mortgage market, and the Farm Service Agency?

■ Can you describe the federal legislation that affects mortgage lending, including the Truth-in-Lending Act (Regulation Z), the Equal Credit Opportunity Act, Community Reinvestment Act (CRA), and the Real Estate Settlement Procedures Act (RESPA)?

MATCHING A   *Write the letter of the matching term on the appropriate line.*

a. *Federal Reserve*

b. *amortized loan*

c. *fiduciary lenders*

d. *Fannie Mae*

e. *Ginnie Mae*

f. *mortgage brokers*

g. *secondary mortgage market*

h. *prime rate*

i. *primary mortgage market*

j. *straight loan*

1. ____ A national system of banking districts designed to maintain sound credit conditions and a favorable economic climate

2. ____ The short-term interest rate charged to a bank's largest, most creditworthy customers

3. ____ Lenders who originate loans by making money available to borrowers

4. ____ Thrifts, savings associations, and commercial banks

5. ____ Intermediaries who bring borrowers and lenders together

6. ____ Investors who buy and sell loans after funding

7. ____ A government-sponsored enterprise organized as a private, stock-issuing corporation that buys pools of mortgages and uses them as collateral for mortgage-backed securities

8. ____ A wholly governmental agency organized as a non-stock corporation that administers special assistance programs and guarantees mortgage-backed securities using FHA and VA loans

9. ____ A type of loan in which the borrower makes periodic interest payments, followed by the payment of the principal in full at the end of the term

10. ____ A loan in which both principal and interest are paid off slowly, over time

TRUE OR FALSE   *Circle the correct answer.*

1. T F The Federal Reserve System is made up of the lenders who originate loans.

2. T F The *discount rate* is the short-term interest rate charged to a bank's largest, most creditworthy customers.

3. T F Income from a loan is generated by up-front finance charges collected at closing, plus interest collected during the loan term.

4. T F The primary mortgage market includes savings associations, insurance companies, and mortgage bankers.

TRUE OR FALSE *(continued)*

5. T F Fannie Mae is a privately owned corporation.

6. T F An *amortized loan* applies each monthly payment first toward the total interest owed over the life of the loan; once the total interest is paid off, each monthly payment is applied to the principal amount.

7. T F In an adjustable-rate mortgage, the interest rate is usually based on an objective economic indicator plus an additional premium, called a *margin*.

8. T F In an adjustable-rate mortgage, the conversion option establishes how often the rate may be changed.

9. T F In a 20-year straight loan of $92,500 at 6.8 percent interest, the borrower's final monthly payment will be $93,024.17.

10. T F The *value* portion of a property's loan-to-value (LTV) ratio is the higher of the sale price or the appraised value.

11. T F The FHA is not a mortgage lender.

12. T F A home equity loan takes first lien priority over the original mortgage loan.

13. T F A *wraparound loan* covers more than one parcel or lot and is usually used to finance subdivision developments.

14. T F In an *open-end loan* the interest rate on the initial amount borrowed is fixed, but the rate on future advances is linked to future market rates.

15. T F Under the Truth-in-Lending Act, consumers must be fully informed of all finance charges and of the true interest rate prior to the completion of a transaction.

16. T F Under Regulation Z, a residential purchase-money borrower has three days in which to rescind a transaction simply by notifying the lender of his or her intent to rescind.

17. T F Under the Community Reinvestment Act, the findings of the government agency review of an institution's reinvestment activities are strictly confidential.

18. T F A computerized loan origination system allows a real estate broker to select a lender and apply for a loan on a buyer's behalf.

19. T F A VA appraisal is referred to as a *certificate of reasonable value (CRV)*.

20. T F Under the Truth-in-Lending Act, a phrase such as *no money down* triggers certain disclosures.

21. T F FHA loans are attractive to lenders because they insure them against loss due to borrower default.

22. T F The VA limits the amount of principal in a VA loan.

23. T F Construction loans usually charge a higher rate of interest due to higher risks of delays or other problems.

24. T F The Community Reinvestment Act requires financial institutions to help meet their communities' needs for low-income and moderate-income housing.

25. T F When a loan is sold in the secondary mortgage market, the purchasing investor always takes over the servicing of the loan.

MULTIPLE CHOICE *Circle a, b, c, or d.*

1. All of the following are roles of the Federal Reserve System *EXCEPT*
   a. help counteract inflationary trends.
   b. create a favorable economic climate.
   c. maintain sound credit conditions.
   d. make direct loans to buyers.

2. A lender who collects payments, processes them, and follows up on loan delinquencies is said to
   a. increase the yield to the lender.
   b. service the loan.
   c. insure loan payments.
   d. underwrite the loans.

3. The primary mortgage market lenders that have most recently branched out into making mortgage loans are
   a. credit unions.
   b. endowment funds.
   c. insurance companies.
   d. savings associations.

4. Name the kind of loan in which the interest rate is tied to the movement of an objective economic indicator.
   a. Buydown
   b. Graduated mortgage payment
   c. Adjustable-rate mortgage
   d. Straight loan

5. The loan in which equal payments reduce the full amount of principal and interest to zero is a(n)
   a. hypothecation.   c. amortized loan.
   b. straight loan.   d. buydown.

6. The borrower who chooses an adjustable-rate mortgage can depend on the margin to
   a. remain constant for the life of the loan.
   b. fluctuate according to some economic index.
   c. only change according to an agreed upon amount.
   d. decrease over the life of the loan.

7. To qualify for most conventional loans, the borrower's monthly housing expenses and total other monthly obligations cannot exceed what percent of his or her total gross monthly income?
   a. 28%   c. 41%
   b. 36%   d. 45%

8. What does private mortgage insurance cover?
   a. Pays the lender if the borrower dies
   b. Reimburses the cosigner if the borrower defaults
   c. Protects the top 25% to 30% of the loan against borrower default
   d. Pays the borrower if the borrower loses the house to a title claim

9. Regulation Z always applies to
   a. a credit transaction secured by a residence.
   b. business loans.
   c. commercial loans.
   d. agricultural loans of more than $25,000.

10. Who is responsible for paying the broker or her salesperson when one of them uses a computerized loan origination system to take the loan application from a borrower?
    a. Lender
    b. Borrower
    c. Seller
    d. Split between the lender and borrower

11. Nguyen's monthly mortgage payment is $665.50. The interest rate on the loan is 6 percent, and the outstanding balance is $111,000. When Nguyen makes this month's payment, what amount of the total payment will be applied to interest, and what amount to principal?
    a. $555 interest; $110.50 principal
    b. $503.50 interest; $162 principal
    c. $497 interest; $168.50 principal
    d. $450 interest; $215.50 principal

MULTIPLE CHOICE (continued)

12. All of the following are characteristics of the Federal Reserve System *EXCEPT*

    a. all federally chartered banks must join the Federal Reserve System and purchase stock in its district reserve banks.

    b. the discount rate set by the Federal Reserve System has little effect on the availability of funds for loans.

    c. by increasing or decreasing reserve requirements, the Federal Reserve controls the amount of money available for mortgage loans.

    d. member banks are permitted to borrow money from the reserve banks to expand their local banking operations.

13. All of the following are lenders in the primary mortgage market *EXCEPT*

    a. endowment funds.

    b. mortgage brokers.

    c. insurance companies.

    d. credit unions.

14. On loans originating after July, 1999, when must a lender automatically terminate private mortgage insurance?

    a. When a new appraisal shows that the property's value has increased by at least 10%

    b. When the borrower has accumulated at least 22% equity and is current on payments

    c. After borrower's equity reaches at least 28%

    d. After loan payments have been paid for at least five years without delinquency

15. A house had a sale price of $240,000. The buyer obtained a loan for $220,000. If the lender charges three points, what will the buyer pay in points?

    a. $5,335 c. $6,950

    b. $6,600 d. $7,540

16. On which type of loan can the borrower prepay without penalty?

    a. Loans sold to Fannie Mae and Freddie Mac

    b. FHA loans

    c. VA loans

    d. All of the above

17. Under the terms of Walt's adjustable-rate mortgage, the interest rate Walt must pay is (1) the U.S. Treasury bill rate as of June 1 of each year, not to exceed 8.95 percent for any period; plus (2) 1.5 percent. What is the term used to describe (2)?

    a. Rate cap c. Margin

    b. Index   d. Payment cap

18. Jessie bought a home overlooking the ocean. The asking price for the home was $585,000; Jessie offered $565,000 and the seller accepted. The appraised value of the home is $560,000. Jessie plans to pay $94,600 in cash and take out a mortgage for the remainder. What is the LTV ratio for this property?

    a. 82%   c. 84%

    b. 83%   d. 85%

19. A borrower took out an FHA-insured loan on a single-family home on November 1, 2005. If the borrower wishes to prepay the loan, what would be the notice requirement and prepayment penalty?

    a. The borrower must give the lender a 30-day written notice of his or her intent to prepay and may be charged a penalty of one month's interest.

    b. If the borrower fails to give the lender a 30-day written notice of his or her intent to prepay, the lender has the option of charging a penalty of up to 30 days' interest.

    c. No written notice is required, but lenders are permitted to charge a reasonable prepayment penalty.

    d. No written notice is required, and there is no prepayment penalty.

MULTIPLE CHOICE   *(continued)*

20. Laura is buying Hilltop House from Ray. Ray bought Hilltop House on December 20, 1989, with an FHA loan and has lived there ever since. Because of its favorable terms, Laura would like to assume Ray's mortgage. Is this possible?

    a. Yes, there are no restrictions on the assumption of this mortgage.

    b. Yes, but Laura will have to go through the complete buyer qualification process.

    c. Yes, but Laura will have to undergo a creditworthiness review only.

    d. No, this FHA loan is not assumable.

21. In 1967, Eldon served for six months on active duty in Vietnam. After winning a medal for bravery and being honorably discharged, Eldon went back to college, received a degree in engineering, and went to work for a large construction company. In 1998, Eldon was killed in a tragic skiing accident. Eldon's widow wishes to use Eldon's life insurance money to make a down payment on a condominium and believes she is entitled to a VA-guaranteed loan. Is she correct?

    a. Yes, the unremarried spouse of a qualified veteran is entitled to a VA-guaranteed loan.

    b. Yes, whether or not she remarries, Eldon's widow is entitled to the same VA benefits as Eldon was during his lifetime.

    c. No, Eldon's death was not service-related.

    d. No, Eldon did not meet the time-in-service criteria for qualified veterans.

22. Which of the following makes direct loans to qualified borrowers?

    a. VA

    b. FSA

    c. Fannie Mae

    d. FHA

23. Marge is purchasing a fully furnished condominium unit. In this situation, Marge would be *MOST LIKELY* to use a

    a. package loan.

    b. blanket loan.

    c. wraparound loan.

    d. buydown.

24. Greta, a real estate broker, has a CLO terminal in her office. Because there are more than a dozen lending institutions in the city, Greta has found that the CLO greatly streamlines the application process for her clients. Greta sits down at the terminal with Boyd, a homebuyer, and the following three events take place:

    1. Greta explains that there is a fee for using the terminal of one-half point, based on the loan amount, and that Boyd may choose to finance the fee.

    2. Greta explains only the different kinds of services offered by the two local lenders who pay Greta a monthly *screen fee* to be included on the CLO system.

    3. Greta helps Boyd answer the on-screen qualification questions.

    Which of these events is an improper use of a CLO system?

    a. 1 only

    b. 2 only

    c. 2 and 3

    d. 1 and 3

25. The Equal Credit Opportunity Act prohibits lenders from discriminating against credit applicants on the basis of all of the following factors *EXCEPT*

    a. religion.

    b. past credit history.

    c. income from public assistance.

    d. marital status.

26. Lenders that make conventional loans to sell in the secondary mortgage market follow the standardized forms and guidelines issued by Fannie Mae and

    a. the FSA.

    b. the FHA.

    c. Ginnie Mae.

    d. Freddie Mac.

MULTIPLE CHOICE   *(continued)*

27. Because some of the principal is still owed at the end of the term, a balloon payment loan is a(n)

  a. negatively amortized loan.

  b. interest-only loan.

  c. automatically-extended loan.

  d. partially amortized loan.

28. A feature of an adjustable-rate mortgage that limits the amount the interest rate may increase at any one time is a(n)

  a. periodic rate cap.

  b. payment cap.

  c. margin cap.

  d. life-of-the-loan rate cap.

29. What is a type of loan in which payments are made by the lender to the borrower and is usually repaid from the sale of the property?

  a. Buydown

  b. Wraparound loan

  c. Reverse-annuity mortgage

  d. Home equity loan

30. What helps lenders reduce the risk on a conventional mortgage loan with a high LTV?

  a. Private mortgage insurance

  b. Flood insurance

  c. Sale-and-leaseback arrangement

  d. Home equity

MATCHING B   *Write the letter of the matching term on the appropriate line.*

a. *blanket loan*

b. *adjustable-rate mortgage*

c. *buydown*

d. *certificate of eligibility*

e. *Equal Credit Opportunity Act*

f. *package loan*

g. *growing equity mortgage*

h. *purchase-money mortgage*

i. *Truth-in-Lending Act*

j. *Real Estate Settlement Procedures Act*

1. _____ A form of loan in which the interest rate fluctuates depending on the behavior of an objective economic index

2. _____ A fixed interest-rate mortgage in which monthly payments of principal are increased over the life of the loan according to an index or schedule; each such increase enlarging the regular monthly payment

3. _____ The document that determines the maximum VA loan guarantee to which a veteran is entitled

4. _____ Form of seller financing whereby the buyer gives the seller a note and mortgage

5. _____ A loan that includes both real and personal property

6. _____ A method of financing the purchase of property that temporarily lowers the initial interest rate through the payment of a lump sum of cash to the lender

7. _____ Lending law prohibiting discrimination based on marital status or sex

8. _____ Type of mortgage used by developers, securing the loan with several parcels

9. _____ Law that is designed to ensure that buyer and seller are both fully informed of all closing costs

10. _____ Law that requires lenders to reveal the true cost of borrowing money

MATH PRACTICE   *Use the Loan Table below to solve the five problems below*

	Amortized Loans							
	Life of Loan (in Years)							
Annual Interest Rate (%)	**(Monthly Payments per $1,000 of Loan Principal)**							
	5	**10**	**15**	**20**	**25**	**30**	**35**	**40**
5.00	$18.87	$10.61	$7.91	$6.60	$5.85	$5.37	$5.05	$4.82
5.50	19.10	10.85	8.17	6.88	6.14	5.68	5.37	5.16
6.00	19.33	11.10	8.44	7.16	6.44	6.00	5.70	5.50
6.50	19.57	11.35	8.71	7.46	6.75	6.32	6.04	5.85
7.00	19.80	11.61	8.99	7.75	7.07	6.65	6.39	6.21
7.50	20.04	11.87	9.27	8.06	7.39	6.99	6.74	6.58
8.00	20.28	12.13	9.56	8.36	7.72	7.34	7.10	6.95
8.50	20.52	12.40	9.85	8.68	8.05	7.69	7.47	7.33
9.00	20.76	12.67	10.14	9.00	8.39	8.05	7.84	7.71
9.50	21.00	12.94	10.40	9.32	8.74	8.41	8.22	8.10
10.00	21.25	13.22	10.75	9.65	9.09	8.78	8.60	8.49
10.50	21.49	13.49	11.05	9.98	9.44	9.15	8.98	8.89
11.00	21.74	13.78	11.37	10.32	9.80	9.52	9.37	9.28

1. John, the borrower, wants to borrow $125,000 for 20 years. He will pay 8.5 percent interest. What will be his monthly principal and interest payments? What will be the cost of interest over the life of the loan?

2. Sandra, a single woman, wants to borrow $200,000 to buy a house. If she must pay 6.5 percent annual interest and can afford a monthly payment of $1,350 (principal and interest), what is the lowest number of years she can borrow the money?

3. A couple plans to borrow $75,000 to buy a condominium. If they obtain mortgage money at 6 percent instead of 7.5 percent for a 30-year loan, how much lower will their monthly principal and interest payments be?

4. Ken can afford $1,175 per month for a payment that includes principal, interest, taxes, and insurance. Annual property taxes are $840 and insurance will cost $480 per year. If current interest rates are at 7 percent and Ken wants a 30-year loan, how much can he afford to borrow?

5. The borrower wants a 15-year mortgage instead of the typical 30-year mortgage. He will be borrowing $300,000 at 6.5 percent. How much more will this cost each month? How much will he save in interest payments over the life of the loan?

Answers:

1. _____   4. _____

2. _____   5. _____

3. _____

ANSWER KEY

Key Term Matching (A)

1. a   **2.** h   **3.** i   **4.** c   **5.** f   **6.** g   **7.** d   **8.** e
9. j   **10.** b

True or False

1. False. The *primary mortgage market* is made up of the lenders who originate loans.

2. False. The *prime rate* is the short-term interest rate charged to a bank's largest, most credit-worthy customers.

3. True

4. True

5. True

6. False. An *amortized loan* applies each payment first toward the interest owed on the loan; the remainder of each payment is then applied toward paying off the principal amount.

7. True

8. False. In an adjustable rate mortgage, the *adjustment period* establishes how often the rate may be changed.

9. True. The principal plus the last month's interest is due at the end of the term: $92,500 × 0.068 = $6,290 ÷ 12 = $524.17. $92,500 + $524.17 = $93,024.17.

10. False. The *value* portion of a property's LTV is the *lower* of the sale price or the appraised value.

11. True

12. False. A home equity loan has a junior lien priority to a first mortgage lien.

13. False. A *blanket loan* covers more than one parcel or lot and is usually used to finance sub-division developments.

14. True

15. True

16. False. Under Regulation Z, a borrower *other than* a residential purchase-money or first mortgage borrower has three days in which to rescind a transaction simply by notifying the lender of his or her intent to rescind.

17. False. Under the Community Reinvestment Act, the findings of the government agency review of an institution's community reinvestment activities *must be made public*.

18. False. A computerized loan origination system allows a real estate broker to *assist a buyer* in *selecting a lender and applying for a loan*.

19. True

20. True

21. True

22. False. The VA limits the amount of the loan it will *guarantee*. Lenders determine the amount of the loan and qualification of the borrower.

23. True

24. True

25. False. The original lender may continue to service the loan and collect payments. The investor is then charged a fee for servicing of the loan.

Multiple Choice

1. d. The Federal Reserve does not make direct loans to consumers.

2. b. Discount points increase the yield to the lender; underwriting is the process that evaluates the risk of the loan; and mortgage insurance insures the lender against borrower default.

3. a. Credit unions were known for short-term consumer loans but have more recently branched out into originating mortgage loans.

4. c. A graduated mortgage payment begins below market rate and increases each year for several years. A lump sum payment to the lender, called a *buydown*, reduces the monthly payment. A borrower makes interest-only payments and one final principal payment when using a straight loan.

5. c. The payment is first credited to the interest owed, and the remainder is applied to reduce the principal.

6. **a.** The margin remains constant during the life of the loan; the interest rate tied to the index fluctuates as the index fluctuates.

7. **b.** Note, however, that Fannie Mae guidelines set this ratio at 33 percent for 95 percent LTV loans.

8. **c.** Private mortgage insurance, usually required for loans more than 80 percent of value, provides security to the lender if the borrower defaults.

9. **a.** The truth-in-lending law, implemented by Regulation Z, does not apply to commercial, business, or agricultural loans of more than $25,000.

10. **b.** The borrower who uses a computerized loan originator must pay the fee to the broker or salesperson who takes the application.

11. **a.** $111,000 × 6% ÷ 12 = $555 monthly interest ($665.50 − $555 = $110.50).

12. **b.** If the Federal Reserve System sets a high discount rate, interest rates for loans increase and fewer loans are made. If the discount rate is low, interest rates for loans decrease and more loans are made.

13. **b.** Mortgage brokers do not loan their own money; they are intermediaries who bring borrowers and lenders together.

14. **b.** Often, a new appraisal may be obtained to determine the current value, but the equity percentage is the primary trigger for dropping PMI.

15. **b.** The buyer will pay $6,600: $220,000 × 3% = $6,600. Points are charged on the loan amount, not the sale price.

16. **d.** Prepayment penalties are fairly unusual in today's market.

17. **c.** The rate set by the U.S. Treasury bill rate is the index in the adjustable rate mortgage. The cost of doing business is the margin which remains constant during the life of the loan and is added to the Treasury bill rate.

18. **c.** The LTV on the loan amount is 84%. LTV = Loan Amount ÷ Appraised Value or Sale Price (whichever is lower), thus: $565,000 − $94,600 = $470,400 ÷ $560,000 = 84%.

19. **d.** For FHA loans taken out before 1985, the lender has the option of charging a prepayment penalty if the borrower pays off the loan without giving at least a 30-day notice. However, since August 2, 1985, no written notice is required.

20. **b.** Because the loan was made after December 15, 1989, assumptions are not permitted without complete buyer qualification.

21. **c.** The widow of a serviceman whose death is service-related may use his entitlements. In this situation, she is not entitled.

22. **b.** The Farm Service Agency will guarantee loans made and serviced by private lenders and guaranteed for a specific percentage; the FSA will also make loans directly to the borrower.

23. **a.** A loan secured by a fully furnished condominium unit is secured by both real and personal property. A blanket loan is secured by several properties.

24. **b.** Consumers must be informed of the availability of other lenders.

25. **b.** Lenders may deny a loan request because of the borrower's previous credit history. Otherwise, lenders may not discriminate on the basis of race, color, religion, national origin, sex, receipt of public assistance, age, or marital status.

26. **d.** Freddie Mac and Fannie Mae are the dominant participants in the secondary mortgage market.

27. **d.** Lenders may extend a balloon payment loan but they are not obligated to. An interest-only loan is not an amortized loan. *Negative amortization* occurs when a payment cap limits payment increases on an adjustable-rate mortgage and the loan balance increases.

28. **a.** A life-of-the-loan rate cap limits the amount the rate may increase over the entire life of the loan. A payment cap sets a maximum amount for payment increases.

29. c. A *reverse annuity mortgage loan* is popular with senior citizens who can tap the equity in their homes without having to sell. *Wraparound loans* are ones where a second lender gives a borrower a new, increased loan at a higher rate and assumes payment of an existing loan. A *buydown* is a way to temporarily lower the interest rate on a mortgage loan by paying a lump sum in cash to the lender at closing.

30. a. *Private mortgage insurance* provides lenders with funds in case of borrower default and encourages lenders to make higher LTV loans. *Sale-and-leaseback* arrangements are used to finance large commercial or industrial properties whereby the owner sells the property to an investor and then leases back the property.

Key Term Matching (B)

1. b   **2.** g   **3.** d   **4.** h   **5.** f   **6.** c   **7.** e   **8.** a
9. j   **10.** i

Math Practice

1. Interest over the life of the loan is $135,400:
   $125,000 ÷ 1,000 × 8.68 = $1,085 monthly
   P&I × 240 = $260,400 − $125,000 = $135,400 interest over the life of the loan.

2. Lowest number of years she can borrow the money is 200: $200,000 ÷ 1,000 = 200.
   $1,350 ÷ 200 = 6.75, which is the factor for 6.5 percent at 25 years

3. The couple's payment will be $74.25 each month:
   At 7.5%: 75 × 6.99 = $524.25
   At 6%: 75 × 6.00 = $450.00
   $524.25 − $450 = $74.25 lower each month

4. $840 ÷ 12 = $70
   $480 ÷ 12 = $40
   $1,175 − $70 − $40 = $1,065 ÷ 6.65 × 1,000 = $160,150 (maximum loan amount)

5. The borrower will have to pay $717 more each month with the 15-year loan but will save $212,220 in interest over the life of the loan, as seen by the following calculations:
   15-year: 300 × 8.71 = $2,613 × 15 × 12 = $470,340
   30-year: 300 × 6.32 = $1,896 × 30 × 12 = $682,560

   In actuality, lenders usually offer a lower interest rate on 15-year loans as opposed to 30-year loans. Therefore, the borrower is likely to have an even lower monthly payment than the one projected here for the 15-year loan term.

16

Leases

BEFORE YOU START...

After completing Chapter 16 of the textbook, you should be able to answer the following "learning assessment" questions. If you are able to answer these questions, then you are ready to move ahead with this chapter of the *Study Guide!* If, however, you are having some difficulty answering any of these learning assessment questions, we advise you to reread key sections of the textbook before attempting to answer the questions in this chapter of the *Study Guide.*

- Do you know the differences between a written lease and an oral lease as they relate to the statute of fraud?

- Can you define the four types of leasehold estates?

- What are the essentials of a valid contract as they apply to a lease?

- Are you able to explain the reasons for other provisions in a lease, including the use of the premises, the term of the lease, and a security deposit?

- How would you explain the legal principles of leases, including possession, recording, improvements, maintenance, assignment and subleasing, options, destruction of the premises, termination, and breach of the lease?

- Can you distinguish the three major types of leases based on how rent is paid?

- Do you know about other types of leases, such as ground leases, oil and gas leases, and lease purchase contracts?

- How would you describe the rights of landlords and tenants in eviction proceedings?

- Are you able to relate the civil rights laws to leasing practices?

MATCHING   *Write the letter of the matching term on the appropriate line.*

a. *actual eviction*

b. *constructive eviction*

c. *tenancy at will*

d. *option*

e. *periodic tenancy*

f. *reversionary right*

g. *sublease*

h. *lease*

i. *tenancy for years*

j. *tenancy at sufferance*

1. _____ A contract between a real estate owner and a tenant

2. _____ A landlord's right to possession of the premises after the expiration of the lease term

3. _____ A leasehold estate that has a specific beginning and a definite end

4. _____ The estate created when a landlord and tenant enter into an agreement that automatically renews

5. _____ A leasehold estate with an indefinite term that may be terminated by the death of either the landlord or tenant

6. _____ The leasehold estate created when a tenant who was in lawful possession of real property continues in possession without the landlord's consent

7. _____ The transfer of some of a tenant's interest, but not his or her obligations

8. _____ A lessee's privilege of renewing a lease

9. _____ The process by which a landlord regains possession of leased premises following a tenant's breach

10. _____ The action by which a tenant may properly abandon premises that have become unusable due to the landlord's conscious neglect

TRUE OR FALSE   *Circle the correct answer.*

1. T F In a lease agreement, the landlord is the lessee and the tenant is the lessor.

2. T F Unlike a freehold estate, a leasehold estate is considered personal property.

3. T F The main difference between a tenancy at will and a tenancy at sufferance is the landlord's consent.

4. T F Although an extension of a tenancy for years requires a new contract, the lease may be terminated prior to the expiration date by either party at any time.

5. T F Periodic tenancies are characterized by continuity because they are automatically renewable.

6. T F The elements of a valid lease are (1) offer and acceptance, (2) capacity of the parties, (3) consideration, and (4) legal objective.

7. T F The *covenant of quiet enjoyment* is a guarantee by the landlord that the tenant is entitled to a quiet building without interference from noisy neighbors.

8. T F A tenant who is leasing only a part of a building is not required to continue paying rent if the lease premises are destroyed.

9. T F When a tenant transfers all of his or her leasehold interests to another person, he or she has assigned the lease.

TRUE OR FALSE *(continued)*

10. T F Under a *net lease agreement*, the landlord pays all the operating expenses of the property, while the tenant pays only a fixed rental.

11. T F Ground leases are generally short-term net leases.

12. T F Except in the case of a tenancy at will or a lease from the owner of a life estate, the death of one of the parties does not terminate the lease.

13. T F To be entitled to constructive eviction, the tenant must show only that the premises have become unusable for the purpose stated in the lease.

14. T F The Fair Housing Amendments Act of 1988 requires that, in leased housing, the same criteria must be applied to tenants with children as are applied to adults.

15. T F All leases must require a security deposit as part of the consideration.

FILL-IN-THE-BLANK *Select the word or words that best complete the following statements:*

actual eviction

actual notice

consideration

constructive notice

estate at sufferance

estate at will

estate for years

Fair Housing Amendments Act of 1988

gross

lessee

lessor

nondisturbance

reversionary right

right of first refusal

sale and leaseback

sublease

triple-net

Uniform Landlord and Tenant Act

1. A type of leasehold estate that gives the right of possession with the landlord's consent for an unspecified term is called a(n) _____.

2. Although rent is the usual _____ given for the right to occupy leased premises, labor could also serve this function.

3. Usually, it is unnecessary to record a lease because possession of the leased premises is considered _____ and anyone who inspects the property receives _____.

4. If the lease allows the tenant the opportunity to buy the property before the owner accepts an offer from another tenant, the tenant has the _____.

5. If the tenant pays all operating and other expenses, such as taxes, insurance, and utilities, in addition to a periodic rent, the tenant has a(n) _____ lease.

6. In a lease agreement, the tenant is called the _____ and the landlord is called the _____.

7. A leasehold estate that continues for a definite period of time is the _____.

8. A mortgage clause that states the lender agrees not to terminate the tenancies of rent-paying tenants in the event the lender forecloses on the building is the _____ clause.

9. The arrangement when an owner of property sells the property and then obtains a lease from the new owner is called _____.

10. A model law that addresses obligations in leases, such as the landlord's right of entry, premises maintenance and protection of the tenants for retaliation by the landlord in the event of complaints is the _____.

MULTIPLE CHOICE   *Circle a, b, c, or d.*

1. Greg, the tenant, pays for his own utilities and makes one payment each month to the landlord who takes care of the taxes, insurance on the building, and maintenance. What type of lease arrangement it this?

   a. Net
   b. Gross
   c. Percentage
   d. Graduated

2. Tenants want to buy the house they are renting. However, they do not have enough money for the down payment. The landlord agreed to put part of the tenants' rent toward the purchase price. The landlord and tenants have agreed to a(n)

   a. lease purchase.
   b. sale leaseback.
   c. ground lease.
   d. option.

3. The expiration date of the lease is September 30. On July 1, the house is sold to a family that wants to live in the rental property. How soon can they move in?

   a. July 1, present year
   b. July 1, next year
   c. October 1, present year
   d. December 31, present year

4. Nan rents an apartment from Rob under a one-year written lease. The expiration date of the lease is May 1. How much notice *MUST* Rob give Nan to recover possession when the lease expires?

   a. 30 days
   b. 60 days
   c. One week
   d. No notice required

5. Two years ago, Marv rented Brownacre to Dan. The agreement stated only that Dan agreed to pay Marv $500 per month. What type of tenancy does Dan have?

   a. Holdover
   b. At sufferance
   c. For years
   d. Periodic

6. Stanley rents an apartment under a two-year written lease from Casimir. Three months after signing the lease, Stanley is transferred to another country for a year. During this period, Stanley leases the apartment to Johann. Johann mails monthly rent checks to Stanley, who continues to make monthly rental payments to Casimir. In this situation, Johann has a

   a. lease.
   b. tenancy at will.
   c. sublease.
   d. periodic tenancy.

7. Carl lives in an apartment building owned by Hal. On Monday during a particularly hot August, vandals break into the building and destroy the central air-conditioning system. Carl's apartment becomes uncomfortably warm. On Tuesday, Carl sues Hal for constructive eviction. Under these facts, will Carl win?

   a. Yes, if Carl's lease promises that the apartment will be air conditioned.
   b. Yes, to claim constructive eviction, it is not necessary that the condition be the result of the landlord's personal actions.
   c. No, to claim constructive eviction, the tenant must prove that the premises are uninhabitable.
   d. No, the premises are not unusable, the condition was not due to Hal's conscious neglect, and Carl has not abandoned the apartment.

MULTIPLE CHOICE   *(continued)*

8. Victoria is a tenant in Bountiful Towers under a one-year lease signed in August. Rent payments are due on the 15th of each month. On December 12, Bountiful Towers is sold to a new owner. On March 14, the building burns to the ground. Which of the following statements accurately describes Victoria's obligations?

    a. Victoria is not required to continue paying rent after March 14, because the premises have been destroyed.

    b. Victoria is not required to continue paying rent after December 12, because the sale voids the preexisting lease.

    c. Victoria is required to continue paying rent for the full lease term, because a tenancy for years cannot be terminated by the destruction of the premises.

    d. Victoria is required to continue paying rent, but the residential lease is converted by law into a ground lease.

9. Judy signs a lease to rent an apartment. Judy's lease runs from October 1 until November 1 of the following year. Kat signs a two-year lease to rent an apartment in a new highrise building that will be ready for occupancy in 15 months. Which of these leases *MUST* be in writing to satisfy the statute of frauds?

    a. Judy's only

    b. Kat's only

    c. Both Judy's and Kat's

    d. Neither Judy's nor Kat's

10. A tenant signed a one-year lease with a landlord on April 10, 2005. On March 1, 2006, the landlord asked the tenant whether the lease would be renewed. The tenant did not respond but was still in the apartment on April 11, 2006. What can the landlord do?

    a. The landlord must initiate eviction proceedings within the first one-month rental period.

    b. The landlord cannot evict the tenant; because the tenant remained in possession of the premises, the lease has been automatically renewed for an additional year.

    c. If the landlord accepts a rent check, the tenant is entitled to a renewal of the one-year lease.

    d. The landlord may either evict the holdover tenant or accept a rent check, creating a holdover or periodic tenancy.

11. If a tenant remains in possession of leased property after the expiration of the lease term, without paying rent and without the landlord's consent, what is his or her status?

    a. Tenant at will

    b. Tenant at sufferance

    c. Periodic tenant

    d. Freehold tenant

MULTIPLE CHOICE *(continued)*

12. Jo wanted to rent an apartment from Diane. Because of a physical disability, it would be necessary for Jo to have all the doorknobs and light switches in the unit lowered to a height of 12 inches from the floor. This would require the installation of new floors and locks, custom-made appliances, and the complete rewiring of both Jo's unit and several neighboring apartments. In addition, the floors in Jo's unit would have to be reinforced by installing steel beams and posts in the apartment beneath and in the basement. Based on these facts, which of the following statements is *TRUE?*

   a. The Fair Housing Act requires that Diane make the accommodation for Jo at Diane's expense; no additional rent may be charged for Jo's modified unit.

   b. Because the modifications demanded by Jo are not reasonable, Diane is not legally required to permit them.

   c. Regardless of the nature of the modifications, Jo's access right is protected by the Americans with Disabilities Act and Diane is legally obligated to permit the modifications to be made at Jo's expense.

   d. Because the proposed modifications would interfere with a future tenant's use of the premises, Jo may refuse to permit them.

13. Norm operates a small store in a shopping center. Under the terms of the lease, the landlord pays all operating expenses. Norm pays a base rent of $1,000 per month, plus 15 percent of monthly gross profits over $10,000. Norm has a

   a. gross lease.   **c.** net lease.

   b. percentage lease.   **d.** variable lease.

14. When a landowner leases unimproved land to a tenant, who agrees to erect a building on the land, the lease is usually referred to as a(n)

   a. lease purchase.   **c.** ground lease.

   b. gross lease.   **d.** improvement lease.

15. Gwen rented a house from Rachel. During the lease term, Gwen had to move out of state. Gwen assigned the lease to Patty, who failed to make any rental payments. In this situation, which of the following statements is *TRUE?*

   a. Gwen has no obligation to Rachel, because the lease was assigned, not sublet.

   b. Patty has no obligation to Rachel, because Patty's lease agreement is with Gwen.

   c. Gwen is still liable to Rachel for the outstanding rent, because Rachel did not release Gwen when the lease was assigned to Patty.

   d. Gwen is still liable to Rachel, because Gwen's arrangement with Patty as described is a sublease, not an assignment.

16. What is the purpose of a security deposit held by a landlord?

   a. Compensates landlord in the event of rent default or premises damage

   b. Functions as the last month's rent on the lease

   c. As an investment option for the tenant

   d. All of the above

17. Who owns the building that is erected on land that has a ground lease?

   a. Testator   **c.** Lessee

   b. Lessor   **d.** Trustee

18. What *MUST* a landlord do before commencing a lawsuit for actual eviction?

   a. Notify the sheriff

   b. Contract with a company to forcibly remove the tenant and possessions

   c. Obtain a judgment from the court

   d. Serve notice on the tenant

MULTIPLE CHOICE   *(continued)*

19. Darla has a lease on a top-floor apartment in a building owned by Cissy. The building is old, and Cissy has been planning to replace the roof. However, she has not yet done it. In spring, a heavy rainstorm created a roof leak that caused the plaster in Darla's living room to become saturated and fall. Darla was left with large holes in the plaster so the lath was showing. Cissy lays a tarp on the roof to prevent more water coming in. But, after two months, Cissy had still not repaired the damage to the ceiling. Darla moves out and claims construction eviction. Can she win this case?

a. No, because the apartment was not uninhabitable.

b. No, because the time period was not long enough.

c. Yes, because Cissy was negligent in not repairing the plaster.

d. Yes, because placing the tarp was an admission of responsibility by Cissy.

20. A lease that provides for specified rent increases at set future dates is called a(n)

a. adjustable lease.

b. graduated lease.

c. percentage lease.

d. interval lease.

TYPES OF COMMERCIAL LEASES

Based on the information given below, write the type of lease and current month's rental beneath each store.

A few years ago, a developer purchased a historic downtown block in the exclusive suburban community of West Flightpath. The developer combined the storefronts into the "Olde Flightpath Commons" shopping mall. Currently, the mall is completely leased to three tenants.

Acrylic Acres pays a base rent of $1,500 per month and 15 percent of property charges, limited to utilities and taxes. Blue Buttons Boutique pays a base rent of $2,000 per month and no property charges. Custom Custards pays a base rent of $1,850 per month and no property charges, but pays 12 percent of its monthly gross sales over $4,000 to the landlord.

Acrylic Acres earned $10,000 in gross profits and netted $4,850. Blue Buttons Boutique grossed $6,500 and earned a net profit of $3,000. Custom Custards had a gross income of $9,542, with profits after expenses of $7,370 for the month.

This month, the Olde Flighpath Commons had to pay $6,790 in utility bills and $495 in regular repairs and maintenance. The month's prorated share of local property taxes was $2,560, and the prorated insurance fee was $900.

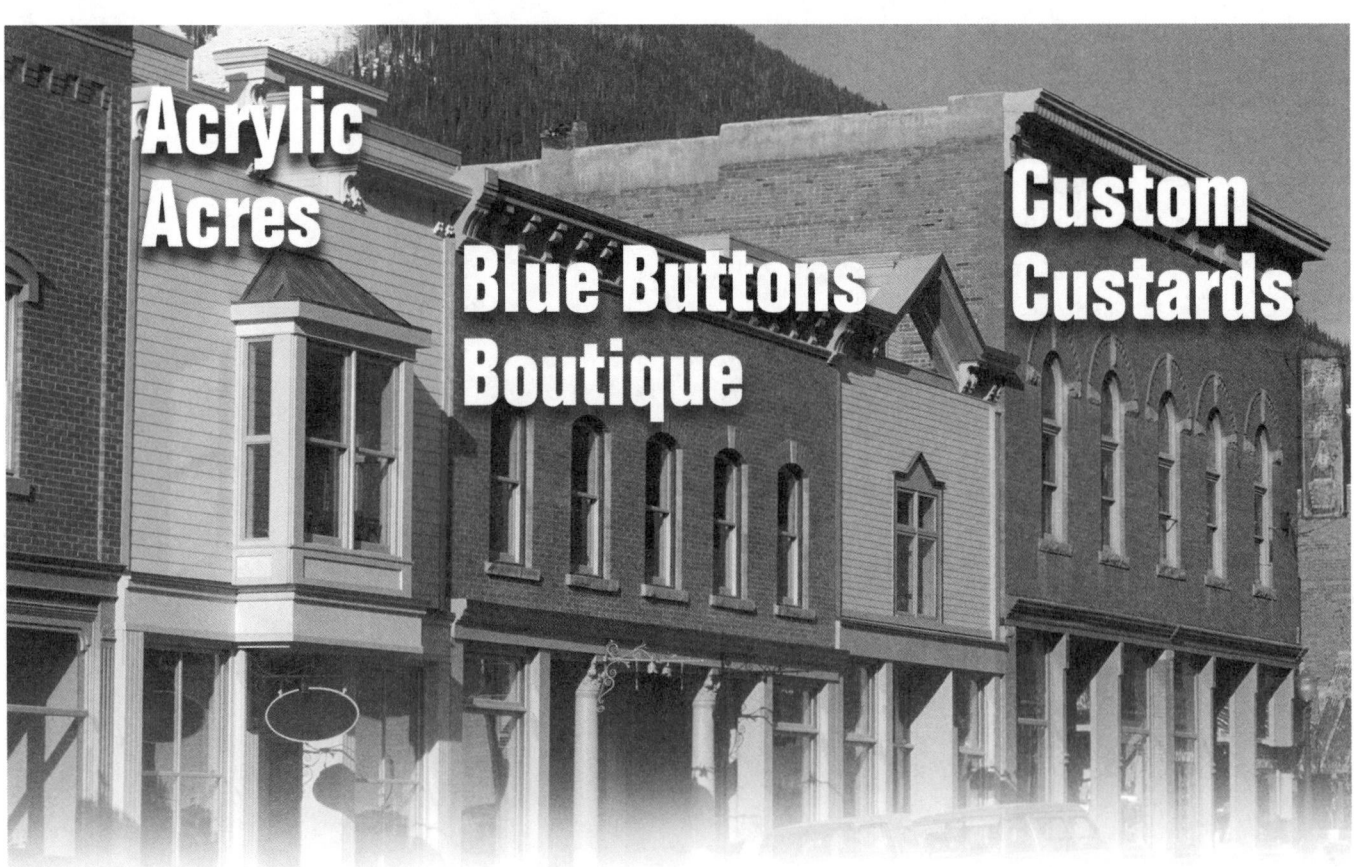

Lease Type: _____   Lease Type: _____   Lease Type: _____

Rent: _____   Rent: _____   Rent: _____

ANSWER KEY

Key Term Matching

1. h **2.** f **3.** i **4.** e **5.** c **6.** j **7.** g **8.** d
9. a **10.** b

True or False

1. **False.** In a lease agreement, the landlord is the *lessor* and the tenant is the *lessee*.

2. **True**

3. **True**

4. **False.** Although an extension of a tenancy for years requires a new contract, the lease may be terminated prior to the expiration date *only if both parties agree or if one party has breached the agreement*.

5. **True**

6. **True**

7. **False.** The covenant of quiet enjoyment is a guarantee by the landlord that the tenant is entitled to *possession of the premises without interference from the landlord*.

8. **True**

9. **True**

10. **False.** Under a *gross lease agreement*, the landlord pays all the operating expenses of the property, while the tenant pays only a fixed rental.

11. **False.** Ground leases are generally *long-term net leases and are often recorded*.

12. **True**

13. **False.** To be entitled to constructive eviction, the tenant must show only that the premises have become unusable for the purpose stated in the lease *due to the landlord's conscious neglect*.

14. **True**

15. **False.** The landlord promises possession and the tenant promises rent; that is sufficient. Security deposits are available for unpaid rent and/or damages to the property.

Multiple Choice

1. **b.** Even though tenants pay their own utilities, the one lump sum every month to the landlord is a *gross lease*. In a *net lease*, the tenant is responsible for paying all or part of the taxes, maintenance, and insurance. *Percentage leases* are generally used by retail establishments and are based on gross sales.

2. **a.** The tenant typically pays a higher *rent* with a portion being applied to the subsequent purchase of the property. It differs from a sale lease-back, whereby the owner of the property wants to pull equity from the building. The owner sells the building and agrees to rent it back.

3. **c.** The tenants have the right to possess the property until the end of their lease. The new owners will have to wait to move in.

4. **d.** This lease will be terminated May 1, an estate for years. By definition, no notice is required. If the landlord wants notice, he or she will have to add a paragraph to override this fact.

5. **d.** Any lease that automatically renews itself is a *periodic tenancy*. It will continue on until either party gives proper notice he or she wishes to make a change.

6. **c.** This is a *sublease* because the tenant has given up possession for some of the portions of the lease. Giving up all of the remaining rights would be an *assignment*. In either situation, the lessee is still responsible for the rental obligation.

7. **d.** *Constructive eviction* is a result of the landlord not providing essential services, such as the place is unsafe or impossible to live in, conditions that are not met in this situation.

8. **a.** Typically, if a residential rental unit is destroyed, the lease is terminated. This is not the case with agricultural land or ground leases.

9. **c.** Both leases are covered by the statute of frauds in that one is more than a year in length and the other will be performed more than a year later.

10. d. This is an example of an *estate for years*. If the tenant does not pay rent, it will be a *tenancy at sufferance*. If the tenant pays rent and the landlord accepts it, it will be a *holdover* or *periodic tenancy*, which could be changed into an *estate for years* if they enter into yet another year-long lease.

11. b. The landlord is suffering because he or she does not have possession and no rent.

12. b. Both the Fair Housing Laws and the Americans with Disabilities Act use the concept of *reasonable* when discussing modifications. The extent of the modifications noted would seem to be beyond the scope of *reasonable*.

13. b. Many retail shopping centers utilize percentage leases. Part of the tenant's success is due to location. Landlords will help with promotional events to draw in customers knowing that the more successful the tenant, the more rent for the landlord.

14. c. A *ground lease* is generally for a long period, sometimes 50 years. The tenant will often record the lease to serve constructive notice of their long-term interest.

15. c. While rights to possession may be assigned or sublet, the obligation to pay rent may not be assigned to another party unless the landlord agrees to the plan.

16. a. Security deposits cannot usually be applied to the final month's rental. This would be an advance rental and the landlord must treat it as income for tax purposes.

17. c. The *lessor* owns the ground. A *testator* is a person who makes a will.

18. d. Depending on the lease and state law, the notice is usually five days or ten days.

19. a. The premises must have become unusable because of the conscious neglect of the landlord. The fact that Darla stayed two more months indicates that the property actually was inhabitable.

20. b. In a *percentage lease*, the rent is based on a minimum fixed rental fee plus a percentage of the gross income received by the tenant doing business on the leased property.

Fill-in-the-Blank

1. A type of leasehold estate that gives the right of possession with the landlord's consent for an unspecified term is called an *estate at will*.

2. Although rent is the usual *consideration* given for the right to occupy leased premises, labor could also serve this function.

3. Usually, it is unnecessary to record a lease because possession of the leased premises is considered *constructive notice* and anyone who inspects the property receives *actual notice*.

4. If the lease allows the tenant the opportunity to buy the property before the owner accepts an offer from another tenant, the tenant has the *right of first refusal*.

5. If the tenant pays all operating and other expenses, such as taxes, insurance, and utilities, in addition to a periodic rent, the tenant has a *triple-net* lease.

6. In a lease agreement, the tenant is called the *lessee* and the landlord is called the *lessor*.

7. A leasehold estate that continues for a definite period of time is the *estate for years*.

8. A mortgage clause that states the lender agrees not to terminate the tenancies of rent-paying tenants in the event the lender forecloses on the building is the *nondisturbance* clause.

9. The arrangement when an owner of property sells the property and then obtains a lease from the new owner is called *sale-and-leaseback*.

10. A model law that addresses obligations in leases, such as the landlord's right of entry, premises maintenance and protection of the tenants for retaliation by the landlord in the even of complaints is the *Uniform Landlord and Tenant Act*.

Types of Commercial Leases

Acrylic Acres has a net lease, with $2,902.50 rent for the current month, calculated as follows:

$6,790 Utilities + $2,560 Taxes × 15% = $1,402.50

Base Rent = <u>1,500.00</u>

Total Rent = $2,902.50

Blue Buttons Boutique has a gross lease, with $2,000 rent for the current month. With a gross lease, no calculations are required. The tenant pays the rent; the landlord takes care of all expenses.

Custom Custards has a percentage lease, with $2,515 rent for the current month calculated as follows:

$9,542 Gross Sales – $4,000 Forgiven Sales =
$5,542.00

$5,542.00 Qualifying Sales × 12% =   665.04

Base Rent =   1,850.00

Total Rent = $2,515.04

17

Property Management

BEFORE YOU START...

After completing Chapter 17 of the textbook, you should be able to answer the following "learning assessment" questions. If you are able to answer these questions, then you are ready to move ahead with this chapter of the *Study Guide!* If, however, you are having some difficulty answering any of these learning assessment questions, we advise you to reread key sections of the textbook before attempting to answer the questions in this chapter of the *Study Guide*.

- ■ Can you define the term *property manager* and describe the objectives of property management?

- ■ Are you able to identify the provisions of a typical property management agreement?

- ■ Do you know the functions of a property manager, including the financial and physical management of the property?

- ■ Why do environmental issues and the Americans with Disabilities Act affect the activities of a property manager?

- ■ Can you describe the risk management activities of a property manager?

MATCHING   *Write the letter of the matching term on the appropriate line.*

a. *management agreement*

b. *consequential loss*

c. *multiperil*

d. *preventive maintenance*

e. *asset management*

f. *risk management*

g. *casualty*

h. *audit*

i. *tenant improvements*

j. *surety bond*

1. ____ The document that creates the agency relationship between an owner and property manager

2. ____ A type of property management specialty that helps owners decide which properties to purchase and when to sell

3. ____ Performance of regularly scheduled activities such as painting and servicing appliances and systems

4. ____ Major alterations to a building's interior to meet a tenant's particular needs

5. ____ Evaluating perils of any risk in terms of options

6. ____ An owner's protection against financial losses due to an employee's criminal acts

7. ____ Insurance policies that offer a package of standard coverages

8. ____ Insurance policies that provide coverage against theft, burglary, and vandalism; specific, not all-inclusive

9. ____ Insurance that covers the results of a disaster

10. ____ An investigation to determine the need for insurance and types of insurance required

TRUE OR FALSE   *Circle the correct answer.*

1. T F One of the key responsibilities of a property manager is to preserve or increase the value of the property.

2. T F The *management agreement* creates a general agency relationship between an owner and the property manager.

3. T F Unlike real estate brokers' commissions, property management fees may be standardized by local associations.

4. T F Rental rates are influenced primarily by supply and demand.

5. T F An example of a readily achievable modification under the ADA is installing a ramp at a building entrance.

6. T F The manager of a residential building should carefully consider a prospective tenant's compatibility with existing tenants.

7. T F A high tenant turnover rate results in higher profits for the owner.

8. T F The four types of maintenance necessary to keep a property in good condition are preventive, repair, rehabilitation, and tenant relations.

9. T F *Corrective maintenance* helps prevent problems and expenses before they arise.

10. T F Tenant improvements are major alterations to the interior of commercial or industrial property, to accommodate the tenant.

11. T F Under Title I of the ADA, all existing barriers must be removed from both residential and commercial properties.

TRUE OR FALSE (continued)

12. T F The ADA requirements for new construction are stricter than those for buildings existing before the law was implemented.

13. T F The four alternative risk management techniques are transfer, control, avoid, and retain.

14. T F In a commercial property, the risk of a shopper suffering a slip-and-fall injury would be covered by casualty insurance.

15. T F A *depreciated value policy* insures a building for what it would cost to rebuild it.

16. T F A cash flow report is the most important financial report because it provides a picture of current financial status of a property.

17. T F Property managers have a responsibility to properly manage hazardous environmental problems, such as asbestos.

18. T F Courts have held that tenants, rather than property owners and their agents, are responsible for protecting against physical harm inflicted by intruders.

19. T F The critical maintenance objective is to protect the physical condition of the property over the long term.

20. T F Examples of variable expenses of property management are employee wages and utilities.

MULTIPLE CHOICE Circle a, b, c, or d.

1. A property manager's first responsibility to the owner should be to
   a. keep the building's occupancy rate at 100%.
   b. report all day-to-day financial and operating decisions to the owner on a regular basis.
   c. realize the highest profit possible consistent with the owner's instructions.
   d. ensure that the rental rates are below market average.

2. The property manager's relationship with the owner is most similar to that of a
   a. partner in a partnership.
   b. cashier in a store.
   c. stockholder in a corporation.
   d. real estate agent.

3. All of the following should be included in a written management agreement EXCEPT a(n)
   a. list of the manager's duties and responsibilities.
   b. statement of the owner's purpose.
   c. statement identifying the manager's creditors.
   d. allocation of costs.

4. If apartment 3B rents for $750 per month and the manager receives a 12 percent commission on all new tenants, how much will the manager receive when he or she rents 3B, assuming that this commission is calculated in the usual way?
   a. $90   c. $1,080
   b. $750   d. $1,800

5. What would be the annual rent per square foot for a 30 foot × 40 foot property that rents for $2,950 per month?
   a. $1.20   c. $24.65
   b. $2.46   d. $29.50

MULTIPLE CHOICE *(continued)*

6. Of the following, a high vacancy rate *MOST LIKELY* indicates
   a. rental rates are too low.
   b. the property is desirable.
   c. building management is effective and responsive.
   d. a defective property.

7. Which of the following is an example of corrective maintenance?
   a. Seasonal servicing of appliances
   b. Picking up litter in common areas
   c. Repairing a hot water heater
   d. Moving a partition wall to make a larger office

8. The ADA applies to
   a. commercial and residential properties and all employers.
   b. commercial properties and employers of persons with disabilities.
   c. commercial properties and employers of at least 15 employees.
   d. new residential construction and employers of at least 15 people.

9. Under the ADA, existing barriers *MUST* be removed
   a. in all public buildings by the end of 2010.
   b. only on request from a person with a disability.
   c. when achievable in a *reasonably inexpensive manner*.
   d. when removal may be accomplished in a *readily achievable manner*.

10. A company was moving from one part of the city to another. During the move, a computer worth more than $750,000 was accidentally dropped into the river. Fortunately, the company was insured under several policies. The policy that would most likely cover the computer during the move from one facility to another is a
    a. consequential loss, use, and occupancy policy.
    b. casualty policy.
    c. contents and personal property policy.
    d. liability policy.

11. All of the following are principal responsibilities of the property manager *EXCEPT*
    a. forcibly remove tenants for nonpayment of rent.
    b. generate income for the owners.
    c. preserve and/or increase the value of the property.
    d. achieve the objectives of the owners.

12. What is the purpose of an operating budget for a property manager?
    a. It documents the month's actual income and expense.
    b. It is a guide for the property's financial performance in the future.
    c. It presents the current cash flows in a standardized format.
    d. It lists the assets, liabilities and equity of the investment property.

13. What type of plan does a property manager implement to deal with renters who do *NOT* pay their rent in a timely way?
    a. Eviction plan
    b. Collection plan
    c. Foreclosure plan
    d. Cash flow plan

MULTIPLE CHOICE *(continued)*

14. One way that property managers meet the goals of ECOA is by

   a. disqualifying tenant applicants on the basis of receiving welfare payments.

   b. not evaluating certain tenant applicants through the use of credit reports.

   c. establishing that certain buildings do not allow children as residents.

   d. making sure to use the same lease application for every applicant.

15. According to the Fair Housing Act, what is *steering?*

   a. Channeling of protected class members to certain buildings or neighborhoods

   b. Encouraging people to rent or sell by claiming that certain protected classes of people will have a negative impact on property values

   c. An appropriate method to manage risks associated with rental property ownership

   d. A method of providing reasonable accommodation for people with disabilities.

TYPES OF MAINTENANCE

Identify each maintenance item listed below as Preventive, Corrective, Routine, or Construction. Mark the approximate location of each item on the floor plan shown in the illustration below.

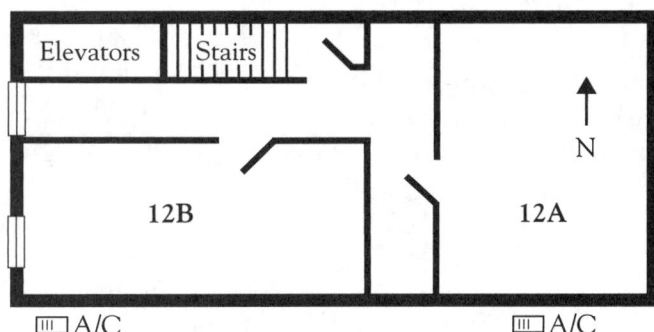

1. Paint 12th floor east-west hallway _____

2. Fix air conditioner in 12B: blows hot _____

3. Repaint exterior brick on west side _____

4. Replace torn carpet on stair landing _____

5. Repair cracked window, hallway-south _____

6. Annual elevator inspection and repair _____

7. Widen doorway in unit 12A and replace door to accommodate tenant in wheelchair _____

ANSWER KEY

Key Term Matching

1. a   2. e   3. d   4. i   5. f   6. j   7. c   8. g
9. b   10. h

True or False

1. True

2. True

3. **False.** Like real estate brokers commissions, property management fees may *not* be standardized by local associations but must be negotiated between the parties.

4. True

5. True

6. **False.** The manager of a *commercial* building should carefully consider a prospective tenant's compatibility with existing tenants, such as traffic counts, noise, etc.

7. **False.** A high tenant turnover rate results in lower profits for the owner.

8. **False.** The four types of maintenance necessary to keep a property in good condition are *preventive, corrective, construction,* and *routine*.

9. **False.** *Preventive maintenance* helps prevent problems and expenses before they arise.

10. True

11. **False.** Under Title III of the ADA, existing barriers must be removed from commercial properties *when this can be accomplished in a readily achievable manner*.

12. True

13. True

14. **False.** In a commercial property, insurance against the risk of a shopper suffering a slip-and-fall injury would be covered by *liability* insurance.

15. **False.** A building is insured for what it would cost to rebuild it in a *current replacement cost* policy.

16. True

17. True

18. **False.** Court decisions have held owners and their agents responsible for physical harm that was inflicted on tenants by intruders.

19. True

20. **False.** Employee wages and utilities are fixed expenses.

Multiple Choice

1. **c.** Keeping the building full could easily be achieved by offering below-market rates, which is not wise. The manager has been hired to spare the owner of day-to-day management. Choice c is most complete.

2. **d.** A property manager is hired as a general agent with broad authority and for a long time. Choices a and c are quasi-owners, and a store cashier rarely has much authority.

3. **c.** A management agreement sets out owner and manager responsibilities, who pays for what, all in keeping with the owner's purpose.

4. **c.** The manager will receive $1,080: $750 per month × 12 months × 12% = $1,080.

5. **d.** The annual rent is $29.50 per square foot: 30 × 40 = 1,200 square feet; $2,950 × 12 = $35,400 ÷ 1,200 = $29.50.

6. **d.** People will rent if the rates are attractively too low, if the building is desirable, and when the manager is responsive.

7. **c.** *Corrective maintenance* is fixing what is broken. Seasonal servicing is *preventive*; picking up litter is *routine*; moving a partition wall is *construction*.

8. **c.** There are some exemptions for small companies.

9. **d.** The key is *readily achievable manner*.

10. **c.** *Contents and personal property insurance* covers building contents and personal property during periods when they are not actually located on the business premises.

    Consequential loss is also known as *loss of rent* or *business interruption*; *casualty* covers theft, vandalism, machinery damage; *liability* covers injuries sustained on the premises.

11. a. Eviction proceedings are carried out by an officer of the court.

12. b. The *budget* is a forward-looking plan that guides and provides expectations. The *cash flow report* is a monthly statement that details the financial status of the property. The *profit and loss statement* documents the actual income and expense.

13. b. Property managers must implement methods to collect rent before resorting to legal action that is costly and time-consuming.

14. d. Equality is the key. It is acceptable to use credit reports, but managers need to require them on all applicants. ECOA prohibits discrimination on the basis of receipt of public assistant such as welfare.

15. a. *Steering* is prohibited under the Fair Housing Act. *Blockbusting* is encouraging people to rent or sell by claiming that the entry of certain protected classes of people in an area will have a negative impact on property values.

TYPES OF MAINTENANCE

Types of Maintenance

1. preventive or routine
2. corrective
3. preventive
4. corrective
5. corrective
6. preventive
7. construction

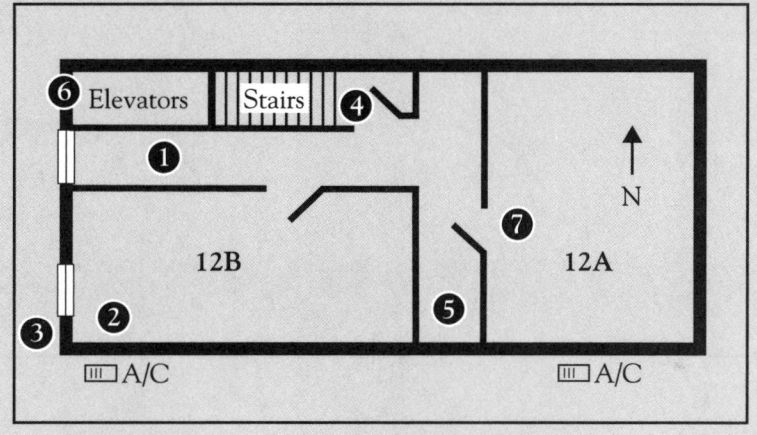

18

Real Estate Appraisal

BEFORE YOU START...

After completing Chapter 18 of the textbook, you should be able to answer the following "learning assessment" questions. If you are able to answer these questions, then you are ready to move ahead with this chapter of the *Study Guide!* If, however, you are having some difficulty answering any of these learning assessment questions, we advise you to reread key sections of the textbook before attempting to answer the questions in this chapter of the *Study Guide*.

- What are the definitions of the terms *appraisal, value,* and *market value?*
- Do you know when a certified or licensed appraiser must perform an appraisal?
- How are an appraisal and a competitive market analysis different?
- Can you define and give examples of the principles of value used when appraising real estate?
- Are you able to describe the steps involved in the *sales comparison approach* to value?
- Are you able to describe the steps involved in the *cost approach* to value?
- How would you explain the differences between *reproduction cost* and *replacement cost?*
- Do you know about the three types of depreciation and the difference between curable and incurable depreciation?
- Can you describe the steps involved in the *income approach* to value?
- How does an appraiser use the process of *reconciliation?*

MATCHING A   *Write the letter of the matching term on the appropriate line.*

a. *anticipation*

b. *appraisal*

c. *appraiser*

d. *assemblage*

e. *change*

f. *conformity*

g. *contribution*

h. *highest and best use*

i. *income approach*

j. *market value*

1. _____ An estimate or opinion of value based on supportable evidence and approved methods

2. _____ An independent professional who is trained to provide an unbiased estimate of value

3. _____ An estimate of value based on the present worth of the rights to future income

4. _____ The most probable price that a property should bring in a fair sale

5. _____ The principle that value is created by the expectation that certain events will occur

6. _____ The principle that no physical or economic condition remains constant

7. _____ The principle that value is created when a property is in harmony with its surroundings

8. _____ The principle that the value of any part of a property is measured by its effect on the value of the whole property

9. _____ The most profitable single use to which property may be put

10. _____ The process of merging two separately owned lots under one owner

TRUE OR FALSE   *Circle the correct answer.*

1. T F Title XI of FIRREA requires that all residential property be appraised by a federally licensed or certified appraiser.

2. T F A competitive market analysis should never be represented as an appraisal.

3. T F The *market value* of a property is what it actually sells for in an open market transaction.

4. T F Cost and market value are the same.

5. T F The value of a property may be affected by events that have not actually occurred.

6. T F The *law of diminishing returns* applies when, no matter how much money is spent on a property, its value will not keep pace with the expenditures.

7. T F According to the economic principle of *plottage*, combining two adjacent lots into a large one will produce a higher total land value than the sum of the value of the two sites if owned separately.

8. T F The economic principle of *contribution* holds that the maximum value of a property tends to be set by the cost of purchasing a similarly desirable property.

9. T F In the *sales comparison approach* to value, the value of a feature that is present in the subject property but not present in a comparable property is subtracted from the sale price of the comparable.

10. T F The square-foot method and the unit-in-place method are both characteristics of the cost approach to value.

TRUE OR FALSE   (continued)

11. T F Depreciation may be curable or incurable, depending on whether the expense required contributes to the property's value.

12. T F External obsolescence is always incurable.

13. T F The income approach to value is based on the future value of the rights to present income.

14. T F A GRM or GIM is often used as a substitute for an income capitalization analysis.

15. T F *Reconciliation* involves averaging the results derived from the three approaches to value.

16. T F The first step in using the income approach to value is to add the debt service to the annual operating expenses.

17. T F The art of analyzing and weighing the findings from the three approaches to value in an appraisal is called *reconciliation*.

18. T F If a property improvement results in a higher value, the law of increasing returns applies.

19. T F To use the sales comparison approach, an appraiser must find a minimum of four properties comparable to the property being appraised.

20. T F An estimate of the rate of return (yield) that an investor would expect for investing in a piece of property is called the *anticipation rate*.

MULTIPLE CHOICE   Circle a, b, c, or d.

1. A property is listed for sale at $235,000. A buyer's offer of $220,000 is rejected by the seller. Six months later, the seller reduces the price to $225,000. Another buyer offers $210,000, and the seller accepts because the seller has found another house to buy and needs to close quickly. The property is subsequently appraised at $215,000. Which of these figures MOST accurately represents the property's market value?

   a. $210,000   **c.** $225,000

   b. $215,000   **d.** $235,000

2. Which appraisal approach would be BEST to appraise a 25-year-old house in a 30-year-old neighborhood?

   a. Sales comparison

   b. Income approach

   c. Cost approach

   d. GRM

3. When appraising a new home in which no one has ever lived, the appraiser will lean toward the

   a. sales comparison approach.

   b. income approach.

   c. cost approach.

   d. GRM.

4. Assuming that all of the following transactions are federally related, the properties would have to be appraised by a state licensed or certified appraiser EXCEPT the

   a. commercial property valued at $2.5 million.

   b. condominium unit with a sale price of $67,850.

   c. residential property valued at $262,500.

   d. commercial property valued over $1 million in a refinance.

MULTIPLE CHOICE *(continued)*

5. What is the role of an appraiser?

   a. Set price

   b. Average value

   c. Determine value

   d. Estimate value

6. The principle that maximum value is realized when land use is in harmony with surrounding standards is

   a. contribution.

   b. conformity.

   c. highest and best use.

   d. competition.

7. Carol plans to build a large house in a neighborhood of smaller homes, so Carol purchases three neighboring lots from their three owners. What is the term for Carol's activity?

   a. Substitution   c. Progression

   b. Plottage   d. Assemblage

8. Lynn buys a small house in a desirable neighborhood of large Victorian homes and pays $390,000. Lynn's friend Murray buys a nearly identical house in a neighborhood of similar homes and pays $290,000. What economic principle *BEST* describes the reason why Lynn paid more than Murray?

   a. Plottage   c. Regression

   b. Substitution   d. Progression

9. If Blandacre were vacant, undeveloped land, it would be worth about $100,000. To build Blandacre Manor and its various improvements today would cost approximately $350,000. As it currently exists, Blandacre Manor's physical deterioration equals about $60,000. If an appraiser were to apply the cost approach, what would be Blandacre's value?

   a. $250,000   c. $450,000

   b. $390,000   d. $480,000

10. In which approach to value are the square-foot method, the unit-in-place method, and the quantity-survey method used?

    a. Sales comparison approach

    b. Cost approach

    c. Income approach

    d. Reconciliation approach

11. The Ghastlie Theatre Building is considered a premier example of external ornamentation. Carved marble gargoyles and granite baskets of glazed terra cotta fruit decorate the entire front of the building. Unfortunately, increased automobile traffic in the downtown area has resulted in air pollution that has dissolved much of the intricate detail work. The cost of restoring the front of the building is roughly five times the building's present value. These facts describe which of the following?

    a. Curable external obsolescence

    b. Incurable functional obsolescence

    c. Incurable physical deterioration

    d. Curable external deterioration

12. The land on which Crumbling Manor was built is worth $50,000. The Manor was constructed in 1982 at a cost of $265,000 and is expected to last 50 years. Using the straight-line method, determine how much Crumbling Manor has depreciated by 2006.

    a. $28,600   c. $127,200

    b. $96,600   d. $145,200

13. Which of the following reports would a salesperson *MOST LIKELY* research and deliver to a prospective seller?

    a. Competitive market analysis

    b. Appraisal

    c. Letter of intent

    d. Cost benefit analysis

MULTIPLE CHOICE   *(continued)*

14. What is the GRM for a residential duplex with a selling price of $234,000 if the monthly rent for each unit is $925?

- **a.** 1.054
- **b.** 10.54
- **c.** 126.5
- **d.** 252.9

15. Which of the following approaches is given the *GREATEST* weight in reconciling the appraised value of a two-bedroom, owner-occupied home?

- **a.** Income approach
- **b.** Sales comparison approach
- **c.** Cost approach
- **d.** Market value approach

16. The very old historical house has a leaking slate roof. The Historical Society demands that the new roof be made of slate. This is an example of

- **a.** reproduction.
- **b.** replacement.
- **c.** regression.
- **d.** substitution.

17. The house has been on the market for several months because most buyers do not want to walk through the master bedroom to reach another bedroom in the back. This floor plan is an example of

- **a.** regression.
- **b.** economic obsolescence.
- **c.** functional obsolescence.
- **d.** physical deterioration.

18. The owner is considering installing a swimming pool. He could spend a fair amount of money. Before he starts, he should consider the concept of

- **a.** change.
- **b.** competition with the neighbors.
- **c.** conformity within the neighborhood.
- **d.** contribution.

19. All of the following formulas are correct for the income approach *EXCEPT*

- **a.** Income ÷ Value = Rate.
- **b.** Income ÷ Rate = Value.
- **c.** Value ÷ Rate = Income.
- **d.** Value × Rate = Income.

20. A beautiful old mansion sits on the corner of a busy intersection. Two of the corners are occupied by gas stations, and directly across from the mansion is a fast food place. The mansion owners have been told that the property would be worth more if the lot were vacant. This is an example of

- **a.** progression.
- **b.** highest and best use.
- **c.** regression.
- **d.** conservation.

21. A two-unit apartment building is being appraised by Sid. In this neighborhood, the accepted gross rent multiplier is 144. The annual income on the building is $16,800 (both units rented). The monthly expenses are $300. What would Sid estimate the market value to be based on the income approach?

- **a.** $201,600
- **b.** $232,500
- **c.** $224,800
- **d.** $258,600

22. An apartment building has $65,000 in potential gross annual income. The vacancy rate is estimated at 5 percent. Total operating expenses are $29,000. The capitalization rate is 9 percent. What would be the value of the building using the income approach?

- **a.** $324,773
- **b.** $363,889
- **c.** $372,895
- **d.** $392,367

MULTIPLE CHOICE   *(continued)*

23. Which of the following applies to every appraisal?

    a. Diminishing returns

    b. Plottage

    c. Highest and best use

    d. Assemblage

24. The property being appraised is called the

    a. lot.

    b. parcel.

    c. subject property.

    d. comparable property.

25. An empty lot is located in a neighborhood of single-family homes. It is the only lot in this well-maintained neighborhood. A busy street with many stores is located three blocks away. An industrial area is about six blocks away. What is the probable highest and best use of this lot?

    a. Store

    b. Factory

    c. Parking Lot

    d. Single-family home

26. What is the process for creating a broker's price opinion?

    a. Broker drives by property, takes picture and fills out BPO form.

    b. Broker engages a certified appraiser to perform an appraisal.

    c. Broker prepares a report compiled from research of comparable properties.

    d. Attorney engages broker to perform a competitive market analysis.

27. All of the following are essential to determining market value *EXCEPT* the

    a. buyer and seller must be unrelated.

    b. payment must be in cash or its equivalent.

    c. buyer and seller must be acting without excessive pressure.

    d. property must be on the market for at least three months.

28. The principle of value that is the interaction of supply and demand is called

    a. anticipation.   c. conformity.

    b. competition.   d. contribution.

29. The most common and easiest method of cost estimation is the

    a. unit-in-place method.

    b. quantity-survey method.

    c. index method.

    d. the square-foot method.

30. Touching up peeling paint is an example of curing

    a. physical deterioration.

    b. functional obsolescence.

    c. external obsolescence.

    d. straight-line depreciation.

MATCHING B   *Write the letter of the matching term on the appropriate line.*

a. *cost approach*

b. *depreciation*

c. *economic life*

d. *sales comparison*

e. *regression*

f. *replacement cost*

g. *reproduction cost*

h. *plottage*

i. *supply and demand*

j. *substitution*

1. _____ The principle that merging or consolidating adjacent lots into a single one will produce a higher total value than the sum of the two sites valued separately

2. _____ The principle that the worth of a better-quality property is adversely affected by the presence of a lesser-quality property

3. _____ The principle that the maximum value of a property tends to be set by how much it would cost to purchase an equally desirable property

4. _____ The economic principle that the value of a property depends on the number of similar properties available in the marketplace

5. _____ The approach that estimates value by comparing the subject property with recently sold similar properties

6. _____ An estimate of value made by determining the value of the land as if it were vacant, adding the current cost of constructing improvements, and deducting accrued depreciation

7. _____ The cost of constructing an exact duplicate of the subject property at current prices

8. _____ The current price of constructing a property similar to the subject property using current construction methods

9. _____ A loss in value due to any cause

10. _____ The period during which a property is expected to remain useful for its original intended purpose

PENNYTREE LANE APPRAISALS

Complete the appraisal problems below based on the five homes on the 1200 block of Pennytree Lane depicted in the illustration below.

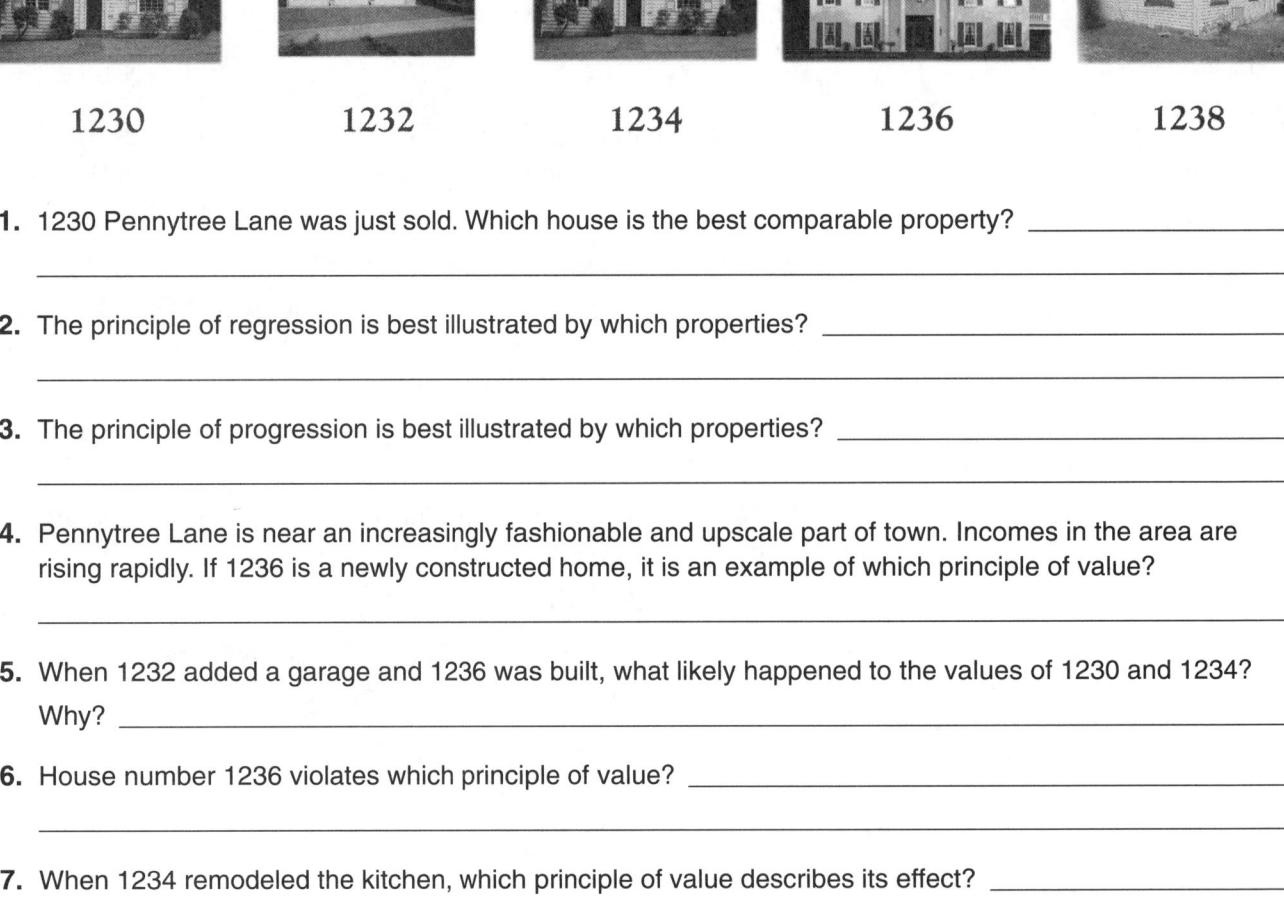

1230   1232   1234   1236   1238

1. 1230 Pennytree Lane was just sold. Which house is the best comparable property? _____

_____

2. The principle of regression is best illustrated by which properties? _____

_____

3. The principle of progression is best illustrated by which properties? _____

_____

4. Pennytree Lane is near an increasingly fashionable and upscale part of town. Incomes in the area are rising rapidly. If 1236 is a newly constructed home, it is an example of which principle of value?

_____

5. When 1232 added a garage and 1236 was built, what likely happened to the values of 1230 and 1234?
   Why? _____

6. House number 1236 violates which principle of value? _____

_____

7. When 1234 remodeled the kitchen, which principle of value describes its effect? _____

_____

ANSWER KEY

Key Term Matching (A)

1. b   **2.** c   **3.** i   **4.** j   **5.** a   **6.** e   **7.** f   **8.** g
9. h   **10.** d

True or False

1. **False.** Title XI of FIRREA requires that all residential property valued at $250,000 or more in a federally related transaction be appraised by a state licensed or certified appraiser.

2. **True**

3. **False.** The *market price* of a property is what it actually sells for in an open market transaction.

4. **False.** Cost and market value may be, but are not necessarily, the same.

5. **True**

6. **True**

7. **True**

8. **False.** The economic principle of *substitution* holds that the maximum value of a property tends to be set by the cost of purchasing a similarly desirable property.

9. **False.** In the sales approach to value, the value of a feature that is present in the subject property but not present in a comparable property is *added to* the sales price of the comparable.

10. **True**

11. **True**

12. **True**

13. **False.** The income approach to value is based on the *present* value of the rights to *future* income.

14. **True**

15. **False.** *Reconciliation* involves a detailed and professional analysis and application of the three approaches to value, not simply an average of the different values.

16. **False.** Debt service (mortgage payments) is not included in the calculation.

17. **True**

18. **True**

19. **False.** The usual standard is three comparable properties.

20. **False.** An estimate of the rate of return (yield) that an investor would expect for investing in a piece of property is called the *capitalization* or *"cap" rate*.

Multiple Choice

1. **b.** The property's market value is $210,000, while its appraised value is $215,000. The seller accepted the lower price because of the pressure to close on the new house. This is an unusual circumstance.

2. **a.** The most appropriate method to appraise an older home in an established neighborhood is the sales comparison approach.

3. **c.** A newly constructed house may be appraised using the cost approach and omitting depreciation.

4. **b.** Appraisals of residential property valued at $250,000 or less and commercial property valued at $1 million or less in federally related transactions are exempt and need not be performed by licensed or certified appraisers.

5. **d.** An *appraiser* estimates value.

6. **b.** *Contribution* is the principle that evaluates the cost of adding an improvement against the value of the property as a whole. *Competition* is the interaction of supply and demand, while *highest and best use* is the most profitable single use to which the property may be used.

7. **d.** The process of merging separately owned lots under one owner is called *assemblage*. *Plottage* holds that merging these lots together into a single larger one produces a greater total land value than the sum of the individual lots valued separately.

8. **d.** Lynn's house benefits from being a smaller one alongside larger, more prestigious ones, i.e., progression. Murray's house is appropriately valued for its neighborhood.

9. **b.** The *cost approach* subtracts the depreciation from the cost of today's improvements and then adds on the value of the land as if it were vacant: $350,000 – $60,000 + $100,000 = $390,000.

10. **b.** The *sales approach* compares values of comparable properties; the *income approach* places a value on acquiring future income.

11. **c.** Air pollution has irreparably destroyed the old design. This is an example of incurable physical deterioration.

12. **c.** The value of the land is not relevant to this problem. The cost of the building is divided by the number of years of its useful life and multiplied to determine the depreciation after 24 years: $265,000 ÷ 50 = $5,300 × 24 = $127,200.

13. **a.** A real estate salesperson often prepares a *competitive market analysis* (CMA), a comparison of the prices of recently sold homes that are similar to a listing seller's home in terms of location, style, and amenities. The CMA helps the owner set an appropriate asking price for his or her property.

14. **c.** Because GRM for one-unit and two-unit residential properties is based on gross monthly rent, GRM = Sales Price ÷ Gross Rent: $234,000 ÷ (2 × $925) = 126.5 GRM.

15. **b.** Most owner-occupied residences are best appraised by comparing them to similar properties, that is, by using the sales comparison approach.

16. **a.** Construction cost at current prices of an exact duplicate of the subject improvement is called *reproduction*, e.g., slate for slate. The roof could be replaced with a modern material at a lower cost and be just as effective at keeping the rain out of the house.

17. **c.** There is nothing physically wrong with the house, but the design is outdated, that is, functionally obsolescent. Perhaps buyers would be more interested if the room were changed to an office use.

18. **d.** Before embarking on installing the pool, the owner should consider its overall contribution to the value of the property, especially alongside his neighbors. Sometimes, the improvement does not add value equal to its cost.

19. **c.** As the rate goes down, the value increases.

20. **b.** The single most profitable use for this property is not a residential mansion; more likely, it would be better suited to another commercial use.

21. **a.** The monthly rental income is $1,400:. ($16,800 ÷ 12 = $1,400) Rental Income × GRM = Estimated Market Value. ($1,400 × 144 = $201,600) The monthly expenses are not included in the calculation.

22. **b.** Gross Income – Vacancy and Rent Losses – Operating Expenses = Net Operating Income: $65,000 × 5% = $3,250; $65,000 – $3,250 – $29,000 = $32,750. Net Operating Income ÷ Capitalization Rate = Value: $32,750 ÷ 9% = $363,889.

23. **c.** The *highest and best use* is the most profitable single use to which a property may be put, or it is the use that is most likely to be in demand in the near future.

24. **c.** *Comparable properties* are properties similar to the subject property. Each comparable property is analyzed for differences and similarities between it and the subject property.

25. **d.** The *highest and best use* is the most profitable or the most likely to be in demand soon. In this neighborhood, the demand is most likely to be for another single-family home. A parking lot is not needed. A store or factory would not be in conformity with the area.

26. **a.** Choice c is the description of a competitive market analysis, which is different from a broker's price opinion (BPO). The BPO is often commissioned by a bank or an attorney handling a divorce or estate matter rather than due to a federally related transaction.

27. **d.** The property must be on the market for a *reasonable time* but no specific time period must be met.

28. **b.** *Anticipation* is the expectation that certain events will occur. *Conformity* says that value is created when a property is in harmony with its surroundings. *Contribution* means that the value of any part of a property is measured by its effect on the value of the entire property.

29. d. With the *unit-in-place method*, the replacement cost of a building is estimated based on the construction cost per unit of measure of individual building components, such as labor. The *quantity-survey method* is so detailed that it is usually used only when appraising historical structures, but it is the most accurate for new construction. The *index method* is useful only as a check of the estimate reached by one of the other methods.

30. a. External obsolescence is always incurable. Functional obsolescence is a loss in value from the *market's response* to the item.

Key Term Matching (B)

1. h   **2.** e   **3.** j   **4.** i   **5.** d   **6.** a   **7.** g   **8.** f
9. b   **10.** c

Pennytree Lane Appraisals

1. The best comparable appears to be 1234 because it is in the same style and condition as the subject property.
2. Regression is illustrated by 1238 because it lowers the value of neighboring properties.
3. Progression is illustrated by 1236 because it raises the value of neighboring properties
4. The new home at 1236 exemplifies the principle of anticipation.
5. The values of 1230 and 1234 increased due to progression.
6. The house at 1236 violates the principle of conformity.
7. Remodeling the kitchen at 1234 illustrates the principle of contribution.

19

Land-Use Controls and Property Development

BEFORE YOU START...

After completing Chapter 19 of the textbook, you should be able to answer the following "learning assessment" questions. If you are able to answer these questions, then you are ready to move ahead with this chapter of the *Study Guide!* If, however, you are having some difficulty answering any of these learning assessment questions, we advise you to reread key sections of the textbook before attempting to answer the questions in this chapter of the *Study Guide*.

- Are you able to describe the ways that the use of privately owned land can be regulated by police power?

- Do you know the purpose and typical provisions of a *comprehensive* or *master* plan?

- How would you explain zoning ordinances, including the purpose of zoning, types of zoning, and zoning procedures?

- Can you define the terms *nonconforming use*, *variances*, and *conditional-use permits*.

- Do you know why *building codes* are used?

- Can you identify the typical provisions of *subdivision and land development ordinances?*

- How is land use controlled through *deed restrictions* and *restrictive covenants*, and can you list procedures for creating and enforcing these restrictions?

- Are you able to explain the major provisions of the Interstate Land Sales Full Disclosure Act?

MATCHING A   *Write the letter of the matching term on the appropriate line.*

a. *buffer zones*

b. *bulk zoning*

c. *comprehensive plan*

d. *conditional-use permit*

e. *enabling acts*

f. *certificate of occupancy*

g. *nonconforming use*

h. *taking*

i. *variance*

j. *zoning ordinances*

1. _____ The device by which local governments establish development goals

2. _____ Document issued by a building inspector after a newly constructed building is found satisfactory

3. _____ Local laws that implement a comprehensive plan and regulate the control of land and structures within districts

4. _____ The legal means by which states confer zoning powers on local government

5. _____ Areas such as parks used to screen residential from nonresidential areas

6. _____ A special type of zoning used to control density by imposing restrictions such as setbacks or limiting new construction

7. _____ The seizure of land through the government's power of eminent domain or condemnation

8. _____ A lot or improvement that is not in harmony with current zoning because it existed prior to the enactment or amendment of the zoning

9. _____ The device by which a day-care center might be permitted to operate in a residential neighborhood

10. _____ The device by which a landowner may use his or her property in a manner that is otherwise strictly prohibited by the existing zoning ordinances

TRUE OR FALSE   *Circle the correct answer.*

1. T   F   *Zoning ordinances* create the broad, general framework for a community; the *comprehensive plan* defines the details and implements the ordinances.

2. T   F   *Bulk zoning* is used to ensure that certain types of uses are incorporated into developments.

3. T   F   Property owners are protected against the unreasonable or arbitrary taking of their land by the seizure clause of the Fifteenth Amendment to the United States Constitution.

4. T   F   The government's payment to a landowner for seizure of his or her property is referred to as *just compensation*.

5. T   F   A *conditional-use permit* allows a landowner to use his or her property in a manner that is otherwise strictly prohibited by the existing zoning.

6. T   F   Zoning permits are usually required before building permits can be issued.

7. T   F   A *subdivider* is a person who buys undeveloped acreage and divides it into smaller lots for sale to individuals or developers.

8. T   F   A detailed map that illustrates the geographic boundaries of individual lots is called a *plan*.

9. T   F   Zoning is a state and local issue; there is no national zoning ordinance.

10. T   F   The average number of units per acre in a development is referred to as the development's *gross density*.

11. T   F   A restrictive covenant is considered a reasonable, legal restraint if it protects property values or restricts the free transfer of property.

12. T   F   The Interstate Land Sales Full Disclosure Act requires developers of any property to file a disclosure statement with HUD.

13. T   F   If a local zoning ordinance requires a 30-foot setback on property and a restrictive covenant for the subdivision calls for a 40-foot setback, the 30-foot setback takes precedence because it is less restrictive.

14. T   F   Clustering housing units can dramatically increase the amount of open and recreational space within a development.

15. T   F   Through power conferred by state enabling acts, local governments exercise public controls based on the state's obligation to protect public health, safety, and welfare.

FILL-IN-THE-BLANK   *Select the word or words that best complete the following statements:*

aesthetic zoning
ordinances

before-and-after method

bulk zoning ordinances

curvilinear

environmental impact
report

Fair Housing Act

gridiron

gross density

incentive zoning
ordinances

Interstate Land Sales Full
Disclosure Act

inverse condemnation

straight-line-depreciation

zones

1. The coding system that outlines how the land may be used (C = commercial, R = residential, etc.) divides the land into _____.

2. Zoning laws that require all new construction be approved by a special board so that the new structures blend in with existing building styles are called _____.

3. Along with an application for subdivision approval, a developer often must submit a(n) _____ to explain what effect the proposed development will have on the surrounding area.

4. The street pattern in a housing development that integrates major and minor roadways so that the development is quieter and more secure is the _____ system.

5. The federal government passed the _____ to help prevent fraudulent marketing schemes when land is sold without being seen by purchasers.

6. When Skyler's home lost value because a new airport was constructed next to it, she filed a(n) _____ action to be compensated for the loss in property value.

7. A developer must keep the average number of units in the development at or below the maximum number, which is also called the _____ _____.

8. A useful method to determine just compensation to a property owner when a portion of the owner's land is seized for public use is the _____.

9. The street pattern in a housing development that features large lots, wide streets, and limited-use service alleys is called the _____ _____ pattern.

10. Zoning laws that control overcrowding by requiring setbacks or limiting building heights are called _____.

MULTIPLE CHOICE   *Circle a, b, c, or d.*

1. A restrictive covenant is included in the deeds for all properties in the Liberty Cove subdivision, which was built in 1970. The covenant bans "all outdoor structures designed for the storage of equipment or as habitations for any animals for 32 years from the date recorded on the original plat of subdivision." In 2006, a resident built a tool shed and a doghouse. Do the neighbors have any recourse?
   a. Yes, they can go to court and sue for monetary damages for violating the covenant.
   b. Yes, they can go to court and be awarded injunctive relief.
   c. No, the restrictive covenant is no longer operative unless the property owners of Liberty Cove have agreed to its extension.
   d. No, restrictive covenants such as this are usually considered to be unenforceable restrictions on the free transfer of property.

2. A state delegates zoning powers to a municipality through
   a. its police power.
   b. eminent domain.
   c. a comprehensive plan.
   d. an enabling act.

3. All of the following would be included in a zoning ordinance *EXCEPT*
   a. objectives for future development of the area.
   b. permissible height and style of new construction.
   c. style and appearance of structures.
   d. the maximum allowable ratio of land area to structural area.

4. Which of the following protects a property owner against being deprived of his or her property by the government without just compensation?
   a. The Preamble to the U.S. Constitution
   b. The *takings clause* of the Fifth Amendment to the U.S. Constitution
   c. The *due process clause* of the Fourteenth Amendment to the U.S. Constitution
   d. The *compensation clause* of Article VII of the Bill of Rights

5. The city of Onion Lake has passed a new zoning ordinance that prohibits all commercial structures over 30 feet high. Roy wants to build an office building that will be 45 feet high. Given these facts, what must Roy do to try to obtain permission for the building?
   a. Apply for a nonconforming use permit
   b. Apply for a zoning permit
   c. Apply for a conditional-use permit
   d. Apply for a variance

6. Lana would like to operate a plant-sitting business in her home, but she lives in an area zoned for residential use only. What should Lana do?
   a. Request that the zoning board declare her home to be a nonconforming use
   b. Ask a court to grant an injunction against the zoning board
   c. Seek a conditional-use permit from the zoning board
   d. Apply to the zoning board for a variance

MULTIPLE CHOICE *(continued)*

7. Chad goes all over the country buying large tracts of vacant land, splitting them into smaller parcels, and building identical communities of single-family ranch-style homes surrounding a central shopping center. Chad sells the homes to residents and leases space in the shopping center to merchants. Chad is a(n)

   a. developer.

   b. subdivider.

   c. developer and subdivider.

   d. assembler.

8. Which of the following *BEST* defines density zoning?

   a. The mandatory use of clustering

   b. The average number of units in a development

   c. A restriction on the average number of houses per acre

   d. A restriction on the average number of acres per parcel

9. Large lots, wide streets, and uniformity are characteristic of

   a. the gridiron pattern.

   b. the curvilinear system.

   c. clustering.

   d. aesthetic zoning ordinances.

10. All of the following are common characteristics of a constitutionally valid zoning ordinance *EXCEPT*

   a. clear and specific provisions.

   b. anticipation of future housing needs.

   c. nondiscriminatory effect.

   d. affects all property owners in a similar manner.

11. Pat owns Heron's Nest, a 2,000-acre tract of undeveloped woodland surrounding a scenic lake in the state of North Virginia. Pat has divided the tract into 106 individual lots, ranging in size from 15 acres to 100 acres. Pat has hired several telemarketers to sell the lots to residents of North Virginia and the three states with which it shares a common border. Based on these facts, how does the Interstate Land Sales Full Disclosure Act apply to the project?

   a. Pat must file a disclosure statement with HUD.

   b. Because Pat's project is not fraudulent, it is exempt from the requirements of the law.

   c. The Heron's Nest project is exempt from the law because of the lot size exemption.

   d. Pat's project is exempt from the law because it is not being marketed outside a contiguous multistate region.

12. Zoning ordinances affect all of the following *EXCEPT*

   a. lot sizes.

   b. building heights.

   c. style and appearance of buildings.

   d. racial composition of neighborhood.

13. The developer has included a playground and running trails between the commercial properties facing the busy street and the houses further back in the subdivision. The recreational area is considered

   a. aesthetic zoning.

   b. a buffer zone.

   c. a taking.

   d. a nonconforming use.

MULTIPLE CHOICE *(continued)*

14. When the area was rezoned as residential, a tavern was grandfathered in and allowed to continue business. This is an example of

   a. a variance.

   b. nonconforming use.

   c. conditional-use permit.

   d. an amendment.

15. A new structure has been completed to the satisfaction of the inspecting city engineer. What documentation MUST be issued before anyone can move in?

   a. Appraisal report

   b. Certificate of occupancy

   c. Certificate of reasonable value

   d. Conditional-use permit

MATCHING B   *Write the letter of the matching term on the appropriate line.*

a. *building codes*

b. *Interstate Land Sales Full Disclosure Act*

c. *clustering*

d. *density zoning*

e. *developer*

f. *subdivider*

g. *building permit*

h. *plat*

i. *police power*

j. *restrictive covenants*

1. _____ The device by which municipal officials are alerted to new construction and alterations

2. _____ A person who buys undeveloped acreage and divides it into smaller lots for sale to others

3. _____ An individual who constructs improvements and sells them

4. _____ A detailed map that illustrates the geographic boundaries of individual lots

5. _____ Ordinances that restrict the average maximum number of houses per acre

6. _____ Standards for building style, setbacks, and use that are included in a deed for property in a subdivision

7. _____ Ordinances that specify construction and safety standards for construction

8. _____ Grouping home sites on lots smaller than normal and designating the remaining land as common areas

9. _____ Act that requires developers to file statements with HUD before the developer can market unimproved lots interstate

10. _____ State's authority to make rules needed to protect the public health, safety, and welfare

ZONING IN METROVILLE

Answer the following questions based on Metroville's zoning map depicted below.

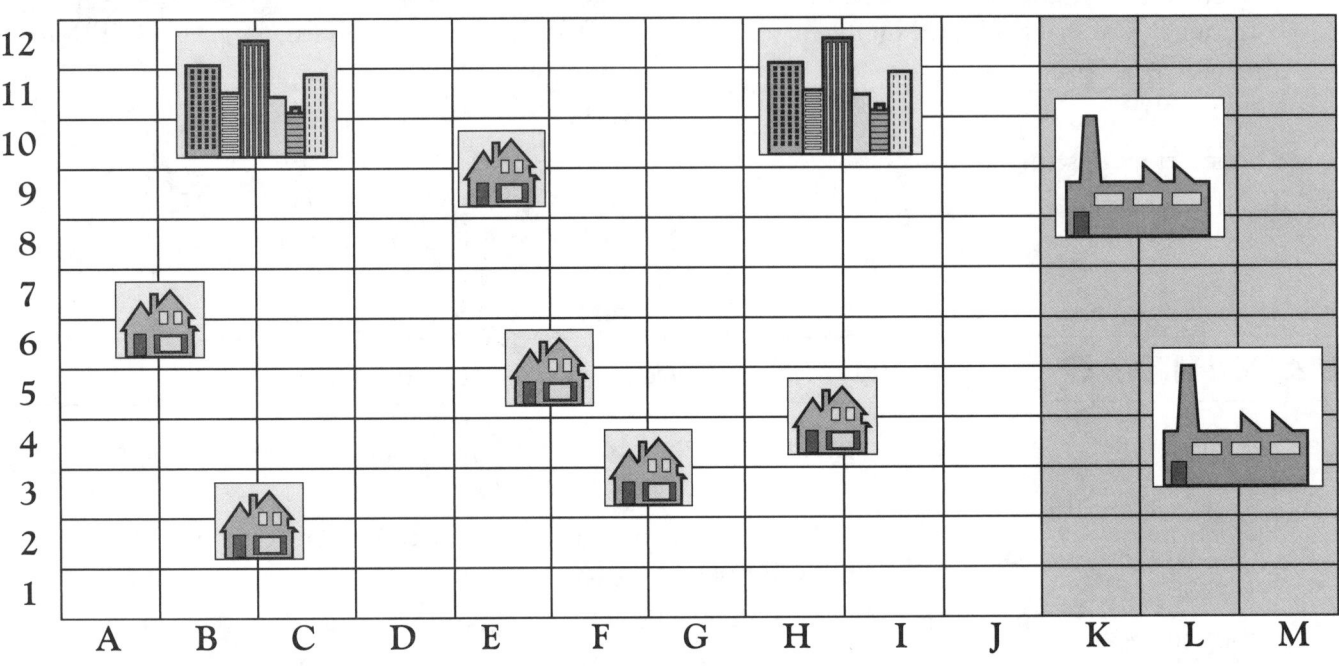

1. What would be necessary before Kiddie Kare, Inc., could legally acquire land in order to operate a day care center in area D5? _____

    _____

2. Where do you think it would be most beneficial for Metroville to locate a new park as a buffer zone? Why? _____

    _____

3. If Metroville rezones blocks G9 and H9 as an historic district with restrictions on the type of architecture for new buildings, what type of zoning is this? _____

    _____

4. The house at E-9 was built prior to Metroville's zoning ordinance. Why is it permitted to continue being a residence? _____

    _____

5. Metroville has asked you where they should locate a new "retail and professional services zone," which will take up to six square units on the map. Where would you locate this new zone. Why? _____

    _____

ANSWER KEY

Key Term Matching (A)

1. c **2.** f **3.** j **4.** e **5.** a **6.** b **7.** h **8.** g
9. d **10.** i

True or False

1. False. A *comprehensive plan* creates the broad, general framework for a community; *zoning ordinances* define the details and implement the plan.

2. False. *Incentive zoning* is used to ensure that certain types of uses are incorporated into developments.

3. False. Property owners are protected against the unreasonable or arbitrary taking of their land by the *takings clause* of the *Fifth Amendment* to the United States Constitution.

4. True

5. False. A *variance* allows a landowner to use his or her property in a manner that is otherwise strictly prohibited by the existing zoning.

6. True

7. True

8. False. A detailed map that illustrates the geographic boundaries of individual lots is called a *plat*.

9. True

10. True

11. False. A *restrictive covenant* is considered a reasonable, legal restraint if it protects property values and *does not* restrict the free transfer of property.

12. False. The Interstate Land Sales Full Disclosure Act requires developers of any *unimproved property offered in interstate commerce by telephone or through the mail* to file a disclosure statement with HUD.

13. False. Because the more restrictive requirement takes precedence, the 40-foot setback would be required.

14. True

15. True

Fill-in-the-Blank

1. The coding system that outlines how the land may be used (C = commercial, R = residential, etc.) divides the land into *zones*.

2. Zoning laws that require all new construction be approved by a special board so that the new structures blend in with existing building styles are called *aesthetic ordinances*.

3. Along with an application for subdivision approval, a developer often must submit an *environmental impact report* to explain what effect the proposed development will have on the surrounding area.

4. The street pattern in a housing development that integrates major and minor roadways so that the development is quieter and more secure is the *curvilinear* system.

5. The federal government passed the *Interstate Land Sales Full Disclosure Act* to help prevent fraudulent marketing schemes when land is sold without being seen by purchasers.

6. When Skyler's home lost value because a new airport was constructed next to it, she filed an *inverse condemnation* action to be compensated for the loss in property value.

7. A developer must keep the average number of units in the development at or below the maximum number, which is also called the *gross density*.

8. A useful method to determine just compensation to a property owner when a portion of the owner's land is seized for public use is the *before-and-after method*.

9. The street pattern in a housing development that features large lots, wide streets, and limited-use service alleys is called the *gridiron* pattern.

10. Zoning laws that control overcrowding by requiring setbacks or limiting building heights are called *bulk zoning ordinances*.

Multiple Choice

1. c. If the neighbors were concerned, they needed to rally support and gain consent to an extension of the restrictive covenant.

2. **d.** *Enabling acts* permit the state to delegate authority to local officials to enact rules to protect the public's health and safety. This *police power* includes creating a comprehensive plan and acquiring private property for public use through the right of eminent domain.

3. **a.** Choices b, c, and d all might be included in a zoning ordinance, while Choice a might be found in a comprehensive plan.

4. **b.** The Preamble to the U.S. Constitution provides for promotion of the general welfare. The 14th Amendment prevents states from depriving "any person of life, liberty, or property, without due process of law."

5. **d.** Because Roy's building does not yet exist, it does not qualify for *nonconforming use;* a *conditional-use permit* is issued for a special use that meets certain standards. A *variance,* if granted, will permit the landowner, Roy, to use his or her property in a manner that is strictly prohibited by the existing zoning.

6. **c.** A conditional-use permit might be granted in this situation because the intended use would not greatly impact the residential nature of the neighborhood.

7. **c.** *Subdividers* buy undeveloped acreage and divide it into smaller lots. A *developer* improves the land, constructs homes, or other buildings, and sells them. Developing is usually more complex than subdividing.

8. **c.** *Density zoning* ordinances restrict the average maximum number of houses per acre that may be built within a particular subdivision. Sometimes a developer will *cluster* building lots to achieve an open effect.

9. **a.** The *gridiron pattern* evolved out of the government rectangular survey system. While it provides for little open space, and many lots may front on busy streets, it is easy to navigate. The *curvilinear system* develops smaller secondary and cul-de-sac streets, avoids the uniformity of the gridiron pattern, but it often lacks service alleys.

10. **b.** Zoning ordinances cannot be static; they must remain flexible to meet the changing needs of society. The comprehensive plan would seek to anticipate future housing needs.

11. **a.** Pat must file the disclosure statement: Her project is being marketed over state lines and is more than 25 lots.

12. **d.** Zoning may not affect the racial composition of the neighborhood.

13. **b.** A *buffer zone* is a strip of land usually used as a park separating land dedicated to one use (commercial) from land dedicated to another use (residential).

14. **b.** Because the tavern had been there legally before the zoning ordinance, it is permitted to continue usually until its use changes or the building is destroyed.

15. **b.** Once the completed building has been inspected and found satisfactory, the municipal inspector issues a *certificate of occupancy* or *occupancy permit.*

Key Term Matching (B)

1. g **2.** f **3.** e **4.** h **5.** d **6.** j **7.** a **8.** c
9. b **10.** i

Metroville Zoning

1. Kiddie Kare, Inc., needs a conditional-use permit to legally acquire land in order to operate a day care center in D5.

2. The most beneficial spot would be J-1 through J-8: A park would serve the residential neighborhoods and provide a buffer between the residential and industrial zones.

3. Rezoning as an historic district is *aesthetic zoning.*

4. The house is a nonconforming use. It was most likely grandfathered in.

5. One possible location would be the square bounded by J-7, I-7, I-9, and J-9: This location would provide retail services near the residential neighborhood and professional services near the commercial zone, and it would not be disruptive to the industrial zone. Other possibilities include A-8 through F-8, or six units between J-1 and J-8 as a buffer. It would probably not be wise to place the new zone in the center of the residential area (due to traffic and noise), or in the industrial zone (it could present hazards to shoppers).

20

Fair Housing and Ethical Practices

BEFORE YOU START...

After completing Chapter 20 of the textbook, you should be able to answer the following "learning assessment" questions. If you are able to answer these questions, then you are ready to move ahead with this chapter of the *Study Guide!* If, however, you are having some difficulty answering any of these learning assessment questions, we advise you to reread key sections of the textbook before attempting to answer the questions in this chapter of the *Study Guide*.

■ Do you know about the various federal laws, including the Civil Rights Act of 1866, the Fair Housing Act, and other federal initiatives and U.S. Supreme Court cases that address housing discrimination?

■ What are the protected classes and acts that are prohibited under federal law?

■ Can you explain how families with children and people with disabilities were affected by the 1988 amendments to the Fair Housing Act?

■ What are the exemptions to the Fair Housing Act?

■ Can you describe the basic requirements of the Equal Credit Opportunity Act?

■ Do you know the major requirements of the Americans with Disabilities Act?

■ How would you relate how *blockbusting, steering,* and *redlining* affect licensees?

■ How do fair housing laws affect appraising and advertising practices?

■ Can you explain the difference between legal and ethical practices and how the industry seeks ethical behavior from its practitioners?

MATCHING A   *Write the letter of the matching term on the appropriate line.*

a. *familial status*

b. *Equal Credit Opportunity Act*

c. *Civil Rights Act of 1968*

d. *disability*

e. *blockbusting*

f. *Fair Housing Act*

g. *ADA*

h. *HUD*

i. *steering*

j. *Jones v. Mayer*

1. _____ A law that prohibits discrimination in housing based on race, color, religion, and national origin

2. _____ The Civil Rights Act of 1968, the Housing and Community Development Act of 1974, and the Fair Housing Amendments Act of 1988, collectively

3. _____ The agency that administers the federal fair housing laws

4. _____ The presence of one or more persons who are under the age of 18, living with a parent or adult guardian

5. _____ A physical or mental impairment

6. _____ A U.S. Supreme Court decision that prohibits all racial discrimination in housing

7. _____ A law that prohibits discrimination against protected classes in evaluating loan applicants (includes nonhousing-related loans)

8. _____ A law that requires accessibility to employment, goods, and services for individuals with disabilities

9. _____ Encouraging the sale or renting of property by claiming a protected class of people are moving into the area and will have a negative impact on property values

10. _____ Encouraging home seekers to limit their search to particular neighborhoods based on noneconomic factors such as race or religion

TRUE OR FALSE   *Circle the correct answer.*

1. T F The purpose of the civil rights laws that affect the real estate industry are to make everyone equal.

2. T F Failing to comply with state and federal fair housing laws may subject a licensee to both fines and disciplinary action.

3. T F The Civil Rights Act of 1968 applies only to race.

4. T F Under HUD regulations, a *dwelling* is limited to single family houses, condominiums, and cooperatives.

5. T F The fair housing laws under the *disabled persons* classification protect persons with AIDS.

6. T F There are no exemptions under the federal Fair Housing Act.

TRUE OR FALSE   *(continued)*

7. T F   The protections under the Equal Credit Opportunity Act are broader than those under the Fair Housing Act.

8. T F   The ADA's specific requirements for making curb ramps, elevators, and other spaces accessible for people with disabilities are contained in the *Accessibility Guidelines*.

9. T F   *Redlining* is the act of encouraging people to sell or rent their homes on the basis that the entry of members of a protected class into the neighborhood will reduce property values.

10. T F   Channeling home seekers to particular neighborhoods based on noneconomic factors is an illegal practice known as *steering*.

11. T F   There are no exceptions to HUD's rules regarding statements of preference or limitations in advertising regarding race.

12. T F   While not valid considerations for the underlying real estate transaction, the following factors may be considered by an appraiser in evaluating a property: race, color, religion, national origin, sex, disability, and familial status.

13. T F   Any individual who believes he or she is the victim of illegal discrimination in a real estate transaction may file a complaint with HUD within three years of the alleged act.

14. T F   Failure to prominently display the Equal Housing Opportunity poster is presumed to be evidence of discriminatory practices.

15. T F   The National Association of REALTORS® Code of Ethics establishes professional standards of behavior that guide real estate brokerage licensees throughout the United States.

16. T F   If a tenant has a visual impairment and needs an assistance dog, the landlord can require a higher security deposit than for other tenants.

17. T F   The Aldeberan Galactic Faith violates the Fair Housing Act if it owns and operates rental housing only for its member employees and others who belong to this religion.

18. T F   One reason that real estate licensees need to be concerned about meeting requirements of the ADA is because their offices are public spaces.

19. T F   If a real estate licensee says to a potential seller that the neighborhood is "changing" and "isn't what it used to be," that message is considered *blockbusting*.

20. T F   The Fair Housing Act prohibits landlords from asking potential tenants for citizenship or immigration documents during the screening process.

MULTIPLE CHOICE   *Circle a, b, c, or d.*

1. Which of the following laws extended housing discrimination protections to families with children and persons with disabilities?

   a. Civil Rights Act of 1866

   b. Fair Housing Amendments Act of 1988

   c. Housing and Community Development Act of 1974

   d. Civil Rights Act of 1968

2. The Fair Housing Act is administered by the

   a. Office of Equal Opportunity.

   b. Department of Housing and Urban Development.

   c. Justice Department.

   d. Federal court system.

3. The Fair Housing Act prohibits discrimination on the basis of all the following factors *EXCEPT*

   a. familial status.

   b. national origin.

   c. religious preference.

   d. sexual preference.

4. The Equal Credit Opportunity Act prohibits discrimination on the basis of all of the following factors *EXCEPT*

   a. amount of income.

   b. source of income.

   c. marital status.

   d. age.

5. Real estate licensees may have a legal obligation to comply with the ADA because they

   a. often have clients with disabilities.

   b. frequently own their own homes.

   c. may be employers.

   d. may need to require *reasonable accommodation* in a home they have listed.

6. Will, a real estate broker, sends a bright yellow flier to all the homeowners in the Grayside Hills neighborhood. The flier contains a reprinted article from a local newspaper describing the future relocation plans of various employers in the region and the following statement, printed in bold red letters:

   "WARNING! THE FAILURE TO SELL YOUR PROPERTY WITHIN THE NEXT SIX MONTHS COULD COST YOU A BUNDLE!"

   At the bottom of the page was printed Will's name, photo, office address, and phone number. Based on these facts, what has Will done?

   a. Will is guilty of steering.

   b. Will is guilty of blockbusting.

   c. Will has committed no offense.

   d. Will has violated the HUD advertising guidelines.

7. In the past six months, a local bank has been forced to foreclose on several mortgages in the suburb of Grand Pasture where mostly Asians live. The bank's board of directors tells the loan department to make no further loans on properties located in the suburb. Based on these facts, which of the following statements is *TRUE*?

   a. The bank is guilty of redlining.

   b. The bank is in violation of the Home Mortgage Disclosure Act.

   c. The bank's action falls under the *reasonable purpose* exception to the Fair Housing Act.

   d. The bank is guilty of discrimination on the basis of race.

8. Under what conditions can someone use race to refuse to rent to an African-American?

   a. Never

   b. If the owner is also living in one of the apartments of a small apartment building

   c. If the owner is handling the leasing without the aid of a real estate agent

   d. A small investor who is selling one of the three houses he or she owns

MULTIPLE CHOICE   *(continued)*

9. Under the Fair Housing Act, what is HUD's first action on receiving a complaint of illegal discrimination?

  a. Investigates for dismissal or reasonable cause to bring a charge

  b. Holds an administrative hearing

  c. Issues an injunction against the offender

  d. Files a civil action in federal district court

10. One of the provisions of the Fair Housing Amendments Act of 1988 is

  a. a repeal of the facilities and services requirements designed to help older persons with physical and social needs.

  b. the addition of sex to the list of protected classes.

  c. a change that made the penalties for violations more severe and added damages.

  d. the addition of religion to the list of protected classes.

11. What is the statute of limitations for housing discrimination complaints filed with HUD under the Civil Rights Act of 1968?

  a. 100 days

  b. 1 year

  c. 2 years

  d. The same as the statute of limitations for torts committed in the state in which the alleged discriminatory act occurred

12. Complaints of discriminatory housing practices filed with HUD will be referred to a local enforcement agency if

  a. the federal law is substantially more inclusive than the state or municipal law.

  b. HUD determines that an administrative law judge should decide the case.

  c. the state or municipal law is substantially equivalent to the federal law.

  d. the complaint involves a licensee who is the victim of a threat or act of violence because he or she has complied with the fair housing laws.

13. The term *professional ethics* refers to

  a. the system of professional standards adopted by the National Association of REALTORS® in 1913.

  b. the requirements of the Fair Housing Act as they apply to real estate professionals.

  c. a system of moral principles, rules, and standards of conduct that govern a professional's relations with consumers and colleagues.

  d. a standard of integrity and competence expected of professionals and licensees in the housing and real estate industry and established by HUD.

14. All of the following people are considered members of protected classes *EXCEPT* a(n)

  a. member of Alcoholics Anonymous.

  b. visually-impaired person with seeing eye dog.

  c. AIDs patient.

  d. person convicted of manufacture or distribution of illegal drugs.

15. To raise a little grocery money, Rayna decides to rent a spare bedroom in her single-family house to a tenant for $50 per month. When a 24-year-old man asks to see the room, Rayna refuses, telling him that she will only rent to women over the age of 50. The prospective tenant threatens to sue for a violation of the Fair Housing Act on the basis of age. Should Rayna be concerned?

  a. Yes, the amount of rent being charged is immaterial for purposes of the Fair Housing Act.

  b. Yes, while Rayna is permitted to exclude individuals on the basis of age or sex, she cannot exclude on the basis of both.

  c. No, the rental of rooms in an owner-occupied single-family home is exempt from the Fair Housing Act.

  d. No, because there was no real estate licensee involved in this transaction, Rayna is free to discriminate on the basis of any of the normally protected classes.

MULTIPLE CHOICE *(continued)*

16. The seller asked the agent to "not show my house to any foreigners." In this circumstance, the agent
    a. must show the house to anyone who wants to see it.
    b. must decline to take the listing with this requirement.
    c. may take the listing and ignore the instruction.
    d. may take the listing and hope that no foreigners ask to see the property.

17. A neighborhood in the west side of town has always been referred to as Little Chinatown because of the large number of Asians living there. When a Chinese couple came to Jon to look for a home to buy, he suggested they look at listings only in this neighborhood. Jon has violated the Fair Housing Act because his actions are interpreted as
    a. stereotyping.   c. redlining.
    b. blockbusting.   d. steering.

18. Hank is the property manager of StarView Apartments. Sue has made an appointment to see a two bedroom apartment. She has two children and is also pregnant. Hank tells her that the rules of the building allow only two children per two bedroom apartment and therefore he can't rent to her. Is this a violation of the Fair Housing Act?
    a. No, rental standards can include a restriction on the number of occupants in an apartment.
    b. No, the Fair Housing Act allows property owners to limit the number of children in a development.
    c. Yes, indicating a preference for a certain number of children as occupants is a violation on the basis of familial status.
    d. Yes, until the third child is born, Sue meets the standards for the number of children in the family.

19. A landlord rented an apartment to a person with a wheelchair. He allowed the tenant to install bath rails and replace the bathroom sink vanity with a pedestal sink with lever faucet handles. However, the landlord required the tenant to sign a restoration agreement that the accommodations would be restored to the former condition at the end of the lease because the vanity provided desirable storage space in the bathroom. In addition, he required the tenant to pay sufficient funds (over a period of time) into an escrow account to restore the bathroom. Has the landlord violated the Fair Housing Act?
    a. No, the landlord can require a restoration agreement and the escrow account.
    b. No, the landlord does not have to allow the tenant to make any of these modifications.
    c. Yes, the landlord cannot require restoration of the modifications.
    d. Yes, the landlord cannot require the escrow account.

20. An occupancy requirement is exempt from familial status protection under the Fair Housing Act if the housing is occupied by
    a. at least one person in each unit who is 50 years of age or older.
    b. persons 62 years of age or older.
    c. persons 55 years of age or older.
    d. at least one person age 60 or older in 80 percent of the units.

21. For fair housing purposes, what is the definition of *disability?*
    a. An impairment of mobility that prevents a person from using stairs
    b. A physical impairment that requires a caregiver's assistance
    c. An impairment that prevents a person from holding a job
    d. An impairment that substantially limits one or more of an individual's major life activities

MULTIPLE CHOICE   *(continued)*

22. How does Megan's law affect real estate licensees?

   a. It adds the protected class of disability to the Fair Housing Act requirements.

   b. It requires education of licensees on how to avoid steering potential buyers to certain neighborhoods.

   c. It may require licensees to disclose information about a released sex offender residing in a particular area.

   d. It establishes a Code of Ethics that licensees can voluntarily adopt.

23. The ADA Notification Act requires commercial facilities and places of public accommodation be given _____ days notice before a lawsuit is filed for alleged ADA violations.

   a. 10   **c.** 60

   b. 30   **d.** 90

24. What is one negative result of redlining?

   a. Appraisers have a difficult time evaluating properties in the area.

   b. It is often a major contribution to the deterioration of older neighborhoods.

   c. The effects test must be applied to determine whether to file a lawsuit.

   d. Licensees are not able to advertise in local newspapers.

25. The resolution of a fair housing complaint by obtaining assurance that the respondent will remedy the violation is called

   a. conciliation.

   b. administrative proceedings.

   c. civil action.

   d. a judgment.

ANSWER KEY

Key Term Matching

1. c   **2.** f   **3.** h   **4.** a   **5.** d   **6.** j   **7.** b   **8.** g
9. e   **10.** i

True or False

1. **False.** The purpose of the civil rights laws that affect real estate is to create a marketplace in which all persons of similar financial means have a similar range of housing choices.

2. **True**

3. **False.** The Civil Rights Act of 1968 applies to housing discrimination based on race, color, religion, and national origin.

4. **False.** Under HUD regulations, a *dwelling* includes single family houses, condominiums and cooperatives, mobile homes, and vacant land on which any of these structures will be built.

5. **True**

6. **False.** There are no exemptions under the federal Fair Housing Act involving race, but there are some for small investors and certain organizations.

7. **True**

8. **True**

9. **False.** *Blockbusting* is the act of encouraging people to sell or rent their homes on the basis that the entry of members of a protected class into the neighborhood will reduce property values.

10. **True**

11. **True**

12. **False.** Race, color, religion, national origin, sex, disability, and familial status may not be considered in any formal or informal appraisal or evaluation of a property.

13. **False.** Any individual who believes he or she is the victim of illegal discrimination in a real estate transaction may file a complaint with HUD within one year of the alleged act.

14. **True**

15. **False.** The National Association of REALTORS® Code of Ethics guides only members of that organization. All licensees are governed by *the states that license them*.

16. **False.** A landlord cannot increase the customary security deposit only for tenants with disabilities.

17. **False.** A religious organization may restrict occupancy of dwelling units that it owns to members of the organization. However, membership in the religion must not be restricted on the basis of race, color, or national origin.

18. **True**

19. **True**

20. **False.** However, HUD provides a specific procedure for collecting and verifying citizenship papers.

Multiple Choice

1. **b.** Choice b, the Fair Housing Amendments Act of 1988, added disability and familial status, and Choice c, the Housing and Community Development Act of 1974, added sex to the list of protected classes found in Title VIII of the Civil Rights Act of 1968. Choice a, the Civil Rights Act of 1866, prohibits discrimination based on race.

2. **b.** The Department of Housing and Urban Development (HUD) handles fair housing complaints on the national level. Most states have enacted *substantially* similar laws, so often it is the state agency that is involved.

3. **d.** Sexual preference is not a protected class under the federal law but has been added to many city and state fair housing laws.

4. **a.** The ECOA prohibits discrimination in lending for eight protected classes; however, people still have to have a source of income in order to qualify for a loan.

5. **c.** In addition, many real estate licensees are brokers who own an office, and the real estate office should be accessible to the public, including a person with a disability.

6. **c.** Although perhaps in poor taste, Will is distributing a published newspaper article to which anyone has access. He is also not making any statements about a protected class of people moving into the neighborhood. In addition, one wonders whom he will find to buy these properties after he portrays such a negative image about the neighborhood.

7. **a.** The bank is refusing to make mortgage loans in a specific area for reasons other than the economic qualifications of the applicants.

8. **a.** Under the Civil Rights Act of 1866, as reinforced by the *Jones v. Mayer* Supreme Court decision, there are no exemptions that permit someone to discriminate in housing simply because of someone's race.

9. **a.** Within 100 days of the filing of the complaint, HUD either determines that reasonable cause exists to bring a charge of illegal discrimination or dismisses the complaint.

10. **c.** Religion has been a protected class since the Fair Housing Act of 1968. Sex was added to the list of protected classes by the Housing and Community Development Act in 1974. The Act was amended in 1995 to repeal the facilities and services requirements designed to help older persons with physical and social needs.

11. **b.** Persons who wish to file a complaint with HUD under Title VIII of the Civil Rights Act of 1968 must do so within one year of the alleged violation.

12. **c.** Many states and some cities have passed Fair Housing Laws that are even more inclusive than the federal law.

13. **c.** The National Association of REALTORS® did adopt a Code of Ethics in 1913, and it has evolved and been changed a number of times in the last 80+ years. The more complete answer, however, is Choice c.

14. **d.** Persons convicted of manufacturing or distributing illegal drugs do not enjoy any protections under the Fair Housing Laws, although disability is a protected class. Individuals who are participating in addiction recovery programs are in a protected class of disability.

15. **c.** The woman, Rayna, is exempt from the law because she will be renting a single room in her home.

16. **b.** This is an instruction to violate the Fair Housing Act. The agent should not take the listing with this requirement. The agent cannot simply ignore the instructions or pretend they don't exist.

17. **d.** Channeling home seekers toward or away from particular neighborhoods based on national origin or any of the other protected classifications is called *steering*.

18. **c.** Occupancy standards must be based on objective factors such as sanitation or safety, not number of children.

19. **a.** The landlord must permit these reasonable modifications, but he can require the restoration agreement and escrow account.

20. **b.** Housing is exempt from the familial status protections if it is intended for occupancy only by persons 62 years of age, or for occupancy in 80 percent of its units by at least one person 55 years of age or older. Strict rules for ongoing verification and reporting are imposed on this second alternative.

21. **d.** The definition of *disability* is very broad and focuses on impairments that prevent or restrict a person from performing tasks that are of central importance to most people's lives.

22. **c.** Megan's law, in effect, creates another category of stigmatized property.

23. **d.** This time period allows property owners time to make necessary changes without having to go to court. However, if no corrections are made in this time period, then a lawsuit is automatically filed.

24. **b.** Redlining is a prohibited practice by lenders and insurance companies. The Home Mortgage Disclosure Act (HMDA) enables the government to detect patterns of lending behavior that might constitute redlining.

25. **a.** *Conciliation* attempts to resolve the complaint without further legal action, such as an administrative proceeding. However, a conciliation agreement can be enforced through civil action.

21

Environmental Issues and the Real Estate Transaction

BEFORE YOU START...

After completing Chapter 21 of the textbook, you should be able to answer the following "learning assessment" questions. If you are able to answer these questions, then you are ready to move ahead with this chapter of the *Study Guide!* If, however, you are having some difficulty answering any of these learning assessment questions, we advise you to reread key sections of the textbook before attempting to answer the questions in this chapter of the *Study Guide*.

■ Can you identify and define environmental hazards an agent should be aware of to protect a client's interests?

■ Do you know the warning signs, characteristics, causes, and solutions for common environmental hazards found in real estate transactions?

■ What does the term *encapsulation* mean in terms of asbestos abatement?

■ What is the potential hazard of underground storage tanks?

■ Can you define the term *landfill* and explain how one operates?

■ Are you able to identify and describe key provisions of CERCLA?

■ Why is it important for real estate professionals to know how to prevent liability under environmental law?

MATCHING   *Write the letter of the matching term on the appropriate line.*

a. *urea formaldehyde*

b. *electromagnetic field*

c. *encapsulation*

d. *capping*

e. *landfill*

f. *Superfund*

g. *radon*

h. *lead*

i. *asbestos*

j. *water table*

1. _____ A highly friable mineral commonly used as insulation prior to being banned in 1978

2. _____ The process of sealing off disintegrating asbestos and chipped or peeling lead-based paint without removing it

3. _____ A material once used in paint that can cause serious brain and nervous system damage

4. _____ A radioactive gas produced by the natural decay of other radio-active substances

5. _____ Chemical previously used in foam insulation that can release harmful gases

6. _____ An effect of electrical currents that may pose a health risk

7. _____ The natural level at which the ground is saturated

8. _____ A site for the burial of waste

9. _____ The process of covering a solid waste site with topsoil and plants

10. _____ Money set aside by the Comprehensive Environmental Response, Compensation, and Liability Act to pay for the cleanup of uncontrolled hazardous waste sites and spills

TRUE OR FALSE   *Circle the correct answer.*

1. T F The Environmental Protection Agency estimates that approximately 30 percent of commercial and public buildings contain asbestos insulation.

2. T F Asbestos removal is a relatively simple, inexpensive process that can be performed by any reasonably intelligent person.

3. T F Under the 1996 regulations published by the Environment Protection Agency and the Department of Housing and Urban Development, owners of homes built prior to 1978 are required to test their properties for the presence of lead-based paint and must fill out a lead-based paint disclosure statement.

4. T F Radon is a naturally occurring substance that is suspected of being a cause of lung cancer.

5. T F Urea-formaldehyde foam insulation can release harmful gases.

6. T F The movement of electricity through high-tension power lines, secondary distribution lines, electrical transformers, and appliances creates electromagnetic fields.

7. T F Groundwater is water that lies on the earth's surface.

8. T F Federal regulations on underground storage tanks do not apply to tanks involved in the collection of storm water or wastewater.

TRUE OR FALSE   *(continued)*

9. T   F   The process of laying two feet to four feet of soil over the top of a landfill site and then planting foliage to prevent erosion is referred to as *layering*.

10. T   F   Liability under Superfund is strict, joint and several, and retroactive.

11. T   F   Asbestos is only harmful when it is disturbed or exposed.

12. T   F   Modern home construction with energy-efficient rooms reduces the potential for radon gas accumulation.

13. T   F   In homes, the mostly likely sources of formaldehyde emissions are pressed wood products such as particleboard.

14. T   F   Homeowners with private wells have little worry about contamination because well water is drawn from far beneath the ground.

15. T   F   Possible causes of mold problems can be roof leaks, unvented combustion appliances, and gutters that direct water to the building.

16. T   F   *Strict liability* under the Superfund means that the owner is responsible to the injured party without excuse.

17. T   F   Today, licensees can feel secure that seller-supplied disclosure forms result in accurate and complete disclosure of environmental issues.

18. T   F   Federal requirements for disclosure of mold contamination in homes are contained in the Home Mold Disclosure Act.

19. T   F   Because CFCs are nontoxic and non-flammable, they are easily and safely disposed of.

20. T   F   To protect against liability due to mold contamination, real estate licensees should ask sellers about leaks, flooding, and prior damage.

MULTIPLE CHOICE   *Circle a, b, c, or d.*

1. Individuals have suffered all of the following health problems due to exposure to formaldehyde *EXCEPT*

  a. asthma.

  b. eye irritations.

  c. brain damage.

  d. burning sensation in the throat.

2. Lead is commonly found in all of the following *EXCEPT*

  a. water pipes.

  b. alkyd oil-based paint.

  c. automobile exhaust.

  d. insulating material.

3. Julie accepts an offer from Kip on her vintage Victorian home, built in 1892. Based on these facts, all of the following statements about lead-based paint are correct *EXCEPT*

  a. Julie must attach a lead-based paint disclosure statement to the sales contract.

  b. if Julie is aware of any lead-based paint on the premises, she must disclose that fact to Kip.

  c. if Kip requests a lead-based paint inspection, Julie has ten days in which to obtain one at her own expense.

  d. Kip is entitled to receive a pamphlet that describes the hazards posed by lead-based paint.

MULTIPLE CHOICE   *(continued)*

4. Where in the United States does radon occur?

   a. Mostly in the western states

   b. Mostly in the warm southern and southwestern regions

   c. In every state in the United States

   d. Only in large urban areas

5. All of the following have been proven to pose a health hazard *EXCEPT*

   a. asbestos.

   b. electromagnetic fields.

   c. lead-based paint.

   d. radon.

6. Harry stores toxic chemical waste in a large steel tank that has only 15 percent of its volume underground. Jena lives far out in the wilderness and has her own gas pump connected to a 1,500-gallon tank of gasoline buried ten feet underground near her garage. Lars keeps three large tanks filled with formaldehyde and battery acid in his basement. Which of these people is (or are) covered by federal regulations regarding USTs?

   a. Harry and Lars

   b. Harry and Jena only

   c. Lars only

   d. Jena only

7. Which of the following is responsible for administering Superfund?

   a. CERCLA   c. EPA

   b. PRP   d. HUD

8. Which of the following would disqualify someone from claiming innocent landowner immunity under the Superfund Amendments and Reauthorization Act (SARA)?

   a. Pollution was caused by a third party.

   b. Landowner exercised *due care* when the property was purchased.

   c. Landowner had only constructive knowledge of the damage.

   d. Landowner took reasonable precautions in the exercise of ownership rights.

9. In 1972, the PKL Co. owned Gray Lake and used both the lake and surrounding woodland as a dumping ground for toxic waste chemicals. In 1985, after many years without use, PKL sold the property to Hetta, who built the Waterland Fun Park. There were no obvious signs that the property contained toxic waste. Hetta borrowed half of the $500,000 purchase price from Big Bank.

   In 1996, the EPA informed Hetta that the Fun Park was built on a toxic dump and that the lake was a stew of deadly chemicals. Cleanup costs would be nearly $1 billion. Based on these facts, who is responsible for cleanup under the Superfund Amendments and Reauthorization Act (SARA)?

   a. PKL and Hetta only; lenders are immune under SARA.

   b. Hetta only; retroactivity does not apply under these facts.

   c. PKL, Hetta, and Big Bank are jointly, severally, and retroactively liable, although Hetta and Big Bank may have innocent landowner immunity.

   d. PKL, Hetta, and Big Bank are jointly, severally, and retroactively liable, and the strict liability imposed by CERCLA prohibits any immunities under SARA.

10. If a potentially responsible party (PRP) refuses to pay the expenses of cleaning up a toxic site, the EPA may

    a. bring a criminal action and have the PRP jailed for up to ten years.

    b. bring a civil action and be awarded three times the actual cost of the cleanup.

    c. bring an administrative action and be awarded the actual cost of the cleanup, plus court costs.

    d. have no legal recourse.

11. Sealing off asbestos instead of removing it is called

    a. encapsulation.   c. irresponsible.

    b. capping.   d. extended liability.

MULTIPLE CHOICE (continued)

12. Lead-based paint is found in about 75 percent of all private housing built before

a. 1978.   c. 1992.

b. 1985.   d. 1996.

13. All of the following can affect the radon levels in a home *EXCEPT*

a. whether the home has a basement.

b. weather conditions.

c. soil density under the house.

d. time of the year.

14. Which of the following is the byproduct of fuel combustion that may result in death in poorly ventilated areas?

a. Radon

b. Lead

c. Urea-formaldehyde foam insulation

d. Carbon monoxide

15. A storage tank is partially buried. At least how much of the tank must be underground to be considered an underground storage tank?

a. 10%   c. 25%

b. 15%   d. 35%

16. How can property owners help avoid carbon monoxide exposure?

a. Have heating systems checked and maintained annually

b. Have the house tested for the presence of carbon monoxide in the basement

c. Encapsulate sources of carbon monoxide emissions

d. Install attic vents

17. What is a source of polychlorinated biphenyls (PCBs)?

a. Large home appliances, such as washers and dryers

b. Small home appliances, such as hair dryers or food processors

c. Fluorescent light ballasts

d. Computers

18. Why is mold a serious environmental problem in buildings?

a. It stains surfaces on which it grows.

b. It destroys property and causes health problems.

c. It has a bad odor.

d. It is deadly to humans and pets.

19. What is the purpose of the Brownfields Legislation that became law in 2002?

a. It restores agricultural areas damaged by toxic waste.

b. It is specifically dedicated to cleaning up PCB spills and dumps.

c. It sets up incinerators to destroy UFFI, DDT, and other persistent chemicals.

d. It gives out funds to clean up polluted industrial sites.

20. What causes mold problems in buildings?

a. Insects

b. Chronic moisture problems

c. Fiberglass building materials

d. Air pollution

ANSWER KEY

Key Term Matching

1. i   **2.** c   **3.** h   **4.** g   **5.** a   **6.** b   **7.** j   **8.** e
9. d   **10.** f

True or False

1. **False.** The Environmental Protection Agency estimates that approximately *20 percent* of commercial and public buildings contain asbestos insulation.

2. **False.** Asbestos removal is a dangerous, expensive process that can be performed only by trained and licensed technicians under controlled conditions.

3. **False.** Under the 1996 regulations published by the Environmental Protection Agency and the Department of Housing and Urban Development, owners of homes built prior to 1978 are *not required* to test their properties for the presence of lead-based paint but must fill out a lead-based paint disclosure statement.

4. **True**

5. **True**

6. **True**

7. **False.** *Groundwater* is water that lies *under* the earth's surface.

8. **True**

9. **False.** The process of laying two feet to four feet of soil over the top of a landfill site and then planting foliage to prevent erosion is referred to as *capping*.

10. **True**

11. **True**

12. **False.** Actually, the practically airtight walls and windows can increase the potential for radon gas accumulation.

13. **True**

14. **False.** Groundwater can be contaminated. The earth's natural filtering systems may be inadequate to ensure clean water. Buyers of homes with private wells should have the water tested.

15. **True**

16. **True**

17. **False.** Licensees should inform buyers of the need to ask and discover and not rely on disclosure forms as warranties or guarantees. Sellers also need to fully disclose problems they are aware of.

18. **False.** There are no federal requirements for disclosure of mold contamination.

19. **False.** Because CFCs deplete the ozone layer of the earth, there is concern about their release. Consumers should be aware of the types of appliances, such as refrigerators and air conditioners, that may contain this chemical so that they can be safely disposed of.

20. **True**

Multiple Choice

1. **c.** Formaldehyde has also been shown to cause cancer in animals and may cause it in humans.

2. **d.** Asbestos is the formerly used insulating material, not lead.

3. **c.** No one is required to test for lead, but the federal law gives the prospective buyer ten days (or any time agreed to or the buyer may waive the right) to have the home tested for lead at the buyer's expense.

4. **c.** Radon has been found in every state, although it's more likely to be found in some states than in others. The only way to know for sure is to have the home tested.

5. **b.** Most electrical appliances create a small or greater field of EMFs, but there is much conflicting advice about whether EMFs pose a health hazard.

6. **b.** Because Harry's tank is more than 10 percent underground, his storage of toxic chemical waste is covered by the law. Jena's tank is completely underground so it is covered. Because Lars's tanks are in his basement, rather than underground, he is not covered.

7. **c.** Superfund is administered by the EPA.

8. c. Landowners cannot claim innocent landowner immunity if they had actual or constructive knowledge.

9. c. Both the present owner and previous owner may be held responsible for the cleanup. Innocent landowner immunity may apply to Hetta and to Big Bank.

10. b. A PRP is a potentially responsible party. If the PRP does not clean up the site, the EPA bills the PRP for the cost. Then, if the PRP still refuses to pay, the EPA can seek damages in court for up to three times the actual cost of cleanup.

11. a. *Capping* is covering over the top of a landfill with dirt and landscaping.

12. b. 1978 was the year the Federal government banned the use of lead in interior paints.

13. a. Radon can occur anywhere in a home, even one without a basement.

14. d. *Carbon monoxide (CO)* is the colorless, odorless, and tasteless gas that is a byproduct of incomplete combustion. High concentrations of CO can lead to death.

15. a. The official definition of an underground storage tank is at least 10 percent is underground.

16. a. Heating systems are prime sources of carbon monoxide if they are poorly vented or poorly maintained.

17. c. Other sources of PCBs are electrical transformers and hydraulic oil in older equipment.

18. b. Mold can trigger allergic reactions and asthma attacks.

19. d. *Brownfields* are defined as defunct, derelict, or abandoned commercial or industrial sites. Many have toxic wastes.

20. b. Moisture, oxygen, and a cellulosic food source feed mold growth. Mold can gradually destroy what it is growing on.

22

Closing the Real Estate Transaction

BEFORE YOU START...

After completing Chapter 22 of the textbook, you should be able to answer the following "learning assessment" questions. If you are able to answer these questions, then you are ready to move ahead with this chapter of the *Study Guide!* If, however, you are having some difficulty answering any of these learning assessment questions, we advise you to reread key sections of the textbook before attempting to answer the questions in this chapter of the *Study Guide*.

- Can you explain the concept of *closing* in a real estate transaction.

- Why should the buyer check the premises before the closing?

- Can you outline the title procedures?

- Who are the participants to a closing and where can it take place?

- What does the term *escrow* mean, and can you describe the escrow procedure?

- Do you know the RESPA requirements?

- Can you describe the items in a closing statement?

- Are you able to solve proration problems?

- Do you know how to prepare a sample closing statement?

MATCHING   *Write the letter of the matching term on the appropriate line.*

a. *accrued items*	**1.** _____ The consummation of a real estate transaction
b. *federally related loans*	**2.** _____ A method of closing in which a disinterested third party acts as the agent of both buyer and seller to coordinate the closing activities
c. *banking year*	**3.** _____ The type of loan governed by RESPA
d. *closing*	**4.** _____ A charge that a party owes and must pay at closing
e. *credit*	**5.** _____ An amount that has already been paid, that is being reimbursed, or that will be paid in the future
f. *debit*	
g. *escrow*	**6.** _____ The division of financial responsibility for various items between the buyer and seller
h. *kickback*	**7.** _____ Expenses to be prorated that are owed by the seller but later will be paid by the buyer
i. *prepaid items*	
j. *proration*	**8.** _____ Expenses that have been paid by and are credited to the seller
	9. _____ A 360-day period used in calculating prorations
	10. _____ An unearned fee, paid as part of a real estate transaction, that is prohibited by RESPA

TRUE OR FALSE   *Circle the correct answer.*

1. T F At closing, the seller receives the purchase price and the buyer receives marketable title to the property.

2. T F Shortly before the closing takes place, the buyer will usually conduct a final inspection of the property, usually called a *spot survey.*

3. T F While the particulars of closing in escrow vary from state to state, the escrow agent is always a licensed attorney.

4. T F When closing in escrow, the seller will deposit proof of a new hazard insurance policy with the escrow agent.

5. T F Real estate licensees often attend the closing to help explain information to their clients and to check that their commission is correctly paid from the proceeds of the closing.

6. T F RESPA applies to all federally related loans, except for those administered by HUD.

7. T F Real estate licensees are exempt from RESPA's rules governing controlled business arrangements and referrals.

8. T F A special HUD information booklet that provides information on settlement costs must be provided to all real estate loan applicants.

9. T F Borrowers have the right to inspect the completed HUD-1 form one business day before closing.

10. T F RESPA's rules prohibit both paying and receiving a kickback.

FILL-IN-THE-BLANK   *Select the word or words that best complete the following statements:*

1099-S

affidavit of title

bring down

buyer

conventional loans

federally related loans

good-faith estimate

HUD-1

payoff statement

proration

seller

settlement and transfer

survey

1. The property *map* that sets out any encroachments and easements is called the _____.

2. The second title search, known as the _____, is done after the closing and usually is paid for by the purchaser of the property.

3. Mortgage loans made by banks, savings associations, or other lenders whose deposits are insured by federal agencies, plus FHA and VA loans are called _____ and are subject to the requirements of RESPA.

4. The form that itemizes all charges to be paid by a borrower and seller in connection with settlement is called the _____.

5. To make sure that an existing loan amount is paid in the correct amount on the date of closing, the lender provides a(n) _____ to the closing agent.

6. Another name for the closing is _____.

7. The closing agent or lender is usually responsible for filing Form _____ to report certain real estate sales to the IRS.

8. A sworn statement, or _____, is completed by the seller and assures the title insurance company (and the buyer) that there have been no judgments, bankruptcies, or divorce involving the seller since the date of the title examination.

9. One of the requirements of RESPA is that no later than three business days after receiving a loan application, the lender must provide the borrower with a(n) _____ of the settlement costs the borrower is likely to pay.

10. Usually the _____ pays for recording charges, such as recording the deed, that are due to the actual transfer of title.

MULTIPLE CHOICE   *Circle a, b, c, or d.*

NOTE: Some state licensing exams use a 360-day year and a 30-day month for proration calculations. Others use the actual number of days. You may wish to concentrate your study on the questions that more closely apply to your state.

For Questions 1 through 4, prorate using a 30-day month and a 360-day year; prorate the taxes as of the close of escrow. Split the escrow fee 50-50 between the parties. Closing is July 31. Use the following relevant facts:

- Purchase price: $25,000 Cash
- Earnest money: $1,000
- Commission rate: 7 percent, split 50-50
- Revenue stamps: $25
- Real estate taxes $350 (paid in full for current tax year of Jan. 1 through Dec. 31)
- Water bill: $90 (six months paid to Sept. 15)
- Title insurance: $153.51
- Recording fee: $2
- Escrow fee: $168
- Loan balance: $9,450 (existing loan including credit for the reserve account)

1. What amount is the buyer debited for the real estate taxes?
   a. $145.83
   b. $146.71
   c. $202.19
   d. $203.30

2. What amount is the seller debited for the broker's commission?
   a. $750
   b. $1,650
   c. $1,750
   d. $2,500

3. What amount of the escrow fee will the buyer pay?
   a. $56
   b. $84
   c. $160
   d. $168

4. What amount is the buyer debited for the water bill?
   a. $10
   b. $15
   c. $17.50
   d. $22.50

5. A sale is closing on August 31. Real estate taxes, calculated on a calendar year basis, have not been paid for the current year. The tax is estimated to be $1,800. What amount of proration will be credited to the buyer?
   a. $1,100
   b. $1,200
   c. $1,485
   d. $1,500

6. A seller would be responsible for providing all of the following items EXCEPT
   a. satisfying encumbrances on title.
   b. affidavits of title.
   c. the deed.
   d. preparation of mortgage and note.

7. How long MUST a lender retain a HUD-1 after the date of closing?
   a. Six months
   b. One year
   c. Two years
   d. Four years

8. Lee owns a fully occupied rental apartment building. If Lee sells the apartment building to Katie, how will the tenant's security deposits be reflected on the closing statement?
   a. Credit Lee, debit Katie
   b. Debit both Lee and Katie
   c. Credit Katie, debit Lee
   d. Security deposits are not reflected on a closing statement

MULTIPLE CHOICE (continued)

9. Tonio is purchasing 345 Minor Street from Sarah. The single-family home is subject to an existing 30-year mortgage of $286,500 at a fixed rate of 6 percent. Under the terms of the sales contract, Tonia will assume Sarah's mortgage at 6 percent interest and pay the federally insured lender's assumption fee of $100. In addition, Sarah will assist Tonio by taking back a purchase-money mortgage in the amount of $25,000 at 8 percent interest. Is this transaction subject to RESPA?

   a. No, because this transaction involves a purchase money mortgage taken back by the seller.

   b. No, because the lender's fee on the assumed loan is more than $75.

   c. Yes, because the seller is taking back a purchase money mortgage at an interest rate higher than that charged for the assumed loan.

   d. Yes, because the lender's fee on the assumed loan is more than $50.

10. Since 1989, Marta, a real estate broker, has had an understanding with two of the five mortgage lenders in town. Marta recommends only those two lenders to her clients and does not tell clients about any other lenders. In return, the recommended lenders pay for the vacations Marta offers her salespeople as rewards for high performance. Based on these facts, which of the following statements is *TRUE?*

   a. Marta is not doing anything illegal.

   b. Because this arrangement has been in existence for more than 15 years, it is exempt from RESPA.

   c. This is a permissible controlled business arrangement under RESPA because Marta is not paid a fee for the recommendations.

   d. Marta's arrangement with the lenders is an illegal kickback under RESPA.

11. All of the following items are usually prorated at closing *EXCEPT*

   a. prepaid general real estate taxes.

   b. interest on an assumed loan.

   c. appraisal fees.

   d. rents.

For Question 12 through Question 14, prorate using the actual number of days in the month and year. Split the escrow fee 50-50. The seller will pay the revenue stamps, and the purchaser will pay title insurance and the recording fee. The purchaser assumes the existing mortgage balance of $127,042.42; the purchaser will pay cash at the closing in the amount of the difference between the purchase price and the loan balance; the present monthly payment on the loan is $1,01.40. Closing is October 15.

Following are other facts:

- Purchase price: $350,000
- Earnest money: $3,500
- Commission rate: 6 percent split 50-50
- Real estate taxes: $2,900 (paid in full for the current year Jan. 1 through Dec. 31)
- Escrow fee: $800
- Title insurance: $1,150
- Insurance policy: $758 (annual premium)
- Revenue stamps: $126.30
- Recording fee: $30
- Interest rate: 8.75 percent (with the next payment due November 1)

12. What are the prorated real estate taxes to be charged to the buyer?

   a. $604.20   c. $690.67

   b. $611.78   d. $728.30

MULTIPLE CHOICE   *(continued)*

13. What will be the amount of commission paid to the cooperating broker?

    a. $8,750   **c.** $17,500

    b. $10,500   **d.** $21,000

14. What amount will the seller receive at the closing?

    a. $201,586.23   **c.** $217,749.28

    b. $205,572.33   **d.** $208,654.34

15. How is earnest money treated if the buyer does not default and shows up for closing?

    a. Credit seller   **c.** Credit buyer

    b. Debit buyer   **d.** Debit seller

CLOSING STATEMENT

Complete the settlement statement worksheet shown on page 211, based on the information provided below. Carry out all computations to three decimal places until the final calculation. Prorate based on a 30-day month. The buyer's and seller's statements should be viewed separately, although many items will appear on both. Although both the buyer's and the seller's total debits and credits must balance, their totals and cash due need not. The selling price for the property is $315,000; the earnest money deposit is $12,000.

Buyers:	Doug and Connie Cornwall	Loan origination:	$7,560 fee (3 points); paid by buyer
Seller:	Cordelia Lear		
Property address:	1604 North Albany	Transfer tax:	$.50 per $500; paid by seller
Closing date:	June 30 of the current year	Recording fees:	$10.00 per document (deed and new mortgage paid by buyer; release of mortgage paid by seller
Broker's fee:	7 percent commission	Attorney's fees:	$500 buyer; $600 seller
Property taxes:	$2,500/year; this year's taxes have not yet been paid	Title insurance:	owner's policy $700 (seller) mortgagee's policy $150 (buyer)
Loan payoff:	$43,000 balance of principal and accrued interest	Document prep:	$50; paid by buyer
Financing:	buyer is obtaining a new $252,000 first mortgage loan	Survey:	$300; paid by seller

CLOSING STATEMENT

CLOSING STATEMENT

PROPERTY: _____

SELLER(S): _____

BUYER(S): _____

SETTLEMENT DATE: _____

SETTLEMENT ITEM	BUYER		SELLER	
	DEBIT	CREDIT	DEBIT	CREDIT
Purchase Price				
TOTALS				
Due from BUYER				
Due to SELLER				

ANSWER KEY

Key Term Matching

1. d **2.** g **3.** b **4.** f **5.** e **6.** j **7.** a **8.** i
9. c **10.** h

True or False

1. True
2. False. Shortly before the closing takes place, the buyer will usually conduct a final inspection of the property, usually called a *walk-through*.
3. False. While the particulars of closing in escrow vary from state to state, the escrow agent may be an attorney, title company, trust company, escrow company, or a lender's escrow department.
4. False. When closing in escrow, the *buyer* will deposit proof of hazard insurance with the escrow agent.
5. True
6. False. RESPA applies to all federally related loans, including those administered by HUD.
7. False. Real estate licensees are *not* exempt from RESPA's rules governing controlled business arrangements and referrals.
8. True
9. True
10. True

Fill-in-the-Blank

1. The property map that sets out any encroachments and easements is called the *survey*.
2. The second title search, known as the *bring down*, is done after the closing and usually is paid for by the purchaser of the property.
3. Mortgage loans made by banks, savings associations, or other lenders whose deposits are insured by federal agencies, plus FHA and VA loans are called *federally related loans* and are subject to the requirements of RESPA.

4. The form that itemizes all charges to be paid by a borrower and seller in connection with settlement is called the *HUD-1*.
5. To make sure that an existing loan amount is paid in the correct amount on the date of closing, the lender provides a *payoff statement* to the closing agent.
6. Another name for the closing is *settlement and transfer*.
7. The closing agent or lender is usually responsible for filing Form *1099-S* to report certain real estate sales to the IRS.
8. A sworn statement, or *affidavit of title*, is completed by the seller and assures the title insurance company (and the buyer) that there have been no judgments, bankruptcies, or divorces involving the seller since the date of the title examination.
9. One of the requirements of RESPA is that no later than three business days after receiving a loan application, the lender must provide the borrower with a *good-faith estimate* of the settlement costs the borrower is likely to pay.
10. Usually the *buyer* pays for recording charges, such as recording the deed, that are due to the actual transfer of title.

Multiple Choice

1. **a.** $350 \div 12$ months $\times 5$ months $= \$145.83$. The seller is credited for five months of taxes.
2. **c.** The seller is debited $1,750 for the broker's commission: $25,000 \times 7\% = \$1,750$.
3. **b.** The buyer's escrow fee is $84: $168 \div 2 = \$84$.
4. **d.** The buyer is debited $22.50: For July 31 through September 15 = 1.5 months prepaid by seller $90 for 6 months = $15 for one month ($90 divided by 6) 1.5 months $\times$ $15 per month = $22.50 (debit buyer)
5. **b.** The buyer's real estate tax proration is $1,200: $1,800 \div 12$ months $\times 8$ months $= \$1,200$.

6. d. Documentation for the new loan—preparation of note and mortgage—is the responsibility of the buyer.

7. c. The lender should retain the HUD-1 for at least two years.

8. c. Lee must pay the security deposit to Katie who will, as the new owner, be responsible for returning the money to the tenant at the end of the lease.

9. d. The transaction would not have been subject to RESPA if the assumption fee had been $50 or less.

10. d. By not telling her clients about the other lenders in town, Marta is limiting their ability to get the best possible financing. That added to the fact that the lender pays for her salespeople's vacations makes her behavior look very suspicious.

11. c. Usually, the lender asks that the appraisal fees and credit report fees be paid outside of closing (POC).

12. b. The buyer's prorated real estate taxes are $611.78: $2,900 ÷ 365 × 77 = $611.78.

The seller pays taxes on the day of closing. There are 16 days left in October, 30 in November, and 31 in December. Thus, the buyer owes the seller for 77 days.

13. b. The cooperating broker's commission is $10,500: $350,000 × 6% ÷ 2 = $10,500.

14. a. Sales price $350,000 – Commission $21,000 + Credit for prepaid taxes $611.78 – Half of the escrow fee $400 – Assumed loan balance $127,042.42 – Revenue stamps $126.30 – Mortgage interest for first half of settlement month $456.83 = Amount to seller $201,586.23. (The seller owes accrued interest on the loan for the 15 days he used the money: $127,042.42 × 8.75% ÷ 365 × 15 = $456.83.)

15. c. The earnest money is brought to closing and credited to the buyer.

CLOSING STATEMENT

CLOSING STATEMENT

PROPERTY: ___1604 North Albany_____

SELLER(S): ___Cordelia Lear_____

BUYER(S): ___Doug Cornwall and Connie Cornwall_____

SETTLEMENT DATE: ___June 30, 200X_____

SETTLEMENT ITEM	BUYER		SELLER	
	DEBIT	CREDIT	DEBIT	CREDIT
Purchase Price	$315,000	$ --	$ --	$315,000
Earnest Money	--	12,000	--	--
Broker's Commision	--	--	22,050	--
Property Taxes	--	1,250	1,250	--
Payoff Existing Mortgage	--	--	43,000	--
New First Mortgage	--	252,000	--	--
Loan Origination Fee	7,560	--	--	--
Transfer Tax	--	--	315	--
Recording Fees	20	--	10	--
Attorney's Fees	500	--	600	--
Title Insurance	150	--	700	--
Document Preparation	50	--	--	--
Survey	--	--	300	--
TOTALS	$318,180	$265,250	$68,225	$315,000
Due from BUYER	--	52,930	--	--
Due to SELLER	--	--	246,775	--
	$318,180	$318,180	$315,000	$315,000